ADVANCE PRAISE FOR
THE RIGHT KIND OF CRAZY

"Emerson's book is a must-read. After rebellious years as a youth, he persevered to become a U.S. Navy SEAL—his journey reads like fiction, but it's a satisfying nonfiction narrative of a credible operator, and besides doing the gritty work of a SEAL in combat zones, Emerson refined the art and tradecraft of sensitive operations elsewhere in the Middle East— a euphemism for high risk, quiet operational work—in the shadows."

—**Chris Costa, Executive Director, International Spy Museum
Deputy Commander SMU, former Special Assistant
to the President for Counterterrorism**

"You have to be a bit crazy to be a SEAL . . . and Clint Emerson takes us on a roller-coaster ride through his career as he demonstrates the 'right kind' of craziness that's required. Buckle your seat belt and be prepared. . . . Clint doesn't mince words or suffer fools kindly, and cares even less about being politically correct. Fortunately, such men still exist, and our country owes Clint and his colleagues a never-ending debt of gratitude."

—**H. Keith Melton, author of *Ultimate Spy***

THE
RIGHT
KIND
OF
CRAZY

ALSO BY CLINT EMERSON

100 Deadly Skills

100 Deadly Skills: Survival Edition

THE RIGHT KIND OF CRAZY

MY LIFE AS A NAVY SEAL, COVERT OPERATIVE, and BOY SCOUT FROM HELL

CLINT EMERSON

ATRIA BOOKS

New York London Toronto Sydney New Delhi

ATRIA
BOOKS

An Imprint of Simon & Schuster, Inc.
1230 Avenue of the Americas
New York, NY 10020

First Atria Books hardcover edition November 2019

ATRIA BOOKS and colophon are trademarks of Simon & Schuster, Inc.

For information about special discounts for bulk purchases, please contact Simon & Schuster Special Sales at 1-866-506-1949 or business@simonandschuster.com.

The Simon & Schuster Speakers Bureau can bring authors to your live event. For more information, or to book an event, contact the Simon & Schuster Speakers Bureau at 1-866-248-3049 or visit our website at www.simonspeakers.com.

Interior design by Jason Snyder
Illustrations by Tom Mandrake
Color Artist Sian Mandrake

Manufactured in the United States of America

1 3 5 7 9 10 8 6 4 2

Library of Congress Cataloging-in-Publication Data is available.

ISBN 978-1-5011-8416-1
ISBN 978-1-5011-8418-5 (ebook)

DEDICATION

MOM
January 1953–January 2019
DAD
February 1951–July 1997

Contents

CONTENTS

CONTENTS

Note to Readers

THE BOOK YOU'RE ABOUT TO READ IS THE CULMINATION OF A TWENTY-year career. To the best of my memory, everything in its pages is true. The text was reviewed for sensitive material by the Department of Defense,* and with the exception of public figures, a few friends and family members, and SEALs whose names have been previously released, names have been changed.

Every SEAL who writes a book takes some degree of shit from the community. "That guy shouldn't be cashing in on the trident." But show me a business run by a special operator who doesn't advertise his service, and I've got a unicorn to sell you.

A lot of those public smackdowns are just bluster, if you ask me. The same guy who gets a million-dollar job in New York talks shit about the guy who writes a book. The guy who writes books talks shit about the guy who teaches shooting and tactics. The guy who teaches shooting and tactics makes fun of the guys running boot camps. The guy with the podcast** makes fun of the guy with a T-shirt company. They're all "cashing in."

Until the guy with the podcast starts selling T-shirts.

I played the role of the silent professional for twenty years, and I've been careful not to reveal information that could compromise my peers

---

* You'll be hearing lots, lots more about this in a bit.

** The guy with the book plugs the guys with the podcasts (check out Mike Drop and the Jocko Podcast), the T-shirts (check out Forged and Industry Threadworks), the gnarly handcrafted knives (check out SH9 Edge Works), and the badass tactical courses (check out AMTAC and Dynamis Alliance).

or future missions. The protocol I used during the second half of my career was unique to me, was developed by me, and, as far as I know, is no longer in use. Same goes for the training programs I stood up— casualties of the shifting priorities of a changing leadership structure.

Some of my peers will hate me for this anyway. But SEALs are hard on one another, and that's nothing new.

To each their own. I don't give a single, solitary fuck about what all the other guys are doing.

Except for the guy who serves for four years and then spends the rest of his life cashing in. Fuck that guy.

Prologue

THERE'S A STRETCH OF THE I-10 IN WEST TEXAS WHERE THE POSTED speed limit is eighty mph, the fastest in the fifty states. Doing the thirty-six-hour drive from San Diego to Fort Bragg had me hitting that stretch in the middle of the night, buzzed on a steady supply of canned Starbucks.

I was going ninety in a new Lexus when some lights popped up in my rearview mirror on one of my trips along that highway. We were the only two vehicles on the road for miles, so when the blacked-out Camaro rolled up right next to me and stayed there, I let off the accelerator. Probably just some idiot teenagers having a bit of fun. Only when I slowed down, the other driver did, too.

I sped back up.

He cruised right back into position next to me.

We repeated that routine several times.

The driver of that vehicle was deliberately trying to fuck with me, a game of cat-and-mouse that kept up for around fifteen minutes. Which, with your cortisol starting to jack up and your heart rate accelerating, can feel like a lot longer. By the time the Camaro started swerving into my lane and forcing me onto the shoulder, my speedodometer needle was deep into the triple digits and I was definitely fully awake.

I kept my foot on the gas and did some quick math. Tinted windows. One to four occupants in the vehicle. Four would be bad. One would be preferable. Two could be manageable. But the car was a two-door. Anyone in the backseat would be delayed in exiting the vehicle. If the occupants of that vehicle were packing heat, odds were pretty good that

I'd have my gun out of my holster before they'd even had the chance to think about drawing theirs.

The other thing was, all the high-speed maneuvering was whittling down my gas supply, and the nearest exit was thirty miles away.

Fuck it.

Without warning, I yanked my wheel over to the right and got out of my car as quickly as possible. A couple of beats later, the Camaro came to a screeching, swerving halt up ahead.

By the time the driver's left foot hit the ground, I was already slamming his car door against his shin. His lower leg might have made a crunching sound when the bone shattered in several places. I wouldn't know, since I was taking in only sounds that represented an immediate threat. By the time I'd thrown him to the ground and landed a couple of punches, passenger number two was coming around from the rear of the car.

I pulled my pistol and stopped him in his tracks.

Before we got the chance to find out how our standoff would play out, the scene was flooded with blue and white flashing lights. Two pairs of state troopers. My tunnel vision had completely obliterated their approach.

When fight-or-flight wakes up the part of your brain called the amygdala, it'll helpfully facilitate your survival by narrowing your field of focus to the threat at hand.

"Get on the ground!"

We were all bad guys until the situation got sorted out. Which didn't take long. Turned out there was a third passenger in the backseat, and a gun for each.

Sounds like the setup for a joke. Three Mexican carjackers out for a joyride ran into a Navy SEAL. One left the scene in an ambulance with a broken tibia, two headed straight to jail. The SEAL was sent on his way with a tip of a hat and "thanks for your service."

SEALs who stay on the right side of the law tend to have pretty good relationships with the police. Especially after 9/11.

PART I

1
NIGHT
MOVEMENTS

IRAQ, 2003

WE'D BEEN SITTING ON STANDBY IN KUWAIT FOR ABOUT SIX WEEKS when the allied forces supporting Operation Iraqi Freedom began the push into Iraq on March 19, 2003. The Air Force kicked things off with a targeted strike on a compound on the outskirts of Baghdad, where Saddam Hussein was alleged to be hiding in a bunker that turned out to be empty. That faulty CIA intelligence gave the allied forces a less than auspicious start, but the mission of Naval Special Warfare remained unchanged: securing the mile-long gas-oil platforms (GOPLATs) and metering stations on the al-Faw peninsula before Saddam's forces could open the spigots or set the platforms on fire. Saddam had dumped millions of barrels of crude oil into the Persian Gulf during the First Gulf War in 1991, and his forces had already gotten to work torching oil fields across southern Iraq. Three pumping stations on land could also potentially be in play.

Taking Iraq's major oil facilities out of commission would be an economic and environmental suicide mission designed by Saddam to keep his nation's most valuable asset out of allied control while simultaneously slowing our progress. To cut that threat off at the pass, headquarters had assembled the largest coordinated effort of Navy SEALs ever deployed on a single operation. Including support personnel, all eight platoons from

SEAL Team 3, manpower from allied partners, and overhead coverage, the operation involved some 250 men.

We were in the midst of our final briefing at the Kuwait naval base when the air raid sirens came blaring through the speakers. Throughout the day we'd been hearing our Patriot antimissile systems blasting off from the base as they intercepted the short-range ballistic projectiles Saddam had started sending our way. We'd haul ass into the nearest bunker, wait until the coast was clear, and then go back to the business of getting ready for war.

We'd been prepping for weeks on a mock-up of the platform in a nearby field, refreshing our muscle memory after a prolonged absence from the simulated environments where we trained, and our gear was ready to go. When the sirens subsided, we broke into a run, piled into our tents, and zipped ourselves into our Nomex flight suits. ████████████
██
██
████████████████████████████████████.*

A fleet of utility vehicles took us to the piers, where we loaded up into MARK-5 jet boats and headed out to sea.

It was a two-hour ride to the transition point. Around twenty-five miles offshore, we'd ditch the MARK-5s for an armada of rigid-hulled inflatable boats (RHIBs)—a smaller, more nimble option that would increase our chances of approaching the GOPLAT without detection.

If we'd had our way, we would have opted for dropping the MARK-5s long before that point and swimming into the target. Motoring over to an elevated target that potentially had eyes on us didn't seem like the smartest move, but our leadership was determined to show the value of the equipment in which they'd just invested upward of $74 million.

* This is the first of many (many) redactions made by the Department of Defense. This will be an ongoing theme throughout the book. Some of the redactions won't make much of a dent in your reading experiences. Others, especially in the second half of the book, might make you want to throw heavy objects across the room or send me hate mail on social media. Proceed at your own risk.

There was plenty of dark humor as we took off.

"It was nice knowing you."

"Nothing like an impromptu visit when the target knows you're coming."

We'd had wildly varying intelligence concerning what to expect aboard the massive GOPLAT, which was the size of several football fields and potentially rigged to explode. One minute, it was three bad guys. The next, more than a hundred armed troops. Then, thirty-five bad guys and a couple of hostages. Video footage captured in late January had shown what looked like a changing of the guard, from oil workers to Iraqi soldiers. Mike Ritland, our platoon's lead intel rep and roving pinch hitter, finally summed up the calculus in terms we could understand: "Hey, fellas, there are gonna be people on board—and we don't fucking know how many."

A chemical attack was another possibility we'd been told to prepare for. But you could forget about the protective Mission Oriented Protective Posture (MOPP) suits we were supposed to be wearing around the clock. Given the context, squeezing yourself into the equivalent of a charcoal-lined rubber fat suit with sixty pounds of gear strapped on top would have been completely moronic. The bulky heat traps would restrict movement to the point of compromise in a close-quarters combat environment. If Saddam really did plan on giving us the same mustard and nerve gas treatment he'd used on the Kurds, the Iranians, the Kuwaitis, and even his own people, we figured jumping into the ocean would work out better as a standard operating procedure. Nature's own decontaminant.

Adding to the threat was the delayed timing of our mission. Our trek out to the GOPLAT was initially supposed to precede any overt action against Saddam's regime, but the mission had been pushed back on the basis of this supposedly infallible tip regarding Saddam's whereabouts. Now we were assaulting a prime piece of real estate in a region buzzing with a heightened sense of awareness and security. The surprise factor that was a central component of any quality frogman operation was starting to feel a little negligible.

Our strategy remained unchanged. The sixteen members of the Echo Platoon, accompanied by a SEAL Delivery Vehicle Team (SVD) and a few other straggler SEALs we'd absorbed from another platoon, would hit the Mina al-Bakr (MABOT) terminal as practiced.

———————

Darkness had fallen by the time we reached the transition point. We waited for our orders for a tense and unexplained two hours. When we finally got the authorization, we pulled our black balaclavas over our heads, strapped on our night-vision goggles, and stepped into the RHIBs.

Not that we needed the NODs. The thing was lit up like a Christmas tree. So much for operating under cover of darkness.

As we pulled in closer with our suppressed M4s pointed at the GOPLAT, the undifferentiated mass began to come into relief. Mentally cross-checking landmarks against imagery collected via helicopter and satellite, we helped guide our boat guys toward the platform's access stairwell. An additional complement of SVD operators in MK5s moved in toward the ends of the terminal ████████████████████████ ██ ██████████████████████.*

We crouched down, coiled like wire springs.

Once the first boat touched down at the sea-level steel grate, the springs went flying. I ricocheted onto the grating, hustling up the stairs with the rest of the platoon directly behind me in a single-file line. We were headed seven flights up, to the berthing station. The most likely spot for a detonator primed to obliterate the pipelines down below.

Bang!

Not the sound of millions of barrels of oil blowing up.

---

* Many of these redactions turned out to be very subjective and often not necessarily related to classified information. If you're not appreciating the disruption of your reading rhythm, feel free to write your congressperson a friendly note.

A gunshot, or maybe something more.

The call came across the radio. "Go dynamic. Repeat. Go dynamic."

No sense in sneaking around now. We scrambled to the top of the stairs. One guy, no gun, responsive to our command to get prone—fast. No one in the next room. But on a grated passageway, twenty-two men in blue mechanic work suits. Their arms were raised in surrender, and any military uniforms were out of sight. Turned out the soldiers had taken them off and stowed them away in their cabins—along with an armory's worth of AK-47s we found tucked beneath their mattresses.

Hell of a way to keep your firearm within reach. But these "soldiers" weren't looking for a fight. Saddam had paid them the equivalent of ten thousand dollars each to blow up the GOPLATs and take their own lives in the process. They still had the money on them, tucked beneath their clothes. Not the banking practice of men who were about to light themselves on fire. If they'd been seriously contemplating doing the deed, that money would have been left with their families, onshore. They weren't hurting for ammo, either. In a nearby room we found a full stash of heavy weaponry—boxes of TNT, blasting caps, AK rounds, antiaircraft guns, and a few shoulder-fired rockets. If the Iraqi soldiers had launched a couple of those RPGs at our boats, we would have been barbecued fish food.

I stayed behind in the berthing area for a while, helping my guys search and zip-tie the Iraqis while the rest of the platoon began to clear the remaining six decks. During rehearsals I'd gone full *Silence of the Lambs* on the fresh-faced sailors we borrowed from the Navy for prisoner role play. "It's going to be over soon," I would whisper into a kid's ear, my gloved hand rubbing his face from behind. "You won't feel a thing." I wasn't above grabbing a bit of Navy crotch to make a point, either. But there's a time and place.

While we cleared the MABOT terminal, our SEAL counterparts and allies were infiltrating their corresponding targets. A couple of nautical miles away, our special forces coalition counterparts and a fire team of SEALs were busy taking down the Khawr al-Amaya terminal, which the

Iraqis had blown up back during Desert Storm. On the mainland, SVD teams infiltrated the port city of Umm Qasr while the remaining SEAL Team 3 platoons secured the manifold and metering stations. The SEAL teams faced some resistance—a moment described by Chris Kyle in his now-famous book *American Sniper*: his platoon got stuck in the mud in their overloaded desert patrol vehicles and was getting hammered by the hordes of Iraqis manning the facility. Things were looking dicey for Charlie Platoon until a contingent of Air Force A10s showed up. Warthogs, as they're affectionately known. Giant tanks with wings, they fly low and slow and mow down everything in their path. They took care of any issues Charlie Platoon was having, with deadly efficiency.

Six hours after we'd landed, Echo Platoon turned over the platform and the prisoners to a contingent of Marines and hopped onto a swift catamaran—a futuristic vessel that combines the dimensions of a ferry and the velocity of a speedboat. The sun was rising as we got back to base. Our objective had been achieved with near-impeccable results—zero casualties, a thousand pounds of explosives and twenty-seven prisoners seized, and zero damage to target infrastructure.

That last part could have worked out very differently.

The mysterious explosive sound we'd heard when we pulled up to the GOPLAT wasn't the sound of enemy fire on deck. It was the sound of a .50-caliber round ricocheting off a thick steel pipeline.

The shooter was one of our boat guys, just a nervous kid. As his RHIB backed away from the platform, he'd accidentally pulled the trigger on the .50-cal Browning machine gun bolted to the bow of his craft, launching a round into the same exact oil-filled pipe we were trying to prevent from spilling into the Persian Gulf. Needless to say, the kid was shitcanned and sent home as soon as we got back to shore.

Taking down the GOPLATs was a classic SEAL mission. Approach by sea under cover of darkness. Clandestine infiltration. A sudden and over-powering blow carrying just the right amount of force. But despite the promising start, our leadership wasn't really sure how to use the SEALs in the early stages of the Iraq War. It took a while for the Naval Special Warfare Command (NSWC), the division of the Navy that oversees most of the SEALs and their associated units, to get into the game.

Compounding the problem were higher-ups who'd done full military careers without seeing any real action. There were more than a few reservists in Iraq who'd come out of corporate cubicle farms for their one last chance at combat. Some of them wound up calling the shots. To say they were con-servative about what the SEALs could or couldn't do is an understatement.

For a while a few of our platoons were headed up by a task unit commander with the look of a sunburned tourist wandering around Disney World in a jungle hat. You'd think my teammates and I would feel bad reaming a family man on chemotherapy drugs that increased his sensitivity to sunlight. But that commander and officers like him were consistently more concerned with the possibility of anything going wrong on their watch than with getting the job done. The sight of his red, peeling face only reinforced our sense that he was a fish out of water, totally unsuited to dry land.

The sign our platoon had hung at the entrance to our tent in Kuwait before we even kicked off operations couldn't have been more accurate:

LIONS LED BY DOGS

From the minute we'd set foot on base, a random assortment of Naval Special Warfare officers we'd never even seen before had been all over our asses about minor protocol like tucking in our fucking shirts. As the LPO (leading petty officer), I was constantly being hounded for shit my guys were doing or not doing. They wanted us clean shaven, wearing our helmets, and in our MOPP suits at all times. Which, for a community used to making its own rules about grooming and gear, was a total affront. Our guys weren't sporting the full beards that became an unspoken SEAL standard as operations in the Middle East continued throughout the decade. But they weren't too concerned about spit-shining their shoes, either.

A lot of experienced SEALs from our team moved on after that deployment. They figured they had better things to do than waste their time and skills on an inept command.

I got lucky when a different kind of opportunity presented itself—one that would take me out of combat and into a specialized role centered on unconventional tactics. I never stopped being a SEAL. But the nature of warfare had changed. And I was more than happy to pursue a different path under a smaller chain of command.

2
A BOY SCOUT
IN THE DESERT

SAUDI ARABIA, 1980s

THE ARAMCO SECURITY GUARDS WERE SHOUTING OUT WARNINGS AS THEY scrambled downhill to the swampy hideaway we called "the puddle." The football-field-size depression in the sand was surrounded by a thick ring of bamboo—a ring of bamboo that we'd just turned into a blazing inferno.

My two best friends and I would regularly burrow our way into our miniature forest oasis and sit around in there sucking on cans of butane. Fire-blowing competitions were a standard way to pass the time. Only that day we'd gotten bored of spitting flames and decided to light a little fire.

In the Saudi Arabian heat, the dry bamboo was a pile of tinder waiting to erupt. We hadn't realized just how combustible the stuff would be.

The can of butane may have had something to do with it, too.

The blaze was just getting out of hand when the guards, driving their regular patrol route on the outskirts of the compound, spotted the smoke.

For a bunch of arsonists we put on a pretty good impression of three terrified little kids as they snatched us away from the flames. But when they turned their backs to assess the damage, we bolted back up the hill. Then we raced back through the tree line to our "headquarters," a small hut we'd built behind my backyard.

13

When I was eight, the Arabian American Oil Company (ARAMCO, for short) shipped my family out to the town of Abqaiq, the location of one of several ARAMCO compounds in the Saudi Arabian kingdom.

Originally a partnership between American oil companies and the Saudi government, ARAMCO had been bought out by the Saudis in 1980. But the North American geologists and engineers who'd built up its infrastructure would be baked into the operation for decades.

Like a lot of the transplants around Saudi, my dad had started working for the company back in Texas before agreeing to the transfer. In those days they were paying a premium to employees willing to haul their wives and kids overseas for a few years, and we'd be upgrading from our duplex to a two-story house surrounded by palm trees.

That first night in Saudi I remember pissing the bed, waking up disoriented with a nose full of sand. We were temporarily stashed in a dressed-up trailer park until permanent housing opened up. Summers back in Texas, I'd sometimes spent the night in my grandfather's RV. But a night under the Texas stars was worlds away from a trailer park in a Middle Eastern desert. That was as good as it got for the Pakistani and Filipino laborers who did the manual work in and around the oil refinery. White-collar engineers and geologists like my dad were eventually moved inside the gated compound at Abqaiq.

The company wasn't cutting corners when it came to recruiting North American talent, and the on-site amenities included a BMX track for the kids, racquetball and tennis courts in the gym, and several Olympic-size swimming pools. Made up to look like a suburban town in Texas or Arizona, our new neighborhood was a miniature American city of green lawns and wide streets.

The granite-colored golf course made of oil-treated sand was one reminder of the landscape outside our fence line. Another was the massive sandstorms that would whip through the Gulf states a few times a year. When a *shamal* hit, you couldn't see farther than about three fee' in front of you, and the Bedouin headscarf known as the *gutra* started

make a lot more sense. The little blue VW Bug we'd bought off a family moving back to the States was sandblasted silver on one side from our first *shamal* experience. You'd see lots of cars like that around Abqaiq, with the side that had been facing the wind buffed to shiny metal.

A half day's drive to the south was the 250,000-square mile expanse of dune-rippled red sand called Rub Al Khali, or "the Empty Quarter"—the world's largest sand desert. Save for the occasional Bedouin town, the place was as desolate as its name implied. It was also the repository of the world's richest oil supply, which got back to the reason they needed engineers like my dad.

It didn't take long for me to find a couple of friends: Cameron, a Canadian kid with an impressive set of biceps, and Ricky, a short, skinny Texan who ran like a bat out of hell. Raising a family on a closed, guarded compound might have given parents at Abqaiq the illusion of safety. What the barbed-wire fence line gave us was several miles of roaming space. In our case, "ARAMCO brat," the nickname for anyone who spent part of their childhood on one of the facilities in Saudi, definitely fit the bill. We were under-stimulated and mostly unsupervised, and we patrolled the facilities, looking for trouble. When we couldn't find any, we manufactured our own.

In the racquetball courts, we ripped the fire extinguishers off the walls. We'd jam their nozzles under the doors so the courts would fill up with bright blue powdered fire retardant. A month or two later, we'd be at it again.

We had some run-of-the-mill pranks like Ding-Dong-Ditch—ringing doorbells and running away. But we liked to bring a sense of creativity to our pursuits. Bats swarmed the camp after dark, and come nightfall we'd sneak out to chuck darts at them. Nailing the creatures as they passed under the streetlamps was surprisingly effective, and we were pretty proud of our success rate. Later we realized the bats' sonar was causing them to mistake the darts for giant bugs. They were impaling themselves in a clear-cut case of bat suicide. Maybe we weren't such great bat hunters after all.

Another one of our favorite tricks was climbing up to the roof of the dining hall to hurl homemade flash-bang grenades down at the other ARAMCO residents.* The sudden bright flash at their feet scared the living shit out of our friends' parents, but thankfully, nobody ever got hurt. Amazingly enough, the three of us never got caught. Which is nuts, considering we did all of this on a regular basis. Maybe we really were invisible in the ninja outfits and camouflage we'd wear during our troublemaking missions. I'd started taekwondo in Texas and kept it up in Saudi, and my obsession with ninjas had survived the trip, too. My sword was a couple of hunks of wood that my dad had helped me sand down and paint black. But my assassin's costume was the genuine article, purchased in Japan.

My dad, Bruce, was a borderline genius with a photographic memory and a gift for fixing anything mechanical. He's technically my stepdad, but neither of us ever considered the other anything less than blood. An industrial engineer who'd gotten his master's at the University of North Texas, he never met a motor or a microwave he couldn't take apart and put back together. No one in my immediate family remembers his title at ARAMCO, but his job boiled down to teaching the Saudis how to pull oil out of the ground. That's what we were told, at least.

He had a dry, slightly warped sense of humor that was definitely passed on to me. One of his favorite vacation mementos was a photo he'd had my mom take, where he was peeing over the bridge on the River Kwai—the "death railway" that took the lives of thousands of POWs. ARAMCO gave its white-collar foreign workers a generous annual travel

---

* To learn more about improvised flash bangs, check out skill 068 in my first book, *100 Deadly Skills, The SEAL Operative's Guide to Eluding Pursuers, Evading Capture, and Surviving Any Dangerous Situation.*

voucher to go back and forth to the States, and my family used it to travel the world on the oil company's dime. Another time he took us to the Hiroshima memorial on a day when Japanese people weren't too happy to see a bunch of grinning American tourists. The son of a World War II paratrooper and brother to a Vietnam vet, he wasn't too concerned about putting any restrictions on his displays of patriotism. Not even on the anniversary of the world's first nuclear attack.

He'd wanted a chance to serve in Vietnam, like his brother did, but couldn't get past the physical after blowing out his knees playing high school and college football.

My biological father, a man appropriately named Dick, was an Air Force sergeant from a military family. His dad ran Lackland Air Force Base, down in San Antonio. Any influence that may have had on my career choice was definitely passed down only through genetics. The whole nature-versus-nurture debate has no place in our story. The guy filed for divorce the day I was born, then dropped me off at a United Way two weeks later. My mother found me the next day, but that was his first and last babysitting gig, as far as she was concerned.

We met just once after that, in Texas. My mom took me to see him at a playground on one of our trips back from Saudi, toward the end of our stay. The first thing out of his mouth was "You feedin' him?"

I was a skinny little runt back then. He was clearly still a dick.

I later heard he became a police officer in Plano, a twenty-minute drive from the town where I live now. Couldn't find a thing beyond some old police reports about a murder he worked in the early 1990s when I looked him up online in search of some family medical history, after retiring from the Navy. Driving over to Plano and asking around at the police station would be a possibility, if I gave a shit about the guy.

When my mom and stepdad, Bruce, first met, he'd been working his way through college as a clerk at the original Howdy Doody, a convenience store in Denton, Texas. My fleabag of a biological dad had hit the road before I'd even had a chance to take my first proper shit, so my mom was sharing an apartment with her sister and scrambling to make ends meet. Their courtship was a slow-burn 1970s romance involving long hair for both of them and letters back and forth. What none of the letters mentioned was little old Clinty. The first few times Bruce came over to her place, my mother even went so far as to hide the stroller, ditch me with a neighbor, and take all my pictures off the walls. Can't say I blame her—a single woman with a diaper bag isn't exactly a college kid's dream. But when she finally found the courage to tell him about her big secret, all he said was "You think I didn't know that?"

He'd seen her driving around town with a car seat in the back. Within a couple of years they were married and he'd all but adopted me as his son. Ten years later my brother, Beej, was born in Saudi. Our dad was just one of those natural caretakers, "Dad" to us both and someone who wouldn't hesitate to help that fatherless kid down the street install a new part in his car. My high school friend Scotty didn't have a father figure in his life, and as a result he spent lots of time at our house back in Texas and formed a pretty tight bond with my dad.

One time Scotty came over to find him floating on a raft in our pool, drinking a beer.

"Hey, Mr. Emerson," Scotty called out, "what you up to?"

"I'm playing basketball, dumb-ass," he replied, taking a swig of his Heineken. "What does it look like I'm doing?"

On another one of those vacations abroad we got swarmed by a bunch of gypsy kids on a bridge near Vatican City. They were begging for money, acting like they were starving, pulling out all the tricks in the street urchin arsenal. All of a sudden he just exploded.

"God damn it!" he barked. "One of these little shits grabbed my wallet."

They'd had their sticky little hands all over us like a bunch of midget detectives frisking a band of suspected perps. That's their game: one kid distracts you by touching your arm while the other slides the wallet out of your back pocket. Dad, who was six foot one, bearded, and darkly tanned by the Middle Eastern sun, spread his arms out like some kind of giant Hulk and backed them all up against the railing, threatening to throw them over the bridge. Eventually the wallet came flying out from the crowd and landed on the sidewalk.

Soon after that he invented his patented comb trick—slipping a comb into the wallet he carried in his back pocket. The comb would catch on the fabric of his pants, preventing any unauthorized attempt at removal.

He also had a few habits that never quite made sense. Anytime we were in the car, before, during, and after Saudi, the guy would be consistently checking all three of his mirrors throughout the ride. Driver's-side mirror, rearview mirror, passenger's-side mirror, repeat. His eyes would sometimes meet mine on their trip through the middle. It's one of those things you notice as a kid, when you're sitting in the backseat and your entire field of view is the back of your parents' heads. That, and the fact that everywhere we went, his .45-caliber, 1911 government-model semiautomatic pistol went, too. When it wasn't in the holster in the waistband of his pants, it was tucked into the passenger seat pocket, for easy access from the driver's seat.

Just before our move to Saudi, he'd started taking me to the shooting range to teach me some marksmanship on a little .22-caliber pistol, before eventually graduating me to a lever-action rifle with one of those Wild West–style loading mechanisms. Having a small arsenal decoratively displayed in your living room gun cabinet certainly didn't make him unique in Texas. But toting around a concealed weapon in the 1970s was unusual, not to mention illegal until 1996. That was long before every Joe, Jack, and Julie started exercising their right to conceal and carry in the great Lone Star State.

It wasn't until I started walking down the path of more surreptitious work that I recognized some of my dad's behaviors as those of a guy with a heightened sense of vigilance. The stories he started to tell me when I got into the military made some sense of that. Either my dad had a past he didn't want catching up to him—or there was more to his ARAMCO oil field job than met the eye. In retrospect, something on that order would help explain his early death from a heart attack at the age of forty-six. Living with jacked-up levels of cortisol running through your bloodstream for years will put a strain on your heart like a layer of cholesterol in your arteries. The man wasn't just outlived by his two brothers. He died before either of his parents did.

But you'd never have known he was going through something internally from the way he doted on us kids, that's for sure.

Kids are fluid when it comes to learning foreign languages, but I didn't pick up a whole lot of Arabic beyond the basics in our time in Saudi. That's mainly because our Arabic teacher, a Lebanese guy called Mr. Hashem, was a giant prick.

He was also one of the main reasons why I hated the place so much. The man was bitter and abusive, and he clearly hated his job—or maybe just the Westerners he was forced to teach. Most of the time he'd just have us sit there in these old-school audio workstations where you'd run a magnetized card with a picture of a dog through a machine. "Kalb, kalb, kalb." The next card would have a picture of a mountain. "Jabal, jabal, jabal." He'd make us do that for an hour straight while picking his nose with the inch-long fingernail he'd grown for just that purpose. When we mispronounced words, he'd throw heavy hardcover textbooks at our heads and call us useless pieces of shit.

Some of the language came back to me later, when I was deployed in that part of the world, but six years of exposure to Mr. Hashem left me with little more vocabulary than what the average tourist would pick up in a monthlong class.

Given the way ARAMCO paid its teaching staff, Hashem was the exception. Most of our teachers were overqualified. You had an actual NASA scientist teaching middle school, along with a couple of buttoned-up government types whose real reasons for being in Saudi may not have been strictly pedagogic.

Outside the classroom, Hashem's attitude toward Westerners was close

to the norm. Americans and Europeans may have been running Abqaiq, but Saudi men believed they were at the top of the social ladder. And regardless of where they stood professionally in the chain of command, they were always finding ways to assert their supremacy. My dad used to get so damn mad when they'd cut in front of him in the commissary line. But we were guests on foreign soil, and there was no way the Saudis were going to let us forget that. The same principle applied to the Saudi state. The residents of our little man-made oasis had special rights they couldn't exercise outside the compound. Women were allowed to drive, which they couldn't do in the rest of Saudi until just recently, and we could all wear whatever we wanted. But even inside our modern suburbia, the kingdom's attitude toward outsiders was made crystal clear time and again. We routinely watched our fathers be humiliated by Saudi men, had our homes subjected to random searches by the Saudi religious police, and had our mail inspected and censored by the Saudi authorities.

That hostile dynamic worked its way down to the relationship between the Saudi adults on the compound and the ARAMCO brats. Getting thrown into the dirt by grown Saudi men was a semiregular event for me and my friends, beginning around the age of ten.

Back then Pepsi cans were made of steel, and some of the Saudi guys would flatten the empty cans into pretty effective throwing stars. Their improvised weapons weren't lethal, but they could definitely pierce the skin. The men were also armed with sandals. Sounds pretty harmless, if you're picturing a pair of floppy rubber shower shoes. These were hard leather, with a slim profile that gave them a knifelike edge, and the Saudis used them to smack us around.

Is it possible we started it? Sure. We definitely provoked them more than a few times. Throwing bits of food at them during the holy month of Ramadan, when all practicing Muslims fast during the day, probably wasn't the smartest thing to do. But we were kids, and these were grown men. When they weren't beating us up, they had their hands all over us. On the day their techniques evolved to include holding us down and sticking us with needles and pushpins, we grew thirsty for revenge. As ten-year-olds, we couldn't take on a bunch of men in their twenties. But we could go after something they held precious—their cats. Come nightfall, we suited up like ninjas, grabbed a couple of boards and some nail-studded baseball bats, snuck onto the part of the base where the Saudis lived, and went to town on the feline population of Abqaiq. Muslims love their cats. The average cat in Saudi probably has more rights than most of its citizens, particularly the women. So the cat carnage was an especially harsh form of revenge.

Listen, I'm aware of the research on childhood animal cruelty. Great predictor for criminality and a mental health diagnosis of "psychopathic antisocial tendencies." Which is just a dressed-up way of saying "budding psychopath." But that phase didn't last long. After a few nights we were back to old tricks, like trying our best to set our lungs on fire.

My accomplices and I were just kids acting out in response to a confusing environment. Kids who definitely could have used a little more parental supervision, that's for sure. But whether you paint me as a highly functioning psychopath or a normal preteen boy with a devious streak and some energy to burn, we can probably all agree it's a good thing I wound up playing for the home team. Until my instinct for troublemaking found an outlet, there were some regrettable casualties.

We found more conventional ways to fill our time through our regional outpost of the Boy Scouts. Partly because there was so little to distract us, we racked up our badges fast. Archery, marksmanship, first aid (taught by the world-class doctors at the compound's medical center), swimming and lifeguarding in any one of the Olympic-size pools . . . The range of on-site facilities made it easy to breeze through the ranks.

My dad was a troop leader for at least part of the time, and each year he would take me to Camp Freedom in Germany. A scouting outpost run by Special Forces and Army guys where a lot of the kids had parents in the military or foreign service, Camp Freedom was like scouting on steroids, without the distraction of school. We'd spend two weeks in the forest racking up merit badges, from forestry and archery badges to basket weaving. Wilderness survival was my favorite. We'd be dropped off in the middle of nowhere with nothing but a poncho and a survival knife. Twelve-year-olds left to spend two nights in the wild on our own, figuring out how to build shelter and find food and water.

Back in Saudi there was a spot to the west of Abqaiq called the Lonely Jabal, after the Arabic word for the single mountaintop in sight. All the different troops in the area (from the larger compound in Dhahran and the outposts in Udhailiya and Ras Tanura) would get together and compete in a jubilee there, just like back home.

Eventually I made it all the way to Eagle Scout, finishing off my scouting career with a community project on water waste on the compound. Environmentalist by day, bat hunter by night. Taking out all those bats might have contributed to an increase in the number of insects around camp. But getting rid of some standing water would have given those insects fewer places to fester. Ecology at its finest.

———

My twisted sense of logic may have been innate, but many of the skills I eventually honed as a SEAL can be traced straight back to scouting. For all the advanced training we get as SEALs, those campouts in the Saudi desert laid a surprisingly useful foundation.

I swam my first mile as a Boy Scout and got SCUBA certified as soon as I was old enough. A friendly Filipino maintenance man taught me how to unscrew a garden hose and use the whole thing as an extended snorkel. The technique worked great until delinquents at the other end would blow into the hose or submerge it underwater.

Escaping the older boys who'd come over and dunk the smaller kids at the Abqaiq pools had already turned me into a pretty fast swimmer, and the lifeguarding certification I'd earn later on involved the same rescue techniques I'd relearn as an aspiring SEAL. I learned to dive in the Persian Gulf, at an ARAMCO-owned beach in Qurrayah.

My most eventful dive, not long after I passed the test, involved a line out to nowhere and some run-ins with a couple of massive *hamours*. Big, ugly, spotted groupers about the size of our family car, those creatures are not afraid of humans, and they'll just sit in the water and stare at you with their beady little eyes.

That day there was also a huge school of migrating jellyfish right off the pier where my adult swim buddy and I were set to dive. We jumped in without paying much attention, realizing only when we looked around that we were surrounded by hundreds of thousands of jellyfish. We'd just swum through poison water. But I was too entranced by the glowing cloud of jellies to mind much when my skin started to sting.

Once we got our bearings, my diving partner grabbed on to a sand-covered rope that was resting on the ocean floor. Permanently tied off to the pier, the line led us out to a man-made reef about a quarter of a mile from shore, a retirement village for the huge tires used on desert excavation vehicles and other heavy-duty machinery. A bunch of old rubber doesn't make the most hospitable habitat for marine life, but it was a cool site for divers to explore. After taking off our masks to chat inside an air pocket our regulators had created in one of the upright tires, we wandered for a bit. I pulled some chopped-up hot dogs out of my dive vest for fish food and found myself surrounded by a school of angelfish.

I was in my own world for a while with the creatures eating out of my hand.

When I looked up, my partner was nowhere to be found. I roamed the reef's perimeter to look for him. But my air supply was running a little low.

Maybe I'd better head back to the pier, I thought.

Only now I couldn't find the rope.

Anxiety sets in fast when things go wrong underwater. The solution seems simple: just head to the surface. But say you pop up and can't see land. You decide to go back down to get your bearings. Quick-moving currents and even a little bit of a wind could make it impossible for you to ever find that reef again down in the dark ocean depths. It's a needle in a haystack down there. One minute you see something, the next it's gone forever. If that something is your buddy, you might be pretty screwed.

Don't forget, all the while the clock is ticking on your air supply. And in this case, you're a skinny twelve-year-old with forty feet of water over his head.

I decided to hedge my bets and swim to the surface. I wasn't exactly lost at sea. But it took a bit of hard kicking before my head and chest were high enough out of the water that I could spot land. Once I washed up on the beach, I spotted my swim buddy messing around with his equipment at a nearby picnic table. This thirty-year-old assistant scoutmaster had left a frightened kid in open waters by himself, and he seemed to have absolutely zero concerns about his actions.

That episode did actually wind up giving me a lot more confidence in the water, which came in handy during the dive and drownproofing sections of BUD/S, the grueling six-month-long training course that all Navy SEALs must successfully complete. Panicking underwater is the enemy of success in a scenario where you've got to swim across the bottom of an Olympic-size swimming pool with your wrists and ankles bound, or when you're bobbing up and down in a thirty-foot-deep combat training tank without any air supply. Nerves will definitely screw you during Pool Comp, when an instructor does everything in his power to fuck with you, from tying knots in your dive apparatus to ripping off your mask and fins. That's just a prelude to making you untangle and reattach all of your gear in a specific order while still underwater with no air supply, until the instructor finally gives you permission to kiss your rig (to show you're still fully conscious) and swim to the surface.

That early experience helped make some of the stupid shit that instructors put us through seem less meaningless. It also made me more sensitized to all the rules we had to follow. There's a reason we swim with buddy lines tethering us to our dive partners through thick and thin. Run into trouble, and you just pull on the line to let your buddy know. 'Cause you sure can't call out for help.

One thing you never want to do is stab your buddy with your dive knife. They don't have to teach you that at BUD/S, but even if they had, I'd already learned the lesson the hard way.

I had accumulated a pretty good collection of knives over the years, and my newest acquisition was a dive knife with a double-edged blade and a skeleton handle. My friend William and I were sitting in the back of the ARAMCO school bus, a shiny black Mercedes model.

The knife came to a razor-sharp, daggerlike point. I held the blade up in the air and pretended to take a swipe in William's direction. I wasn't aiming to actually cut him. But he flinched and reflexively swung his forearm up as a block. The point of the knife punched right through the space between the knuckles of his index and middle fingers, then came out the other side of his palm.

Oh, shit.

It took a minute before the blood really started to gush. The driver did a U-turn and took us straight back to Abqaiq while I ran water over William's hand and the blood spiraled down the drain. Luckily the blade hadn't hit any tendons, and William was sent home from the hospital with a couple of stitches. The fallout for my dad lasted longer than it took for that wound to heal.

Stir a pot long enough for it to boil over at Abqaiq, and it wasn't the line cook the authorities would come looking for. If a kid misbehaved, if a wife got written up by the Saudi police for immodesty, the fathers were the ones who got brought in for questioning. Women and children are considered the property of their husbands and fathers in Saudi, and the male guardians charged with enforcing the rules sometimes take the brunt of the discipline when there's an infraction. Not that the kids were exempt from punishment, either. A kid we knew at the Dhahran compound got the full Saudi police caning treatment in front of the whole school for spelling his name in pee on the sidewalk. When a teenage girl tried to sneak some weed into Abqaiq after a family vacation to Amsterdam, her entire family was deported on the spot.

Sure enough, rumors that I'd stabbed my friend began working their way around the compound, and it wasn't too long before my dad got pulled in by Saudi police. The whole thing died off when they realized I wasn't a knife-wielding murderer. But that was a typical reminder of the way a schoolyard incident could escalate in Saudi. The fences surrounding the ARAMCO compound were no protection against the laws of the land— and we were still living in a country where punishments were dictated by the Quran. Torture by the police was a routine occurrence, and back then petty thievery could still leave you with a stump where your right hand used to be. Public beheadings, death by stoning, lashings, and years-long jail sentences for petty offenses were some of the ways the kingdom was inclined to part you from appendages or pieces of your hide.

The threat of three hundred lashes didn't stop ARAMCO parents from partaking in a little at-home fermentation, though. In the famously dry kingdom, making your own moonshine was a time-honored tradition. Like many of his friends, my dad had converted one of our guest bathrooms into an amateur winery using a set of hacked-together filters and hoses. The risk level was medium-high, but we were protected by a network of informants who'd send word down the line whenever the Saudi police conducted their raids. We'd come home from school and our parents would shout, "Grab the bottles!" The entire family would start dumping wine down every available drain and toilet. The whole house would smell like wine, but the evidence was gone.

For all the freedom my friends and I enjoyed on the compound, we all got a taste of how differently things worked in the kingdom when we first landed just outside Dhahran. You immediately got the sense that you weren't in Kansas anymore when they separated the men from the women and children on the tarmac. Then the Saudi version of the TSA literally took your suitcase, dumped the contents right onto the floor, and pushed your stuff around with sticks, looking for contraband like alcohol, drugs, or pornography. I guess the function of the sticks was to prevent them from being tainted with our infidel smut. As for their definition of smut, it ran the gamut from *Playboy* to the bra-and-panties section of the JCPenney catalog—we'd get ours three months late because they had to take the time to go through every single page and black out the women's bodies with markers. They did this for every publication mailed into the compound.

The irony was that despite all their religious rhetoric, they were more than happy to drive over the bridge to Bahrain to get their nut off with Russian and Filipino hookers. I guess they thought Allah couldn't see them there.

My family and I lived in Saudi for six years, and I don't have much of anything good to say about the place. The kingdom functions on a system of bribes, and corruption is an accepted way of life. Nobody gets too worked up about it, since the monarchy appeases its constituents by putting a huge number of them on the dole. As a result, you've got a population so used to government handouts that they sit around unemployed while cheap labor from Pakistan or the Philippines does their dirty work.

The women are still treated as a subservient class with a limited set of rights. And the men have loads of bullshit rhetoric that goes along with an interpretation of Islam so literal and backward that it often contradicts the rules of basic human decency. They'll force a bunch of middle school girls back into a burning school because they aren't fully covered. Or they'll skirt their own fucked-up rules against the mixing of the sexes by targeting young children. Young boys get used as sex toys so frequently in that part of the world that there's even a saying for it: "Women are for children, boys are for pleasure."

And we wonder why they grow up to crash planes into skyscrapers.

Let's not forget, Saudi Arabia is the birthplace of Osama bin Laden, the architect of the worst terror attack in U.S. history. Fifteen out of the nineteen hijackers who blew up the twin towers of the World Trade Center and a corner of the Pentagon, killing 2,977 innocent people in one day, were his fellow countrymen. Yet the United States considers the country an ally.

If you ask me, not enough Americans know Saudi Arabia as one of the world's biggest exporters of terrorism. The Saudi government has actively financed the spread of the extreme form of Islam called Wahhabism for decades, to the tune of billions of dollars. For years the state has spent its oil money building fundamentalist mosques, sponsoring extremist imams and scholars, and distributing controversial translations of the Quran all over the world.

On the bright side, spending some time in Saudi sure will make you grateful for the freedoms we sometimes take for granted over here in the free world.

You encounter about three hundred and fifty frauds for every actual Navy SEAL, the saying goes. In retrospect the first one I met probably fit into the category of make-believe. It was on a layover in Frankfurt, one of my last trips back to Texas for Christmas at the grandparents' before we moved back. Running into other Americans overseas often led to a certain degree of chitchat, and once we started talking I asked the burly older guy next to me about the tattoo on his bicep.

"That's a trident, son," he responded, pushing up his sleeve to give me a better view.

"What's a trident?" I asked. Greek myths had never been my strong suit.

"It's a symbol. Ever hear of an outfit called the Navy SEALs?"

I knew a little about the Navy SEALs from a kid's book I'd been given in Texas. But I hadn't realized just how cool they were until the man at the airport started describing them. An elite group of soldiers who dropped down from planes, swam onto islands most of the world had never heard of, and crept up on our enemies in the dead of night was just the kind of thing that set my imagination on fire.

I learned later that the man's trident wasn't strictly authentic. The full Navy SEAL trident is a composite featuring a trident, a bald eagle holding an anchor, and an old-fashioned firearm called a flintlock. The national bird symbolizes both our ability to drop in from the sky and our devotion to our country. The anchor reflects our military mothership, the United States Navy. The trident recalls the power of Poseidon, god of the seas. The weapon's significance should be obvious. Taken together, the symbols represent a class of amphibious warriors who fight over sea, air, and land—the three terrains that make up the SEAL acronym.

When I pressed him for details, he said he'd recently operated in Libya, "taking out antiaircraft guns" to clear the way for American bombers.

I actually knew what he was talking about.

A year earlier, in 1986, Vice President George Herbert Walker Bush had stopped by Abqaiq in the midst of Operation El Dorado Canyon, and my scouting troop had played a role during his ceremonial visit. As one of the color guards standing watch over the flag, I'd been steps away from our future president when he made his speech.

The reason for his visit was a surprise air raid on Libyan forces and terrorist training camps—a retaliation for Muammar el-Qaddafi's involvement in attacks on Israeli and American targets in Rome, Vienna, and what was then West Berlin. Gunmen armed with assault rifles and hand grenades had taken nineteen lives during airport attacks on Israeli terminals in Rome and Vienna in late 1985. The subsequent bombing of a West Berlin disco known for attracting American soldiers had killed three people (two of them U.S. service members) and injured more than two hundred (among them seventy-nine of our soldiers) just a few months later. All three attacks had been publicly praised by the Libyan president, and intelligence pointed to the Libyan government as the source of planning and funding.

Bush was there to trumpet the success of our counterattack and to reassure American citizens in Saudi that the U.S. government had C-130s ready to fly us out in case of retaliation. We were a tempting bull's-eye for any local enemies who might have relished the notion of rubbing out an American stronghold and derailing the global oil supply in one fell swoop. The concern wasn't misguided—Abqaiq wound up being the target of an al-Qaeda attack in 2006. And the antiaircraft guns studding the barbed-wire fence line around the compound were manned by Saudi troops, which in retrospect probably made them somewhere around 100 percent unreliable.

I asked the man with the trident tattoo what he meant by that thing about the antiaircraft guns.

"Well," he replied with a casual shrug, "you shoot everybody manning the guns and then you blow the damn things up."

That was the day my dreams of becoming a ninja got left in the dust.

A few months later I was given a computerized career assessment test at school back in Saudi. The printer had spit out one of those old green bar reports pointing me toward careers in marine biology, deep-sea diving, or underwater demolition.

Pretty clear-cut.

All of those choices seemed like a sign from above about those men who blew shit up and snuck up onto dry land to surprise their enemies.

Ironically, like most SEALs, I came to hate the water.

Once I joined the community I asked around about any undercover SEAL ops in Libya in 1986. No one had heard a thing—Operation El Dorado Canyon was an Air Force job, as far as we could see. I guess it's possible the mission was so secret that command wouldn't divulge the info. But then what are the chances the guy would be blabbing about it to some kid at the airport?

Somewhere around three hundred and fifty to one.

3
MAGIC TRICKS

PLANO, TEXAS, 1990S

"GET OFF MY PROPERTY!"

I was dousing my face with paint thinner when my patented cleansing technique was interrupted by the sound of my mother screaming at somebody on our front porch.

The solvent left a temporary sting, but it did a good job of burning away the excess oil that had settled on my skin ever since our return from Saudi in 1988. Peering out onto the driveway from my bedroom window, I could see a blue-eyed blonde around my mom's age. Instead of getting lost like my mother told her to, she opened up her trunk and grabbed a bunch of papers, and after some more discussion she brought her folders into the den. Once my mom stopped yelling at the top of her lungs I couldn't hear much of what was said. But hours later, after the uninvited visitor had gone, my mom told me why she'd gotten so upset.

"I'm sorry about all that commotion," she said, her hands shaking as she lit up another Marlboro Black. "But Clinty, you're never gonna believe this. That woman says she's my sister!"

Between the raspy smoker's voice and a deep Texas drawl, you'd never know my mother was born in Germany or that she'd grown up all over the world. But now she'd been unexpectedly plunged thirty years back into her past.

She didn't know much about her biological lineage. After being given up by her birth mother as an infant, she'd been adopted by an American Air Force colonel and the German woman he'd fallen in love with while stationed in Wiesbaden, just after World War II. When they found out they couldn't have children of their own, they'd picked up a pair of fraternal eighteen-month-old twins—my mother, Meta, and her sister, Mila. After Germany came France, Iran, Iraq, Spain, plus a few other stops in a series of administrative service posts. The twins grew up speaking German, French, and English. They also grew up knowing next to nothing about where they'd come from. They didn't even find out they were adopted until they were sixteen. So when this mysterious blonde showed up at our door with her stack of papers, claiming to be a long-lost half sister who knew of four other half siblings out there in the world, my mother's grip on reality was a bit shaken.

The other piece of information in my new aunt's pile of papers was even less welcome.

The twins had been raised like little princesses—French lycées, gymnastics, fencing, ballet, the works, almost as if my grandparents were overcompensating for their humble orphan origins. So to be told that their birth mother was a German prostitute traded back and forth among Nazi and American officers during World War II was quite the shock. The long-lost half sister had spent ten years following leads and tracking down siblings all over the world. The materials in the stack of evidence she presented were convincing. Despite her initial resistance, my mother had to admit that it seemed probable, more than probable, that she'd been given up for adoption by a wartime prostitute. Which would make me the grandson of a German whore—potentially with some SS blood thrown into the mix.

According to a genetic test I took a while back, my DNA is 50 percent German. Who knows how accurate those things are, but it makes for a nice bedtime story.

Surprises like this were kind of business as usual in my family. I was six years old when my mom first broke the news that the guy I'd known my whole conscious life as my dad wasn't biologically related to me. Her questionable decision to break the news through an open bathroom door left behind a memory no amount of therapy could erase—she was sitting on the crapper, with a cigarette dangling between her lips.

It was lucky Bruce never considered me anything less than his own son, because the visit from my mom's half sister lit a fuse to a bomb she had been harboring for who knows how long. In a matter of months she'd made the decision to end the marriage, follow her new boyfriend out to Palm Springs, and enroll in a high-speed auto-racing school—leaving me, my dad, and Beej behind.

The boyfriend and the racing were connected. An out-of-state contractor she'd met through her secretarial job at the insurance company where they both worked, he flew in once a month from California. He was unavailable, he wasn't local, and he had a racing hobby—all of which apparently made him irresistible to a married woman in the grip of a midlife crisis. Bruce found out about the affair after getting suspicious about a supposed late-night meeting and tracking her to a restaurant. He came home late that night and teared up as he told me their marriage was in trouble. First time I ever saw him cry.

The Isuzu my mother drove would have made her an outlier among the Porsches and Ferraris on the SCCA road-racing circuit, the wealthy hobbyist's version of NASCAR. But within the space of a year, her transformation was complete. She went from housewife in Plano to silver-medal-winning race car driver with a sponsorship and some trophies, at a time when there weren't a lot of women on the racing circuit.

A race car–driving mom sounds cool in retrospect, but it was an extended shitty period for the family. My dad was teaching engineering at Texas A&M, five hours away in College Station. Back when he'd first taken the job, my mom hadn't wanted to move to a sleepy college town, so they'd settled on a compromise that had my dad living in College Station during the week, then driving home to Plano on weekends. In light of recent developments, this meant our single-parent household became a zero-parent household during the week, when I turned into the primary caregiver for Beej.

Sunday night, Dad would set me up with grocery money and take off from Monday through Friday. That meant teenage Clint was on big-brother duty for five-year-old Beej—a fifteen-year-old without a driver's license dropping this tiny tot off at kindergarten each day and picking him up each night. Helping with homework, cleaning the house, rustling up makeshift dinners, all of that now fell to me.

My teenage parenting style had its limitations. My dinnertime specialty was bologna in a muffin tin topped with an egg-and-cheese and oven baked, and Beej got stuffed into a dryer and tossed around for a partial cycle a few times after pushing my buttons. He was definitely the first kid at school every morning, waiting outside the gymnasium in his snow boots for almost an hour because high school started before kindergarten did. But he got to ride there on the back of a Honda Goldwing, one of the bikes my dad had hanging around the garage. A hundred-and-forty-pound teenager without a license zigzagging through traffic on a huge old-man's touring bike, classic rock blaring through the built-in stereo system, and a five-year-old riding on the back. That was our car pool.

Between football practice, schoolwork, and Beej, my plate was full to the brim. But I'd always been entrepreneurial, mowing lawns and washing cars around the neighborhood, and somehow I still found some excess energy to burn. So every weekend, with my dad back on Beej duty, I'd suit up in my black polo shirt and jeans and head out the door with an assortment of magician's props.

I'd gotten my first taste of sleight of hand on a family trip to Thailand during middle school. There were street magicians all over the place in Bangkok. On every block you'd find a guy selling the props for one specific trick, and by the end of our vacation I'd convinced my dad to shell out for a dozen. Soon I was spending hours practicing tricks in front of my bedroom mirror.

I'd kept it up in Texas, eventually getting decent enough to make a run at magic as an after-school gig.

My tricks were nothing special, but after trying them out on Beej, I knew they were good enough for little kids. By sophomore year I'd professionalized, making up a business name ("Party Magic") and printing a pile of business cards ("Warning: Cannot make your children disappear").

Once I took out ads in the Plano paper and word started to travel, I had my pick of children's birthday parties. I'd usually bring along a magician's assistant, one of the girls from the drill team who hung around my crew, and I packed my props in an old government briefcase I'd inherited from my grandfather. My signature move was the grand finale, an "appearance trick" with a cheeky twist. I'd start by tying two handkerchiefs together and asking the birthday boy or girl's mom to slide them through her shirt at chest level. That was the first cue for a bunch of little kids to start cracking up. Then I'd ask the man of the house to hold the knot, dead center on her sternum. More laughter from my underage audience. On my count of three, two of the kids yanked on the ends of the handkerchiefs—and the setup came apart, with a bra attached to the middle. *Tada!* The bra wasn't Mom's, but even she stopped to check.

At fifty bucks for twenty minutes of magic, I was putting money in the bank. But as any illusionist will tell you, it's never about the cash.

The first thing I stole was a pack of gum from a 7-Eleven. Without much forethought, I walked up to the register and stuck my hand into the clear plastic globe at the counter.

"How much for a pack of gum?" I asked, one pack tucked into the palm of my hand and the other jutting out between my index and middle fingers.

"Fifty cents."

I dropped the visible pack like a cheapskate, palmed my fifty-cent prize, and strolled right out the door. A classic sleight-of-hand, sticky-fingered trick.

I moved on pretty quickly from petty thievery to outright plunder. Maybe I started robbing my high school classmates as a distraction from all the shitty family drama. Or maybe I just liked the high. Either way, my career as a thief really took off when my friends and I started attending house parties around Plano. I didn't turn out to be much of a drinker, and a lightbulb went off in my head as I watched my classmates lose all awareness of what was going on around them. Drunk people are naturally distracted. And the loot—Mom's finest jewelry, Dad's best watch, the odd billfold—was right there for the taking, as long as the mechanism that regulated your tolerance for risk was faulty enough. My technique wasn't complicated. I'd just wait until that point in the evening when things started to go sideways, then sneak upstairs into the master bedroom and get busy plundering. Walk right out the front door, then turn around and pawn my stash for up to a thousand bucks a pop.

This wasn't something I did just once.

My core group of friends knew what was going on, but nobody else ever found out. At one point a huge football player whose party I'd pillaged did start shaking people down and got close to finding out who had ransacked his house, but I never got the pat on the back. Twenty years later, I heard that same guy got his head blown off in Philly while breaking into a residence. It's lucky I ended up finding an outlet for that itch or I could have ended up just like him. I knew even then that my little capers weren't financially motivated. It was the risk itself I craved. And the worse the potential consequences, the bigger the payoff.

As the months went by, occasionally my mom would come home, beg my dad for rent money, then hightail it out of town with a twenty-thousand-dollar check in her pocket. One time she came back and told him she'd stay if he installed a swimming pool. So he put in a pool. She left again.

No one but the two people involved ever really knows what goes on in a relationship, but from my perspective, it sure seemed like my mom was toying with my dad. I probably could have worked a little harder to shift my point of view. But that's the SEAL mindset for you. Betrayals aren't something we come back from easily.*

Another time she called and told him she was ready to come home. Somehow I got deputized to fly out to Palm Springs and help her drive back. Once I got over there, the two of us got a U-Haul trailer, hitched it to the back of her car, packed up her shit, and prepared to hit the road. She wanted to see the man she'd been living with one last time, so against my objections we stopped by his work. From my seat in the lobby, I could see into his glass-walled office. He was a regular-looking, corporate kind of guy, not physically impressive as far as I could tell. But their voices carried, and what I heard was my mother pleading with him to take her back—some variation of the same speech she'd just been giving my dad.

Part of me can see that she was clearly out of her mind at that point. But in some ways, I'm still the angry teenager watching his mother betray her family. Apparently the conversation didn't go the way my mother had been hoping, because we got back into the car.

We hadn't even made it out of California when she had me pull over so she could use a pay phone.

"I'm sorry, Clinty," she said, shaking her head as she got back into the car. "I'm not coming back."

"Good for you," I told her, adding a few other choice words. At that point, I was done. I remember calling my dad and just telling him, "Dad, this woman is *not* coming home."

* Most SEALs I know come from broken homes.

The pattern continued through high school. My dad commuted, I raised my brother during the week. Occasionally we'd get home from school and Mom would be there in the kitchen, the two of them laughing like everything was back to normal. Eventually they did get back together and remarry, just before the end of my senior year. That was probably the craziest part of the whole thing.

During one of their failed attempts at reconciliation, my mother left one of her race cars behind in our driveway. The Isuzu Impulse wasn't a showy ride straight off the lot, but she'd had it tricked out with a racing engine, a souped-up suspension, and premium analytics. All through high school I'd been driving my paternal grandfather's tank, a gold 1970 Oldsmobile 98—the classic box with a 455 rocket under the hood. The trunk alone was so big it had room for a mini mattress and a big old rebel flag.

That patriotic hideaway got a lot of use once I scored my first girlfriend, my junior year. The prettier half of a set of fraternal twins, she took my virginity in my bedroom after a party I'd thrown for my high school friends. No one could have been more surprised than me. There was still a collection of throwing stars and knives hiding in a secret cache behind my encyclopedias. Kylie claimed to be a virgin herself, but she had a whole lot of confidence in the bedroom for someone who'd allegedly never done the deed. She was also the glue that held me together my junior and senior year. I loved her like a kid can only love his first, and during the period when my mom was away her family would have me and Beej over for dinner several times a week, and even occasionally pick him up from school. I wouldn't have made it through that time without her.

Despite the Oldsmobile's roomy trunk and its notoriety on campus, I was pretty excited when the white Isuzu arrived toward the end of our summer break. I'd already cemented my reputation as a lunatic behind the wheel of the tank. For such a massive ride, the Olds was surprisingly

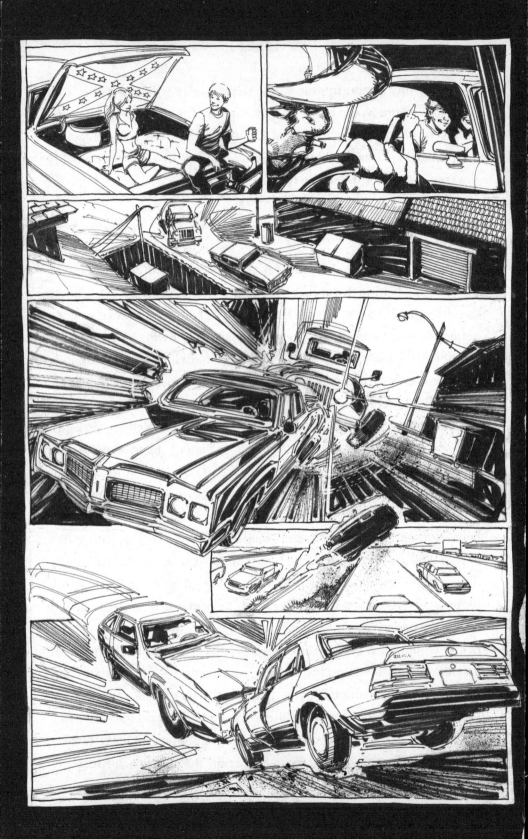

fast. The car was also bulletproof, a quality I took serious pleasure in abusing. I'd swing the door open to purposely scrape paint off neighboring vehicles, or floor the gas through strings of stop signs in residential neighborhoods on the way to football practice. Pissing people off and running away continued to be a specialty of mine, and drag races with strangers, especially this one angry dude in a red Jeep, were routine. I'd flipped him the bird in traffic just for the fuck of it while riding in Scotty's white Camaro, and every time he spotted us driving around in the tank we knew we'd be in for a chase.

His older-model Jeep must have had a V-8, because that red box could haul ass. Maybe I should have been afraid the night I ran into him on my own after midnight, but my main concern was getting home to bed. Eventually I dragged him through a series of alleyways near my house, where I knew the lay of the land. But I couldn't lose the guy. Finally, with his car right on my tail, I decided to put an end to it by slamming to a sudden stop.

On most vehicles, the front brakes tend to engage more aggressively than the brakes on the rear tires, and the shocks on the Oldsmobile were a little loose. So the abrupt transition, from seventy miles per hour to a standstill, caused the front end of my car to nose down and the tail to rise—conveniently negating the height difference between our cars and allowing the Jeep to crash straight into my massive chrome bumper. In my rearview mirror I could see a shattered headlight and steam pouring out of his radiator. It was game over for that guy and his car. The trusty old tank was undefeated.

Things didn't work out quite so well for my new set of wheels. Within two weeks of the Isuzu's arrival in our driveway, the car was reduced to a smoking heap.

I'd been on my way to Kylie's house, driving down a wide-open three-lane road that runs through the center of north Dallas. Despite my feelings about my mother's new racing hobby, there was no denying that the speedy little car she'd left behind was fucking cool. I couldn't wait to see my friends' faces when I rolled onto the school parking lot at the end of summer break.

Turned out I'd never get the chance.

Despite my bumper-car hijinks in the tank, I was still an inexperienced driver. So when I tried to thread the needle between three cars in a chevron formation and one of the drivers balked, I veered to the left, overcorrected—and launched right over the median and into an oncoming vehicle. If I'd hit that car head-on, someone would have died that day. Instead I ripped the axle, the oil can, and a bunch of the undercarriage out from under the Isuzu, popping the front tires for good measure.

I was expecting to get into some kind of trouble when my dad arrived on the scene. But things between my parents were so dicey then that he just looked at the car, laughed, and said, "Well, you ready to go home?"

It doesn't take a degree in psychology to read into the subconscious motives I might have brought to that little caper, and that was the end of the Isuzu. But it's the old clunker with the motel room in the trunk I still think about. That was the tinker car for me and my dad, an excuse to spend a Saturday afternoon working on it together. Those Saturdays also gave me a decent foundation in some basics that proved useful when it came to retrofitting a civilian vehicle for surveillance.

4
SEE YA!

MY FEW FRIENDS IN THE KNOW DIDN'T PAY MUCH ATTENTION TO MY BIG dreams of becoming a SEAL. If they'd stopped to think about my future at all, they would probably would have guessed that I was heading for a life of petty crime or a permanent gig as a low-rent magician. Technically I'd been athletic and even played some high school football. But I was a benchwarmer for the B-team, the kind of scrawny kid who kept a set of weights in his bedroom and prayed for bigger biceps. Long runs around the neighborhood after putting Beej to bed helped me blow off steam and kept me in decent cardiovascular condition. But the only thing I really had going for me on a physical level was some diving experience and a pretty unremarkable aptitude for swimming.

Scotty made it abundantly clear that he thought I was full of shit. He'd heard me talk about joining for years, and he'd even come along when I got a shark tattooed on my ankle at eighteen. The menacing shark ended up looking more like a dolphin. Not that a shark made much sense in the first place. No Navy SEAL has ever been bitten by one—the sound of our Draeger rebreathers could be the reason—and sharks aren't part of the community's visual vocabulary the way tridents, pirates, and frogs are. Scott's dismissal of my plans may have had something to do with the fact that we hadn't spoken for two years. Which *may* have had something to do with my having pulled a gun on him the summer after our senior year.

Working as a lifeguard and counselor at the YMCA, I'd gotten a place in Plano with our mutual friend Ty after graduation. By then I'd moved on from house party robberies to clearing our apartment with live fire. Acting out a nut-job hostage rescue scenario, I'd stage thick phone books all over our apartment and wait until Ty was drinking a beer on the couch. Then I'd scare the daylights out of him by jumping out of dark corners, shooting live rounds at my targets. The bullets always stopped inside the yellow pages, long before they hit the drywall. Ty would jump so high off the couch he'd practically hit the ceiling.

"You're fucking insane, you motherfucker!"*

It was hysterical, if you ask me, and a lot more interesting than the shooting range where Ty, Scotty, and I sometimes messed around with my dad's guns. But my little jokes didn't always land.

One night I answered Scotty's knock on the door by pointing the business end of one of my dad's guns at him through a crack in the blinds. I'd just wanted to mess with him, but instead I'd scared the fuck out of him. And for a while, that was that. I'd taken a dumb prank too far and almost lost a friend for good.

———————————

After that summer I went on to community college in Plano. I'd purposely stayed close to home at first to feel out the situation between my parents. I met my future wife, Carrie, there that fall in an intro-level composition class. She was an all-American cheerleader—pretty, sweet, athletic, and blonde, with big Texas hair and an indecisive streak that would dog me for years. She caught my eye from day one, partly because she came to school dressed for work. In her fitted pantsuits and heels, she was a

---

* I was a real dumbass at this point in my life.

standout in a classroom full of sloppy college kids. You would never have guessed that she came from a devout Pentecostal family who spent their Sunday mornings speaking in tongues. The first time she brought me to church and the congregation broke out into their crazy gibberish, I burst out laughing uncontrollably. That didn't go over so well with her parents.

Our relationship progressed in fits and starts, a weird hybrid between a friendship and something more. Not so unusual in a college scenario, except for the fact that we carried on for years without things getting physical. Good churchgoing girls in Texas didn't put out back then, and I guess they were on to something because Carrie had me wrapped around her little finger. She was having trouble juggling school and her part-time job at a real estate office, so I started writing her papers for her. Though I'd never been able to sit still enough to become much of a reader, I'd always liked to write.

Our friendship was real enough, though, and we grew closer when we both transferred to University of Houston after the first semester in Plano.

Only a few people knew that I'd been harboring dreams of doing something bigger with my life. But I'd spoken to Carrie about my semi-secret ambitions, and it turned out she had a friend named Gary who'd gone through BUD/S but hadn't made the cut.

The first part of the BUD/S acronym stands for "Basic Underwater Demolition," and the S stands for "SEAL." The four letters together represent a brutal six-month-long training course that kicks the ass of 100 percent of aspiring frogmen and graduates only 20 percent every year. There's a lot of mystique surrounding BUD/S, and back in those pre-Internet days there wasn't as much freely available information about the curriculum.

Gary was a few years older than we were. A giant Dolf Lundgren look-alike with a chip on his shoulder, he'd been medically rolled back from BUD/S on account of a knee injury before the grueling test known as Hell Week. Whether you quit, drop out with an injury, or get kicked out for performance issues, when you leave BUD/S without graduating you're sent back to the Navy to finish out your four-year military contract swabbing decks and cleaning toilets with the regular fleet. It's a humiliating outcome for someone whose dream involves parachuting out of helicopters and mowing down bad guys with a select group of warfighters.

Despite the fact he was now basically unemployed and living with his mother, Gary was charismatic. A badass martial artist and former gymnast who got off on doing backflips at parties, he was a great source of information on what to expect, and how to prepare. Like anyone who was interested in the community, I'd read the grandfather of all SEAL books, Dick Marcinko's *Rogue Warrior,* soon after it came out during my senior year of high school, and seen the Charlie Sheen movie *Navy SEALs* around the same time. The founder of the secretive counterterrorism team that goes by several names, Marcinko had introduced modified grooming standards to Naval Special Warfare and pretty much defined the term "unconventional warrior." His dark, bushy beard was ahead of its time in 1980, but after he left the Navy to spend some time in prison writing his memoir, it had become part of his brand and seemed a little theatrical. Just like his descriptions of some of his feats.

Like Marcinko, Gary played outside the lines in a way that wasn't without appeal. Through his martial arts connections, he'd gotten himself heavily involved in an insurance scam headed up by some Chinese mafia out of Houston. They'd stage car accidents, then pocket the two-thousand-dollar insurance deductible with the help of a network of crooked lawyers and chiropractors. After the mafia got its cut of the take, drivers like Gary could walk away with a pretty decent chunk. Out of curiosity I took the Oldsmobile for a spin-and-crash experiment as a one-time thing. Fortunately the gambit didn't stick.

More important, Gary was my first concrete link to the SEAL community, and getting to talk with him was exactly what I needed.

With his input, I started running, swimming, and doing bodyweight exercises to get up to speed for the boot camp test. I'd bulked up some after my teenage metabolism finally slowed down, and a bodybuilder I'd met had given me some pointers. But weights aren't a great idea when you're preparing for BUD/S. Overdoing it can increase your chance of injury. Instead of bulk, pound-for-pound Bruce Lee–style strength became my goal. The guy was the size of an ant, but he could lift twice his weight. With one semester left to go, I enlisted at a run-down recruiting office in Houston.

Gary had been training along with me, and he decided to head back to boot camp to give BUD/S a second try.

Even though both of my parents came from military families, I kept my plans close to the vest. Aspiring to crack one of the world's most elite military units isn't a dream to share widely—you're just setting yourself up for a chorus of voices trying to get you to ratchet down your goals. I didn't tell anyone I'd signed on the dotted line until two weeks before we took off.

My mother flew into a full-blown panic, imagining either my immediate defection from the Navy or my equally immediate death. She was on full standby to "rescue" me if I wanted to come home. My dad wanted me to finish school first. But he was quietly supportive, and not too surprised. It wasn't the first time either of them had heard me talk about joining up. But he'd understood that I was serious. Maybe what the two of us had been through together gave him confidence in my ability to rise to the occasion.

As for me, I was riding off the anticipation those last few weeks.

In an uncharacteristically assertive move, I even told Carrie that her wait-and-see game was coming to an end.

See ya!

Find somebody else to play with. Time to move on to bigger and better things.

On the plane ride over to the Great Lakes, where the Navy holds its boot camp in the dead of winter, the enormity of what I'd committed to punched me in the gut. I actually welled up for a minute, and when Gary caught me with tears in my eyes he took way too much pleasure in mocking me for it. Looking back, he probably did me a favor by stripping me of that security blanket. From that point forward, I was on my own.

5
HOOYAH!

GREAT LAKES, CORONADO, 1994-1995

BOOT CAMP IS A PLACE WHERE YOU REALIZE PEOPLE HAVE ALL KINDS OF motivations for joining the military—many of them financial. I can't speak for what it's like now, but the boot camp I experienced was one of the most depressing corners of the military. You spend all this time stenciling your name on your shirt exactly so many inches down from the collar, your biggest task of the day is achieving ninety-degree hospital corners on your bed, and the physical conditioning is such a joke that many come out in worse shape than they came in. Aspiring SEALs pretty much have to start over from zero to get back into reasonable shape for BUD/S.

I'd say it's a fair guess that less than 5 percent of the United States military actually go in to serve their country and do something selfless and for the greater good. The rest are there for the paycheck and the benefits, the free college degree, or the chance to get out from under whatever crap life they had the bad luck to be born into.

With some distance it's clear that they were the ones who'd drawn the short straw. But at the time it was a rude awakening to the realities of the U.S. military at large. For those of us who'd been dreaming of proving ourselves worthy of access to an elite world only a couple of hundred men a year would be allowed to enter, basic training was a

serious letdown. Your dreams are on steroids when you show up and pull on that first shitty uniform. You quickly find out that "America's finest" is really a random collection of extremely young men and women from every walk of life. On the bright side, at least they're doing something to better their lives and serve their country. But the kicker is that you get a bunch of dudes joining the Navy who literally don't know how to swim.

The general level of commitment increases once you show up to BUD/S, even before the cuts are made and the quitters start ringing the bell. You also get a bunch of white guys—they tend to be the ones who show up to anything that has to do with killing people and blowing things up. I've always wondered whether it's a coincidence that most serial killers are white males, the same demographic that dominates the SEAL teams.

After the first couple of weeks of boot camp you start being able to receive mail. In my stash there were dozens of letters from Carrie telling me she loved me, that she'd made a mistake. When I first told her I loved her, all she'd said was "Thanks." I should have taken the hint. Instead I swallowed the bait.

I passed the timed screening test that allows you to go on to BUD/S without issue—a 500-yard swim, push-ups, sit-ups, pull-ups, and a 1.5-mile run—and my ASVAB scores (the military's general aptitude test) were squared away. That meant I'd move on to BUD/S after a three-month stop at A-school, where you train in the secondary "rates" or jobs you choose as you enter the Navy. I'd selected corpsman, the Navy's term for medic, after hearing that there was a shortage that year. A-school's basic first-aid course was just a prelude to the advanced medical training I'd receive later, in San Antonio, and the skills were nothing I hadn't picked up as a Boy Scout. But the job would become my default in the Navy if I didn't make it through BUD/S.

The course involved a fair amount of classroom time. Luckily there was a seasoned SEAL there with us who'd already been through BUD/S and deployed. He led us through the many hours a day of brutal physical conditioning we'd need to shed the flab we'd accumulated in boot camp.

Everybody's already done enough talking about how hard BUD/S is, and I'm not the first SEAL to say that the training is 90 percent mental, 10 percent physical. But I might be the first one to say I'm not going to bother describing it in much detail. At this point the stories are getting as repetitive as the training itself. If you want to read about the three-mile log runs, the obstacle courses, the near hypothermia, the sleep deprivation, the endless ratcheting up of the physical and psychological stakes, read one of those other books. Hell, look that shit up on the World Wide Web. Anyway, I'm not the most reliable narrator when it comes to a six-month-long period of my life that was followed by nineteen years of operations in frequent proximity to explosives.

Honestly, my main memory of BUD/S is sneaking around with my video camera and laughing through the most challenging "evolutions," the torturous building blocks that fill up our daily training schedule. The random inappropriate laughter was actually useful as a form of stress release, but secretly carting a camera around BUD/S was just a bone-headed move. I'd been given a Sony Handycam for Christmas, one of those old-school models with the little cassettes and the clamshell viewing screen, and starting around dive phase I took every opportunity to use it. Dumb stuff, like chow hall shots of us messing around for the camera dribbling food out of our mouths, or outtakes from our explosives training. If I'd been caught by an instructor, that would have been the end of my big dreams. But there was no rhyme or reason to half the pranks I pulled back then. My best footage came from the roasts at the end of each phase, where we would give our instructors a taste of their own medicine. During that particular BUD/s class, all the diving instructors were East Coast SEALs who loved to talk about how much character they'd built in the frigid waters of the Atlantic. We had a lot of fun with that skit—"When I was a SEAL, we used to duct-tape chunks of steel radial tires to our feet, and that's how we got around."

BUD/S was and is a kind of lawless torture chamber where anyone who signs on the dotted line can be subjected to six months' worth of ceaseless violence and persecution. But outside of Hell Week, they do actually let you sleep. And for me, knowing that every day had an end was a key component of my coping strategy. You spend most of your time living for your next meal. You're burning such a heavy caloric load that most of the guys would add on a fourth meal after we got back from the debrief at the end of the day, huge plates of spaghetti and meat sauce from the local pasta joint or entire large pizzas. If I could get through the next five minutes, the next hour, the next evolution, make it to the next meal, then I could wrap my head around the size of the challenge we were facing. As the course went on, I started learning how and when to take breaks, to regulate my output so I had enough steam to make it through the day.

I'm not trying to say that BUD/s was some sort of a cakewalk. When my parents flew in to see me in that two-day pause after Hell Week, they found a catatonic blob, bloated like a corpse that had been sitting in salt water for a few days. You're chafed in places you didn't even know existed, your eyes are swollen shut, your legs are blown up like tree trunks, and your feet are so huge you have to buy sandals two sizes up just to get around for the next couple of days. To complete your swollen couch potato look you've got a big old bald spot from running around carrying a fucking boat on top of your head for five days.

One of my first calls during that break was to Scotty. We hadn't spoken in months, but I still couldn't wait to tell him that I'd made it through the hardest part of BUD/S.

"Guess what?" I shouted into a pay phone in the barracks. "I'm gonna be a fucking SEAL!"

And just like that, our friendship was reinstated.

The joys of BUD/S weren't quite over yet. The punishment of Hell Week is strategically followed by hydro-reconnaissance training, a week of measuring ocean depths to identify landing opportunities for larger vessels. The low-tech training block harks back to the Navy SEALs' origins as UDT, the Underwater Demolition Teams that cleared the way for the Normandy invasion during World War II. You're out in the ocean with a slate board, depth-reading using a lead line fitted with knots in three-foot increments. You count the knots until you hit bottom, reel in the line, mark the depth on your slate, then swim fifty meters and repeat. At the end you can create a contour map of the sort that would allow amphibious crafts to land contingents of marines. Satellite technology gets the job done nowadays, but it's a piece of the training in which we're all proud to take part. It's also the one time you appreciate spending large portions of your day in 55-degree water, because the ocean becomes your own personal cryotherapy chamber. The cold takes care of the swelling and aches, and salt water is great for all those pesky open wounds.

Most aspiring SEALs bite the dust long before they get to experience that brief reprieve. Gary was medically rolled back once again on the basis of his knee, calling it quits the second or third day of Hell Week. After starting out as a mentor, he'd gradually turned on me when I outpaced him, throwing out this jealous, competitive vibe that was actually a rarity in the environment. The insurance scams he'd been doing back in Houston caught up with him when a law enforcement official showed up and pulled him out of BUD/S to ask him about the Chinese mafioso running the operation. Getting caught up in a federal investigation might have had something to do with his increasingly shitty attitude, but I think it was mostly a personality thing. Still, he wound up giving BUD/S one last chance after going back to the fleet and finally made it through on his third try. He was determined—I'll give him that.*

---

* Gary and I had our differences, but in the end he turned into an excellent SEAL.

One thing I can't recommend to any prospective SEAL is having a common last name. Emerson isn't my birth name—it's an alias I adopted to keep my family safe. But my real name is just as common, and there were a bunch of other BUD/S students with the same one in our class. Several of them, one in particular, happened to suck. The shitty Emersons were a long shadow that followed me throughout the first phase of BUD/S. But no one did more damage than that one POS.

At the end of every day of training, you wind up in the classroom for a debrief of the day's evolutions and some prep on what gear you'll need for the next cycle of torture. You also sign off on any deficiency chits for poor performance. Students can be written up for each individual exercise (from pull-ups to running to swimming), and the Emersons made a habit of doing just that. At the end of each day there'd be a dozen deficiency chits for the shitty, poor-performing Emerson and his friends, and guess who went up to the front of the classroom and signed every single one? An unlucky guy named Clint, whose first name put him at the top of the alphabet.

Only a sucker for punishment is going to argue with an instructor. They could tell you that the sky is brown and the earth is blue, they fucked your mother last night and tongued her dumper, too—and if you don't enthusiastically agree you'll be dropping and giving them a hundred. They don't really give a shit who's wrong or right. Once you become a SEAL and get a few deployments under your belt, insubordination becomes a mark of your experience and individuality. But as a young aspiring frogman, there's no such thing as "That wasn't really me." Your scripted, one-word response to any question under the sun is simply "Hooyah!"

Each night as the other students went back to the barracks to drink a gallon of watered-down Gatorade, eat another huge helping of starch and protein, or pass out, an instructor would lead me and another student named Rodriguez in three-hour sessions of "remediation training"—another name

for pounding your ass so hard that you'd hopefully give up and quit. For *many* weeks this little mix-up caused me to get my ass violently reamed on a nightly basis. We'd get back to the barracks well after nightfall, wet, sandy, and miserable with the other students all tucked away in their racks. The other guy, Rodriguez, had definitely been earning his own chits, because he truly sucked. The instructor, a dead ringer for Richard Gere, was superfit and straight from DEVGRU, ███████████████████████ ███████████████████.* He liked to lie out on his lawn chair catching the last rays of sunlight while we rotated PT with buddy carries late into the night. It was push-ups, pull-ups, eight-count bodybuilders on the grinder, then pick up Rodriguez and haul ass the two hundred yards to the surf zone. Get wet and sandy enough to increase the whole-body chafing, then repeat.

"Why can't you do this during the day?" he'd holler at me. "Emerson, why do you suck so much during the day?"

An enthusiastic "Hooyah!" was the only response I could give.

As Rodriguez started losing energy, his already patchy technique would go down the toilet. One night as he crossed his feet and wobbled through an extra-pathetic set of push-ups, Richard Gere jumped out of his lawn chair and started barking at him like an angry pit bull on methamphetamines.

"What the fuck are you doing?"

We kept up our rhythm as he approached. The last thing you want to do in a situation like that is give an instructor more cause for rage.

"You call those push-ups?" Richard Gere bellowed, getting right up into Rodriguez's face.

Then he took a couple of steps back and landed a Muay Thai kick straight to the poor kid's ankle. It wasn't until our next trip back into the surf zone that Rodriguez told me he thought the bone was broken. The next day he went to medical, and sure enough, he was dropped. He came up with some story to tell the doctor, but something about his

---

* Another pointless redaction suffocating my First Amendment rights.

delivery wasn't convincing. He might have hinted that he'd tripped over an instructor's foot. The issue didn't work its way up the line until I was the last of the Emersons standing and my trail of deficiency chits had vanished into thin air.

Leadership still didn't know exactly how Rodriguez had hurt his ankle, but they had a feeling there'd been a witness. They hammered us as a class, but I wasn't saying shit, even when the whole class was repeatedly pounded with extra PT. (Sorry, fellas.) Eventually enough suspicion built up to have Richard Gere put into instructor purgatory for a while. He'd crossed that fine line between squeezing and actually breaking government property.

As for me, I started and finished with BUD/S Class 203, and graduated in February 1996. It's rare that guys graduate from the same class they started in. In my year there were 28 out of an initial 180 who didn't quit, get dropped, or get rolled back for injuries. Including the second- or third-timers who rolled in at different phases, BUD/S Class 203 finished with 40 or so men. I don't actually remember seeing anyone ring the bell during Hell Week. But the group had noticeably thinned out by the last day.

It's a little twisted, but I freely admit to *wanting* people around me to quit or get injured. It fueled me—every guy who disappeared was a jolt of energy for me. *That will never be me,* I remember thinking when I spotted a bunch of guys dressed in the Dixie cup sailor hats and denim the command forces all quitters to wear.

I wasn't the greatest athlete. Or, by a long shot, the biggest guy. I could do pull-ups for days, but I was a middle-of-the-pack runner with underdeveloped leg strength. In the water, my skills weren't anything to write home about. It helped that some of the swimming and diving skills were already familiar to me from my scouting days. But any advantage

I'd racked up as a teenage diver evaporated in the face of collegiate swim champions, a hundred pounds of equipment, and violent trips through the surf zone that turned us all into human tumbleweeds.

The overemphasis on BUD/S in the public imagination puts too much attention on the physical demands of the job. If that were all there were to it, the only requirement would be a CrossFit certification. The truth is, being able to do a hundred push-ups a minute doesn't count for dick on the battlefield. You're breeding warriors. What you want is the guy who's going to show up when you need him with his weapon ready, instead of crapping his pants in the corner. And it helps if he's not some dipshit you're going to have to spend months with in very close quarters.

Having the mental and emotional fortitude to get through the toughest training on earth is a pretty good indicator of suitability for the job. But the specifics of the actual training don't really matter so much. What's more interesting is that by the end of the course, you all become the same guy. You could take a kid who came out of a trailer park and a Harvard graduate, put them through BUD/S, and by the time you come out on the other end into a SEAL platoon, they're the same person. Physically, the big guys get smaller and the small guys get bigger. Performance-wise, everyone's at the top of their game. And after making it through a course designed to break you, you have this confidence that's borderline cocky, combined with a humbleness that comes from knowing you're never going to be the best man in the crew. The smartest guys realize they're not that smart, and the dumbest guys realize that they've actually got some brains. Anybody who counters that attitude usually doesn't make it through.

If anything, what I had was an ability to tune out distractions, a refusal to quit, and not just a tolerance but an appetite for risk. On some level I just knew that the rewards of getting through BUD/S would be worth the blood, sweat, chafing, potential injuries, and bone-deep exhaustion. Whatever discomforts and physical extremes the course could dish out, pushing through was worth it to me. The image of the trident and everything that was associated with it had been fixed in my imagination ever since that chance encounter at the Frankfurt airport. With college behind me, a career that could channel my proven capacity for trouble-making to the greater good became all the more appealing.

Last but certainly not least—my personal experience of a restrictive, intolerant, and ass-backward culture had only reinforced my sense that ours was worth fighting for. I should probably thank Saudi for playing an important part in getting me to the finish line, by the sheer force of how much that place sucked.*

---

* If you haven't figured it out, I am not a fan of the Kingdom.

6

THE GREATEST BROTHERHOOD ON EARTH

SAN ANTONIO, FORT BENNING, 1996-1997

AFTER BUD/S I WENT ON TO SIX MONTHS OF ADVANCED MEDICAL SCHOOL in San Antonio through the Army's special operations branch. The "short course," as it was then known, was the first leg of the Army's two-part 18 Delta Course, and it focused mostly on paramedic medicine. The students were Special Forces guys and a few SEALs who mostly kept to themselves. I quickly became friends with a couple of the other frogmen: Eric, a half-black, half-white SEAL from California who was always shaking his butt to the music in his head, and Steve, a Kansas City Chiefs fan from Missouri with some Native American blood to match his football affiliation.

When the course was done, Carrie and I tied the knot in front of two hundred of our closest friends, parents, siblings, and extended family. Scotty was my best man, and a few SEAL friends I'd made during BUD/S were standing up at the front of the church beside him.

As the pastor started reading our vows, my groomsmen kicked off their countdown in a very loud whisper.

"It's not too late to walk away, buddy."

"Ten, nine, eight . . ."

Just another innocent frogman tradition meant to cap off a momentous day.

My relationship with Carrie had been in overdrive since our tearful post–boot camp reunion. I'd popped the question at my very next opportunity, after A-school and before even going off to BUD/S. Now I was about to turn twenty-three, making a lifetime commitment to a woman I'd never technically dated in any other capacity but long-distance.

Maybe the fact that we'd never logged time together in an actual relationship wasn't such a problem, since I was simultaneously signing on for a military career that would have me training and operating all over the globe. In retrospect, distance was the only reason our marriage lasted as long as it did.

After finding us a rental in San Diego, I moved her in with a friend, where she'd stay until our new place was ready. She was working in telecom and had found a new job along similar lines. Meanwhile I went on to jump school at Fort Benning, right on the border between Alabama and Georgia.

Jumping out of a plane for the first time definitely tickles the brain. I was surrounded by a bunch of other first-timers, mostly fresh Army recruits, and none of us was feeling too confident. Watching the plane full of uncertain eighteen-year-olds line up for their turn to leap while anticipating my own step out the "hellhole," it was hard not to imagine a twisted scene out of some Road Runner cartoon—each guy jumping straight into an early grave, followed by a cartoon cloud. It got a lot easier after the first few jumps, once we'd gotten to know and trust the equipment.

The next order of business was six months of SEAL Tactical Training (STT) back in San Diego. With the selection-geared trials of BUD/S behind us, the training block now known as SEAL Qualification Training (SQT) would allow us to drill down on the more advanced skills and equipment used in real-world operations. Graduating from the Vietnam-era radios we lugged around during BUD/S to the smaller, better, faster comms we'd actually be using to operate, we got comfortable with an armory's worth of advanced weaponry and learned many more ways of blowing shit up, both underwater and on land. We finessed our understanding of how to use our weapons in tight spaces during close-quarters combat (CQB) training, and added fast-roping and rappelling to the skill sets we'd picked up in jump school during air phase. Visit, Board, Search, and Seizure (VBSS) training applied combat diving and air phase skills to the task of boarding and seizing a naval craft or gas-oil platform, and dive phase had us putting our Draegers back on to master advanced combat diving skills.

After you passed your competency tests and your Chief's Boards (a pop quiz from a room full of master chiefs), STT was technically done. But back then, you still had to prove yourself to your new teammates before you earned your bird. When the training was still managed by the individual teams, graduates were moved into their assigned platoons to join a predeployment workup in a probationary capacity. Nobody was handed a trident until senior members of that platoon had determined that the new guys were ready. That could take anywhere from three months to more than a year. Or never. Your senior peers had the power to shitcan you back to the regular Navy for performance issues. Eventually centralized through Naval Special Warfare, today's SQT is more of a standardized pipeline, automatically awarding its graduates the trident once they've passed through the course.

Now you've got guys with no real-world experience showing up to their platoons with birds on their chest—along with a sense of entitlement that could be a real liability in the middle of a gunfight. The last thing you want on the battlefield is some asshole whose first priority is himself, his personal kill tally, or some combination of the two. A lot of the older SEALs think a valuable vetting and teaching tool was lost when the command got rid of that period of subjective peer evaluation when they started cleaning things up in the name of objectivity.

Whatever the timing, in my day you weren't *really* a member of the team until you'd been indoctrinated into your platoon the good old-fashioned way: through some ceremonial hazing. I'd selected SEAL Team 3 as the first choice on my wish list during BUD/S. Back when the teams were still geographically specialized, ST3 owned all of the operations in the Middle East, putting that team at the top of many new frogmen's wish lists since there was always a good chance of things heating up in its area of operations.

I happened to get lucky and draw my first choice.

In the spring of 1997, Eric, Steve, and I checked into SEAL Team 3's Foxtrot Platoon. Our workup took us through dozens of locations. The loss of our innocence didn't occur until later in the year, just before Christmas leave, as we were finishing a session at a shooting school outside Memphis.

Platoon leaders like to take care of any unfinished administrative business before going on leave. In our case that meant stripping me and Eric down butt naked outside our training quarters to kick off a timeless ritual that inevitably involves nudity. Even in the dead of winter. Eric and I were wrapping up the day and cleaning our weapons when we realized that the other guys had slowly trickled out of the room. Suddenly the entire platoon rushed inside in their flight suits. For added drama they'd pulled balaclavas over their heads.

"You're going down, motherfuckers!"

We tried to give them a good fight, just as a matter of honor. But our fates had been sealed for months.

Our brothers in arms threw us to the ground, restrained our arms and legs, arranged us into a sixty-nine position, and duct-taped our faces to each other's balls.

"Jesus," I mumbled, directly into Eric's ball sack. "What the fuck is wrong with you people?"

They just laughed diabolically in response.

"Let it happen, boys. You might even enjoy it."

---

* Let's all take some comfort in the fact that the turds at the Department of Defense were forced to closely review the image on the opposite page.

They had a point in that squirming around was useless. Our noses were tucked into each other's assholes, which made breathing just as refreshing as it sounds. To make the whole situation even more enticing, they brought out a couple of mini blasting machines, the hand-cracked devices that use an electrical charge to set off ordnance. They stuck the leads on both of our asses, cranked the shit out of the machines, and laughed their faces off as our ass cheeks gripped in response to the electroshock therapy. Why, yes, the gripping *did* clamp our butt cheeks that much tighter around each other's faces. Did I mention that the whole time we'd also had beer bottles stuck up our asses and catheters rammed up our urethras?

Luckily, Eric and I were both good-natured guys who were able to laugh through our screams. The two of us were wrapped in that sweet embrace for several hours before we were finally set free, left to reclaim what was left of our dignity on the freezing asphalt beside the pool. The burn from Tabasco sauce being dripped down your urethra lasts about a week. The feeling of brotherhood is forever.

We're still friends twenty years later, so that tells you something.

Two medics is the standard in a platoon, but the Navy's call for recruits during a shortage had created a temporary surplus among the new guys. Our third, Steve, wasn't around for that special event in Tennessee, but he was treated to a party of his own later on back in California. There's a problem with rats on the island of San Clemente, where we would occasionally return for additional training, and glue traps are everywhere. So naturally Steve had a bunch of wriggling, half-dead rodents glued to his body and head.

There's lots to say about hazing and its usefulness as a team-building tool, if you ask me. But here's the short version: if you go your whole career as a SEAL without ever being hazed, then nobody really ever gave a shit about you.

The weekend after I finally got my trident, in July 1997, my parents came out to San Diego for Naval Special Warfare's Fourth of July demonstration. Before we got too busy fighting wars, the NSWC used to put on a big, ceremonial show of force, with SEALs parachuting in from the sky, divers emerging from the sea, and massive explosions out on the water. Family and friends would come out to watch, and the show attracted a devoted fan base. Certain unmarried SEALs had been known to print their phone numbers on laminated cards they'd hand out to women in the crowd as they came crawling out of the water.

As a graduation gift, my dad had refurbished his old 1970 Triumph Trident. The same kind of bike Evel Knievel used when he jumped the Caesars Palace fountains in 1967 and wound up with a bunch of broken bones and a concussion. Dad had painted the bike black, refinished it with chrome, and attached two golden tridents to either side of the gas tank. After the two and a half years of studying, training, and focus, he was so damn proud to see me at the finish line.

Dad, Mom, and Beej had arrived in town a couple of days before the ceremony to spend some time hanging out with me and Carrie in our condo on 28th Street. The day before the show, my dad woke up with a headache and told us he was going out for some aspirin and a newspaper. The trip should have taken him ten minutes max. When a half hour turned into forty-five minutes, we were starting to think he'd gotten lost. Eventually I decided to drive around the neighborhood and look for him.

On my second round back to the house I found my mother in tears. My uncle Drew had called to say Dad was in a local hospital—a nurse had found my uncle's business card in Dad's wallet. Uncle Drew didn't have much information, but he thought he'd heard Dad's voice in the background of the call.

As far as we knew, he was in a hospital, but conscious. We figured he'd fallen, or maybe gotten hit by a car.

But when we got to the emergency ward, a nurse started walking us to the room with a cross on the wall. The room you walk into for one sole purpose—which is finding out that your loved one has died. I'd spent enough time in hospitals to know you don't want anything to do with that room. Instead of following in her footsteps, I veered right, pushed open a set of swinging doors, and walked straight into the ER, yanking open the first closed curtain I found.

My dad was already in a body bag with an endotracheal tube sticking out of his mouth. He'd had a heart attack and died before even making it to the hospital.

Later, hoping to reconstruct what had happened, I found the paramedics who'd brought him in. I'd just been through paramedic school and needed to understand the sequence of events for myself. Mainly I wanted to make sure they hadn't mistaken my dad for an older guy who'd fallen on hard times and was living on the street. He was wearing one of the regulation military brown T-shirts I'd get for him at the Navy Exchange on base and hadn't had his morning shave.

It turned out he'd died right there on the street. He'd fallen between two parked cars, where nobody saw him for a while. One of the paramedics told me he might have had a chance if he'd been found sooner. A woman who lived in an adjacent condo thought she heard someone cry for help, but couldn't see anything when she looked out her window. She'd come down later, when the paramedics were out front, to find out what was going on.

We skipped the Naval Special Warfare show, flew him back to Dallas in a steel box, and buried the best person I'd ever known with a simple graveside ceremony. His life had ended just as mine was beginning.

I still had the mark of the trident on my chest, in the spot where my new teammates had taken turns punching it in as hard as possible. They'd left a spreading purple bruise around the outline I would now symbolically wear over my battered heart.

7
BIG SHIPS

PERSIAN GULF, 1998–1999

MY FIRST DEPLOYMENT TOOK ME TO INTERNATIONAL WATERS OUTSIDE Iran with SEAL Team 3's Foxtrot Platoon. Embedded with a small group of giant warships as part of an Amphibious Ready Group (an ARG), we roamed the oceans on standby, ready to deploy to potential hot spots in the Middle East at a moment's notice. With a detachment of Marines and Navy sailors five thousand strong and various airborne assets, tanks, and amphibious vehicles on board, the floating task force was an all-purpose, ready-to-launch war delivery system containing a landing force (the Marines), a waterborne attack force (the Navy), and a small direct-action unit (the sixteen-man SEAL platoon).

At the time, the Pentagon's focus for maritime ops in the region was Visit, Board, Search, and Seizure (VBSS) missions targeting noncompliant boats running dark in the Persian Gulf. Smugglers were illegally exporting huge quantities of Iraqi oil from Saddam's regime onto the black market, and we were tasked with enforcing the United Nations sanctions they were flouting. Originally imposed during Saddam's invasion of Kuwait, the sanctions were meant to pressure Saddam into giving up his suspected stockpile of "unconventional" weapons—a gray war that would eventually turn bloodred. But the bigger picture behind the sanctions or Saddam's regime didn't occupy much of our headspace.

All we knew was that the shipboardings kept us busy. Busy was good. We could count on the smugglers to engage us in a complex bit of moonlit choreography nearly two nights out of three.

Those rogue captains carrying embargoed contraband had been working their routes for years, smuggling a combined total of nearly half a million barrels of oil over the decade. Their trade was profitable, so they were highly incentivized to dodge our interdictions.

Hugging the twelve-nautical-mile mark that divides territorial waters from international domain, boats carrying contraband would sail the narrow international shipping lane after nightfall. Foxtrot Platoon would spread ourselves out in international waters, small, dark, and inconspicuous in our RHIBs. Typically we wouldn't be sitting out in the water for too long before our radars detected the arrival of a big, suspicious-looking fish barreling along the edge of the shipping lane with its lights out.

When our radars pinged, we would motor into formation and approach at a clip. And if the captains saw us coming, they would veer their tankers into Iranian waters. The U.S. Navy isn't allowed to wander into territorial waters on a whim, particularly not those of America-bashing regimes looking for any excuse to fire off a warning shot. If the captains reached Iranian waters it would be game over. We'd have to retreat back into our lane and wait for the next big fish to come along.

But more often than not, we caught up with them. And then it was game on.

As our boat teams steered the RHIBs toward the ships, we'd jock back up, doing last-minute checks on our weapons and tech. Since the captains clearly weren't in the mood for a friendly visit, we were gearing up for the "boarding" portion of our VBSS routine.

██

███████████████████

██

██

███

███
███
███
███
███
███
████████████████████████████████████
███
███

████████████████████████████████.* Once we were on the boat we found that a little shouting in the international language of "Hey, buddy, you're totally fucked!" didn't hurt. and was usually enough to get the guys to comply pretty quickly.

"Get on the ground, motherfucker!"

After restraining the crew and taking control of the steering, we'd begin the process of search and seizure. If our searches turned up oil or weapons contraband (or any of the other trade items on the list of sanctioned goods), we'd hand them over to NATO forces, who would take custody of the ship and steer it to Bahrain.

We'd honed the skills we needed during our yearlong predeployment workup back in Coronado. Every workup rotates through our full complement of sea, air, and land warfare capabilities, with extra emphasis on the scenarios the platoon is most likely to encounter at its next destination. Training on GOPLATs in an offshore oil field near Santa Barbara, we'd spent an additional two weeks for just this purpose. It helped that I'd met the two other new guys, Eric and Steve, during 18 Delta. But by the time we deployed, we'd logged so many hours together as a platoon that all of the guys felt like a second family—with a few weirdo stepbrothers thrown in the mix. In that category was a SEAL named Donny,

---

* Similar material has been published without redaction in at least one other Pentagon-reviewed SEAL book.

who lived and breathed the lifestyle of the Bruce Willis character in *The Jackal.* His hair was dyed a pure platinum white, and when he wasn't in his cammies, he wore black from head to toe. He drove a friend's 1985 Ferrari and lived in a small houseboat, but told everyone his house was a yacht. Carrie and I always felt a little funny socializing with him and his wife, like they were subtly trying to recruit us to the swinging life. After leaving the Navy he moved to Vegas and was never heard from again.

Two of the men in our platoon were former Marines: our point man, Ray, a barrel-chested, clean-cut quiet professional; and our hard-as-nails, equally low-key chief. Winning the chief's trust was a significant milestone for us all. The guy was such a badass even dolphins perceived him as a threat.

We got so aggressive in the frequency of our stings that the bad guys started nailing barbed wire or makeshift spikes to the sides of their boats to impede our progress. The captains and crew would even weld themselves into the bridge. Since the smugglers' goal was to slow us down long enough to get over to Iranian waters, every second counted. A couple of times, their stalling tactics worked, and we had to hop onto our RHIBs in a hurry. The Iranian fleet was small but would have liked nothing more than a chance to fuck with the American Navy. We weren't looking to give them any excuses.

SEALs tend to complain about being attached to ARGs and spending the bulk of a six-month deployment at sea. The nature of the beast is that, as a roving readiness force that basically roams around looking for trouble, you might spend a good amount of time twiddling your thumbs, crammed into tight racks and sharing small spaces with your entire platoon. I'll never forget the night I woke to the sound of crunching, intermingled with episodes of heavy breathing, and caught Ray in the middle of a weird werewolf ritual in the tiny bit of floor space between our racks.

Instead of howling at the moon, the guy was butt-ass naked, alternating sets of push-ups and eating Doritos out of a giant bag under the dim red glow of the lights used to light the way for the night crew. But for all its charms, in the late 1990s, being loaned out to a Big Navy ARG for maritime interdictions and sanctions enforcement in the waters around the Middle East was your best chance of seeing some action.

My left nut wound up seeing more than it had bargained for the night it got caught on the side of a ladder somewhere off the coast of Iran. Water, sand, and balls don't play well together, so SEALs generally go commando to avoid chafing. Well, that day I found out there were worse things than a raw, chafed nut sack. ███████████████

██

██

██

██

█████████████████.* Things might have worked out differently on a colder night. But it always stayed hot as hell over there after sundown, so the temperature had the family jewels hanging low. As I climbed, my pants and left nut somehow got twisted up in the spot where the rung connected to the ██████████████ rail. And when I reached up with my right foot and hoisted myself onto the next rung, I felt a shooting pain worse than a kick in the nuts from an elephant in steel-toed combat boots. There was nothing to do in the moment but just think to myself, *Holy crap, my left nut might be broken,* take a moment to detach my junk, and keep on climbing.

That's the story of how I strangled off my left testicle's blood supply, permanently turning its contents into a mangled bag of worms.

Another time Eric and I were the first two men on board the bridge of a massive tanker. Normally, ████████████████████████

---

* I'm starting to think the reviewer has some kind of personal vendetta against nut sacks.

███████████, the unexpected sight of a bunch of Navy SEALs materializing in full commando gear on the deck of their ship was enough to stop the captains and crew in their tracks. On this occasion the two massive bearded dudes we confronted on the bridge were totally unimpressed by our automatic weapons and our sudden appearance. Their response to our orders to get down on the ground was something on the order of "Fuck you," and their heavily Eastern European–accented voices betrayed a general lack of attention to the rule of law.

We couldn't just shoot them unprovoked, as they clearly seemed to know. So Eric and I slung our rifles behind our backs and pulled out our pistols.

The pistols would help us wrestle them to the ground. In the way that a muzzle strike to the forehead tends to get someone's attention in the middle of a fistfight.

Even on less eventful boardings, you never knew what you were going to find. One night we pulled up alongside a fifty-foot-long fiberglass dhow, the traditional working boat of Asia and the Middle East. Through our NODs we could see a huddled mass of some twenty sleeping people beginning to stir. Once we boarded the craft, our support helos came in close, shining their lights into the boat as they hovered. In the massive spotlight we saw rats the size of housecats intermingled with the boat's unlucky occupants—probably Pakistanis being smuggled to some equally cramped quarters to become part of the semi-enslaved workforce that packs the world's tuna and cleans its toilets. The same population who'd done the dirty work at ARAMCO, and another form of contraband we occasionally encountered in the Persian Gulf.

Those dhow seizures became so common that we eventually started to facilitate our boardings. Though the ships were a whole hell of a lot smaller than trawlers or container ships, they were still taller than our RHIBs. Too tall to hurl ourselves over, too short for our ladders. So we ██ ████████████████████████████████. SEAL innovation at its finest.

It was a busy deployment, all the more enjoyable for its link to the activities of our World War II forebears, the Underwater Demolition Teams (UDT) who'd made history on the beaches of Normandy. We weren't clearing mines or booby traps, but like them, we were small groups of men using unconventional methods out at sea. Combat diving and shipboardings are embedded in our identity and our training, but in today's real-world operations SEALs are much more likely to insert by helicopter than swim up on a target. We all liked the element of historical throwback that made the missions seem that much more authentic. For me it was close to ideal as a first deployment that allowed me to apply a bunch of the skills I'd learned in a real-world context.

With war a remote concept during the Clinton administration, Naval Special Warfare would deploy its platoons to potential hot spots around the world, shuffling its assets in the hopes of getting its men actionable experience. Embedded in waterborne task units or stationed in far-flung bases, we were like freelancers, waiting for a gig. Soon our dance card would be full.

8

BIG SHIP, LITTLE SHIP

GULF OF ADEN, YEMEN, 2000

BETWEEN MY FIRST AND SECOND DEPLOYMENTS THERE WAS DRAMA ON the home front. My brother, Beej, was turning into a dick of a teenager.

My dad's sudden death three years earlier had left my mom a single parent, and without a male presence around to tame him, Beej had started getting into fights as he entered his teen years. He was slipping away to friends' houses for days at a time, coming home drunk, letting schoolwork slide, an angry fifteen-year-old who'd mouth off to anyone who got in his way. Nothing too extreme, but it wasn't good news, either. The real issue was that my mom's midlife-crisis disappearing act had left a lasting mark. As a result, Beej didn't have a lot of regard for her authority. Behavior that could have been managed in a two-parent household was going unchecked. After several hysterical calls from my mother it was clear that the situation was getting out of control.

My early experience as Beej's caretaker had left me as the lone male authority figure. Eventually I made the executive decision to step in.

"Pack your shit," I told Beej when he came home from school one afternoon in the spring of his sophomore year to find me sitting on the back porch. "You're moving to California."

I wasn't that interested in his protests. They seemed halfhearted, as if part of him appreciated being rescued from his self-destructive spiral. He admitted as much years later.

"Here's the deal," I said as we pulled onto the highway the next day. "You're coming to live with me and Carrie. You're going to follow my rules, and you're going to straighten your shit out."

No stopping by his girlfriend's house to say good-bye, no going-away party with his friends. I drove us straight to San Diego. Then I took off to lead dive and GOPLAT training for incoming members of SEAL Team 3. At twenty-six, only three years out of BUD/S, I was a little young to be an instructor. But the teams were running their own trainings back then, and at the time they happened to be understaffed on the instructor front.

In retrospect I should have consulted Carrie before making the decision to move Beej into our home. Especially since she was about to become his main caregiver. But when you sign up to become a SEAL, your time is no longer your own. Whether you're leading dive training on an island a stone's throw from your house or anchored to an ARG many thousands of miles from home, you're in the wind for most of the year. In those rare periods of time when you're actually sleeping in your own bed, there's a crapload of shit to deal with around the house, and you learn to make decisions quickly. You can accrue a lot of responsibility pretty quickly in the military, and particularly within the SEAL teams, on a timeline that doesn't necessarily match up with your emotional maturity.

I was busy in Coronado and San Clemente for most of the spring of 2000—but not too busy to notice that the dynamic between Carrie and Beej wasn't great.

A few months later I was reassigned to a new platoon and shipped back off to the Middle East, where I expected a repeat of the same kind of ops Foxtrot Platoon had seen in the Gulf. After a stop in Hawaii, we made our way to Australia, where we spent a month testing a new high-speed, lightweight catamaran.

After that a detour took half the platoon a little ways up north through East Timor, an island that had bounced between Portuguese, Japanese, and Indonesian occupations before coming under the supervision of the United Nations in preparation for its eventual independence. Starting in the fall of 1999, an allied peacekeeping force had been working to tamp down an anti-independence militia. A year later, things had gotten hairy. We'd been called up to clear a beach so that any Americans in the area could evacuate, a short mission that went off without issue.

SEAL Team 3's Golf Platoon was temporarily stationed seven hundred miles away in Bahrain when we got word of the attack on the USS *Cole* on October 12, 2000.

An 8,300-ton destroyer designed to defend a Navy fleet had been felled by a surprise attack in the Port of Aden. Two terrorists in a fiberglass speedboat with four hundred pounds of explosives on board had blown a hole in the galley of the destroyer just as the crew was eating lunch. Seventeen American sailors had lost their lives. Forty others were seriously wounded.

All deployed ships in the area sprang into action. Other detachments were on-site within hours to help triage the injured and take away the most gravely wounded. Two days later, we boarded a Navy assault ship and began working our way toward Yemen. That a tiny rubber boat could wreak carnage on that scale against a behemoth of modern wartime engineering was hard to comprehend, and it set into motion a reckoning that would eventually alter the Navy's security protocol.

When we arrived, we found a heavily traumatized crew. Pumping bilge from the listing ship, they'd been putting out fires and standing watch for days without relief. In the lingering October heat, with the ship's power and refrigeration systems blown out, the bodies and the food in the hold had started to rot.

I immediately approached the ship's corpsman to offer my assistance in my capacity as a medic. The most seriously injured had been taken to a local hospital and were on their way to being life-flighted to Europe. The rest were under his care. He asked me to look out for any member of the crew who needed to talk. Some crew members who'd been presumed dead were discovered many hours after the attack, immobilized by shock in various parts of the ship. Others had been trapped in rooms on upper decks by compartments that had blown up through the floor. Because the compartmentalization used to ensure watertightness creates a closed environment for shock waves to ricochet through, explosions on board a ship are especially violent. One kid had both legs broken when one of the ship's sixty-pound steel doors blew off its hinges. Others had been deafened in one or both ears. Each and every one had lost close friends in the attack. And for the moment they were trapped at the site where the trauma had occurred.

Golf Platoon slept aboard the ship for the first couple of nights, the silence punctuated by the sound of crew members crying out in their sleep as they relived the incident in their nightmares. We were sleeping in dead men's racks, pictures of their families all around us.

The Navy custom of honoring fallen soldiers by removing your hat as you walk through the galleys had never seemed so apt. In this case, the galley—the site where any sailor who loses his life at sea is stowed until a burial can be arranged—had become both a crime scene and a temporary morgue.

The attack wasn't the first of its kind. In 1993, a group of jihadists attempted to take down the World Trade Center with a 1,200-pound bomb packed into a rental van. In 1996, the Saudi branch of the terrorist organization Hezbollah took nineteen lives and injured many hundreds with a truck bombing of an Air Force housing complex in the Saudi Arabian city of Khobar. In 1998, al-Qaeda had killed two hundred people with simultaneous truck bombings of U.S. embassies in Kenya and Tanzania. And in January 2000, al-Qaeda had set the stage for this most recent attack with an attempt on a U.S. ship in the harbor of Aden.

This time they'd succeeded.

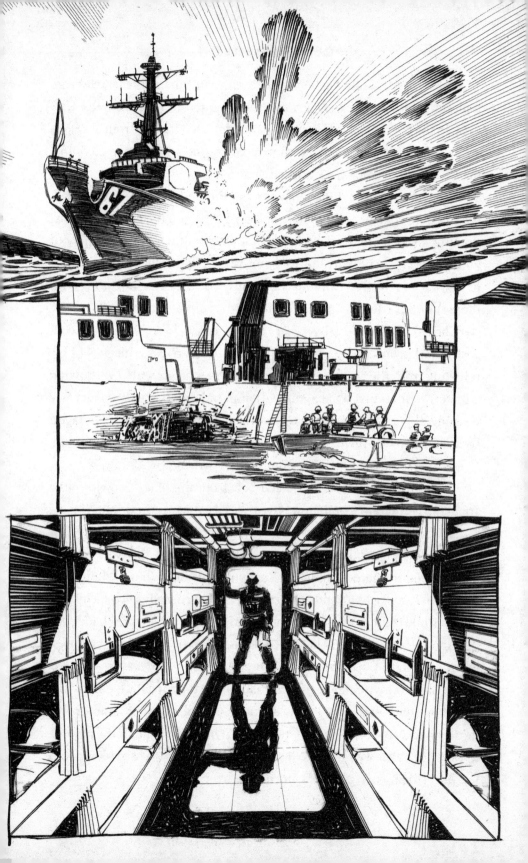

The terrorists hadn't achieved their ultimate goal, however. Not content with the damage they'd done, they wanted to fully sink the USS *Cole*. In the coming days U.S. intelligence detected threats from al-Qaeda affiliates over unencrypted maritime radio channels. They were planning, they claimed, to come back and finish the job.

Given the potential for a follow-on assault, Golf Platoon set up round-the-clock surveillance on board to stave off further damage to the vessel. Rotating in "dead man" rounds, we took the night watch, swapping out with a contingent of marines from our ARG. At dawn we would ride our RHIBs back to the USS *Duluth,* which had set down its anchor along with the rest of our ARG a couple of miles farther out at sea.

Chosen by the Navy two years earlier as an alternative to the congested harbor in nearby Djibouti, the Port of Aden was a dicey spot for refueling from the start. Yemen was a violent, chaotic state overflowing with terrorist groups. That similar attempt in January had been an early warning about the lack of security in the harbor. But as the Pentagon commander in charge of the Middle East put it soon after the hit on the *Cole:* "Aden was the best out of not many good choices."

At the time the attack felt like a bolt from the blue. Knowing little about the perpetrators or their motives, we all wondered how much inside assistance the suicide bombers had received. The harbor at the Port of Aden had been eerily quiet the day the *Cole* came in to refuel, a noteworthy detail that pointed to the possibility of Yemeni collusion. When a significant American ship docks in a third-world country, you usually get a sprinkling of locals lining up in the harbor for free MREs and other Navy handouts.

Another interesting detail that got passed around through the ranks: when a military vessel moors in a foreign harbor, it's Navy custom for the captain to invite the harbormaster aboard for a meal. Generally the harbormaster jumps at the chance. But on October 12, 2000, rumor was he declined. Must have had a better invite. Or an inkling that the guided-missile destroyer was about to have a forty-by-sixty-foot hole blown into her port side by two al-Qaeda suicide bombers.

Whoever was involved, the attack had been diabolically well planned, with a hit to the galley timed to inflict maximum damage, and the harbor was a tense stew of unknowns and potential threat. We'd been assaulted during peacetime, immediately escalating our security posture from standby to full throttle.

Aside from a few small boats occasionally testing the five-hundred-meter perimeter we'd established, however, the area surrounding the ship was relatively quiet after the attack. Most of our company as far as seacraft consisted of a bunch of abandoned Iraqi tankers, left to rust in place since the retreat of Saddam's forces from Kuwait during the First Gulf War, nine years earlier.

The biggest threat seemed to come not from the sea but from the docks, where a number of Yemenese army troops had spread themselves out with antiaircraft guns. They'd supposedly shown up to help secure the harbor.

Strange thing was, their guns were pointed *toward* the USS *Cole*.

At best the Yemenese soldiers pointing antiaircraft guns toward a distressed ship docked in their harbor with full permission of their government were ass-backward. At worst they were al-Qaeda recruits who'd help plan the attack from the inside.

Maybe they were just jumpy. A battery of battle-ready Navy ships had joined our ARG on-site, and the imposing flotilla loomed in the distance. Some serious American military power was being projected onto the poorest country in the Middle East.

From our point of view, we'd just been attacked on the banks of a country whose politicians regularly urged their followers to commit jihad against America on national TV.

So, logically, we occasionally whiled away the hours by pointing our infrared lasers directly into the Yemenese soldiers' eyes. Over time, exposure to the lasers, visible only through our own night-vision devices, would definitely have fucked with their vision. Not an action sanctioned under the rules of engagement of any land. Then again, we were at sea.

In the coming weeks, the FBI agents who investigated the attack repeatedly found themselves in similarly confusing situations. Greeted on the runway by a bunch of Yemenese special forces soldiers with AK-47s pointed their way, they were perpetually an inch away from armed conflict with the guards supposedly securing their hotel.

We were still getting the lay of the land when I received an urgent Red Cross message from the operations room: "Contact home, family emergency."

I called Carrie from the deck of the USS *Cole* on one of the ship's mobile satellite phones, expecting to hear that another parent had passed or that she'd fallen seriously ill. Instead I got a reminder that the word "emergency" can have very different meanings in the civilian and military worlds.

"Your brother is out of control," she said in her steeliest voice. "And I need you to come home."

Carrie knew as well as I did that nothing short of a death in the family would have prompted the U.S. military to send a soldier home in the middle of an active deployment. Especially in the middle of an international crisis. She was also a twenty-six-year-old bride who'd been unexpectedly saddled with sole responsibility for an increasingly out-of-control teenager. Deployed soldiers were a lot more disconnected back then, with the Internet in its infancy, and connections at sea were as slow as molasses. To a certain extent, any problems back home were out of sight, out of mind. But the dynamic between Carrie and Beej, not great from the start, had worsened in my absence. I'd left her alone with a simmering pot, and the pot had boiled over.

Beej had added a few new tricks to his usual pattern of insubordination. Walking around shirtless with scratch marks all over his back after losing his virginity in our guest room was just the start. The little fucker had also somehow managed to convince his girlfriend's parents that he was being mistreated at home. He failed to mention the reason Carrie had taken away his lunch money. (He'd been blowing it all on weed.)

The authority issues he'd had with my mom were amplified, partly because Carrie was so young and wasn't working so hard to hide her resentment at being stuck dealing with him. A big chunk of that resentment would have been turned my way, if I hadn't been eight thousand miles from home.

Eventually, it would.

"Put him on the fucking phone," I told her.

I let him have it, told him he could expect to have his skull beaten in the next time he saw me—a threat I wound up making good on more than a couple of times.

We had dead American sailors below deck or in the process of being dredged out of the water, scores seriously wounded, a crew in shock over the most serious attack on American forces in years . . . and here I was, dealing with a fifteen-year-old's crap. Couldn't this kid see that there were bigger things going on in the world?

There wasn't much else I could do from a ship on the other side of the world, so Carrie reached out to the nearest male authority figure we could think of to arrange for a man-to-man talk. The SEAL Team 3 command master chief had been a mentor to me. Maybe a visit from him could help straighten Beej out.

What happened instead was that Beej blew up and threatened to punch the master chief's wife in the face. The kid was a mess.

Despite Carrie's entreaties I still had to close out the rest of the deployment with my platoon, guarding the listing destroyer as the MV *Blue Marlin* drifted our way. We spent an excruciatingly long forty-five days awaiting her arrival, then standing guard as the *Cole* was slowly loaded and fastened onto the gigantic heavy lift ship that would bail her home.

With the U.S. military on high alert, the Navy had halted the resupply of ships around the world as it reviewed regional threat levels and assessed the probability of similar attacks. With food supplies dwindling on board the *Duluth,* a Vietnam-era amphibious troop transport ship that was one of the older ships in the fleet, the situation got grim. Breakfast, lunch, and dinner was mystery stew from boxes of frozen meat rumored to be labeled "For Veterinary or Military Use Only," powdered mashed potatoes, MREs, and whatever protein powders we had left in our lockers. As the shock of the attack faded into the reality of working the vampire shift over a two-month-long surveillance gig, the guys started getting antsy. What we really wanted was an opportunity to strike back. We'd felt the weight of our uselessness ever since our arrival on scene.

But it would be a few months before the CIA and FBI completed their investigations and decisively attributed the attack to al-Qaeda.

A lot of dumb shit went down aboard the *Duluth* as we awaited our deliverance in the belly of the ship. Glen Doherty, a fellow medic and a sniper who was becoming my closest friend in the platoon, was lifting weights down in the gym when he somehow managed to smash the head of his dick between two forty-five-pound plates. Nothing ice, over-the-counter painkillers, and a lot of teasing couldn't cure, but it sure wasn't pretty. Glen had joined the teams in his mid-twenties, a free spirit who'd racked up nine lives' worth of experience before getting into the military. He'd grown up wrestling and boxing, done time as a semipro-level ski bum, hitchhiked around the United States following the Grateful Dead, and worked on a fishing boat in Alaska. Along the way he'd collected a lot of great stories, which is always an asset when you're stuck on board a ship cutting squares across the ocean with thousands of other men.

We spent so much downtime in our festering racks that at one point Shane Hyatt, an explosives specialist who liked to roam the ship's passageways half-naked, decided to try to see how many times he could squeeze off a nut without leaving his bunk. After thirty-nine hours and fourteen separate incidents of self-pleasuring, he declared himself the victor of the Beatoff Olympics. A piss jug and an easy-to-reach locker full of Oreos and Myoplex protein powder were key components to his win. It helped that he was competing only against himself.

When the *Blue Marlin* finally arrived, the *Cole* was towed back to the Mississippi shipyard she'd launched from just five years earlier to be completely rebuilt. Golf Platoon hopped on a U.S. Naval Service ship to Dubai, where we joined some marines in securing the Port of Jebel Ali.

Until the DOD could confirm that the threat of further attacks had passed, the Navy would restart its resupply process at a single, secured replenishment point in Dubai's busy, modern harbor. Golf Platoon was tasked with harbor overwatch, vetting incoming shipping trucks and tugboats hauling food and fuel.

The interlude had a covert flavor that we all embraced, some of us more than others. Given the recent attack on U.S. service members and a mistrust of our shaky alliances in the region, nobody was keen on deploying a full SEAL platoon in broad daylight without taking precautions. Using a service ship as our center of operations, we improvised a cover to reduce our visibility during daytime operations. In the blue zip-up jumpsuits worn by the service ship's skeleton crew, we looked like a harmless bunch of machinists and technicians. Of course we were strapped underneath our coveralls, and a sniper in the ship's superstructure was scanning the horizon for potential threats.

Several other team members milled around on the deck, a few more had eyes on the resupply warehouse, and a cluster of divers surreptitiously examined any approaching tugboats that looked like they might be riding heavy or towing suspicious loads. We kept up our routine for about a month, jumping into position every few days as ships came into the harbor. Eventually the Navy set up a larger security unit with a full-time, permanent presence in the port.

After spending Christmas in Bahrain, we headed to Thailand for a few days' leave. What happened there is too gnarly to print. Let's just say we blew off a substantial head of steam. At our next stop, in Hong Kong, I parted ways with the men. That brush with our domestic situation had convinced the SEAL Team 3 master chief to send me home early on a military bird. The rest of the platoon had a monthlong boat ride to Hawaii before they'd catch a flight back to San Diego.

Back in the States, Beej continued to dish out his bullshit, working himself under Carrie's skin like it was his full-time job. When his girlfriend broke things off, he'd posted a seminude selfie she'd given him all over their school. Now my little brother had a restraining order against him. Apparently the fat lip I'd given him on my return from deployment hadn't done the trick. One night we woke to the sound of him hurling his guts all over the bathroom, so Carrie started lighting him up for driving home drunk. Maybe Beej was just planning on getting in her face when he lunged toward her. But it sure seemed like he was fixing to hit her. I threw him in the bathtub, punched him, choked him out, and left him there to cool off.

The very next morning he came down to the kitchen and immediately started cursing Carrie out. The idiot had been so drunk, he thought *she* was the one who'd given him that little bathtub beatdown.

Either way, it didn't seem like he'd gotten the message. So I kicked his legs out from under him, slammed him into the floor, and choked him out again. As far as I could see, he had two options: start respecting the other members of his household, or get his ass beat every goddamned day. Not being a total moron, he chose the first. It took a while for the tough love to take effect, but eventually things quieted down in our house, and Beej got his shit together. After a year living under our rules, he was able to go back to Texas to finish out high school with his friends.

That early parenting experiment wasn't quite so successful for Carrie. Any deployment is hard on any military wife, but she'd inherited an angry and confused teenage boy before we'd even gotten around to having a baby of our own.

Every SEAL's wife understands that the job will always come first. But there are times in a marriage when that pill can be an extra-bitter one to swallow. For Carrie, the moment when I foisted Beej on her without her consent was a clear demotion from second to third place. She ended up using that deployment against me for the rest of our marriage.

I understood her point of view, to an extent. But I wasn't about to let my little brother turn into a piece of shit if it was preventable.

For the rest of us, the events of October 2000 would take on a different significance. Terrorist attacks of the past had targeted embassy buildings, the occasional airplane, or hotels and cafes crowded with Westerners. Sowing fear and chaos by randomly butchering innocent civilians and diplomats was their cowardly stock in trade. Now they'd struck directly at the American military, nearly sinking a billion-dollar guided-missile destroyer and killing seventeen of our sailors. It was the kind of surprise attack that would have been called an ambush if it had taken place on a battlefield. But it hadn't.

As SEALs we'd been trained to fight over any terrain and under any conditions. But we'd always figured we would be the ones locating the threat, protected by top-of-the-line weapons and technology and our allegedly superior intelligence. Now the threat was anywhere we were, our fleet had been made to look vulnerable, and our intelligence agencies appeared to have been caught completely off guard. The world was a war zone, the threat a couple of men in a tiny boat. Or, as we'd eventually come to learn, a few passengers on a commercial aircraft, a single driver behind the wheel of a rented truck.

The attack was simple, but the planning and intelligence behind it were complex. The terrorists had known where and when to strike for maximum carnage. And they didn't mind blowing themselves up to meet up with those seventy-two virgins on the other side, a fucked-up belief system that just added to the unpredictability of the assault.

Its perpetrators, like the leader we'd all come to know in the years ahead, were mostly Saudi born and bred.

That piece of information doesn't get nearly enough attention, if you ask me.

A certain Saudi Arabian–born militant named Osama bin Laden had declared war on the United States of America all the way back in 1996. One of his central grievances? The presence of U.S. troops in Saudi Arabia, closely followed by American support of Israel. Saudi oil fields had always looked like a tempting target for Saddam Hussein. In the aftermath of his invasion of Kuwait in 1990, Bin Laden, the radicalized son of a wealthy Saudi family, had offered the royal family the protection of his militant followers. They'd decided to go with the United States instead, to the tune of half a million troops over the course of Operation Desert Shield.

The Saudis, who'd go on to revoke his citizenship in 1994, hadn't taken him seriously, and neither had we. What could this bearded, sandal-wearing exile hiding in the mountains of Afghanistan do to us? Unfortunately it would take an attack on an even greater scale than the *Cole*, designed to demonstrate our vulnerabilities and make the world take notice, before we did.

There were signs missed on all sides, by the intelligence community, the military, and the press. None of us had recognized the threat posed by the attack on the *Cole* and the previous attempt at Aden, because we were still in the mindset of perceiving war as a contest between nations, involving huge numbers of soldiers, tanks, and weapons. The last entity we'd perceived as a direct threat was the Soviet Union, which had collapsed while I was still in high school. But now our world order had irrevocably changed, and our days of pining for action on ARGs were behind us for good.

9
LIVE TISSUE
TRAINING

FORT BRAGG, NORTH CAROLINA, 2001-2002

IN THE SUMMER OF 2001, A BREAK IN NAVAL SPECIAL WARFARE ACTIVities allowed me to follow up my medic training with the second part of 18 Delta training, the "long course." Seven months of advanced medical training out at Fort Bragg in North Carolina.

Now consolidated into a single block, the long course was a full-fledged medical school at light speed. What regular medical students learned in four years, we learned in about half the time, with an emphasis on treatment over theory. We went through civilian paramedic classes; lab training that enabled us to read our guys' blood work in a combat theater or a jungle miles away from any decent hospital; trauma medicine; and advanced field training that prepared us for worst-case-scenario mass-casualty situations. Then, like med school graduates in their residencies, we were embedded in a number of hospitals for supervised rotations. The difference was, none of our patients knew we were members of the military.

Preparing Army Special Forces medics and a handful of SEALs for a spectrum of eventualities, from chemical warfare to dengue fever to emergency amputations, our condensed, hands-on training has its quirks. To speed up our absorption of the material and ensure that we get real-life experience as quickly as possible, we use one another as guinea pigs. That

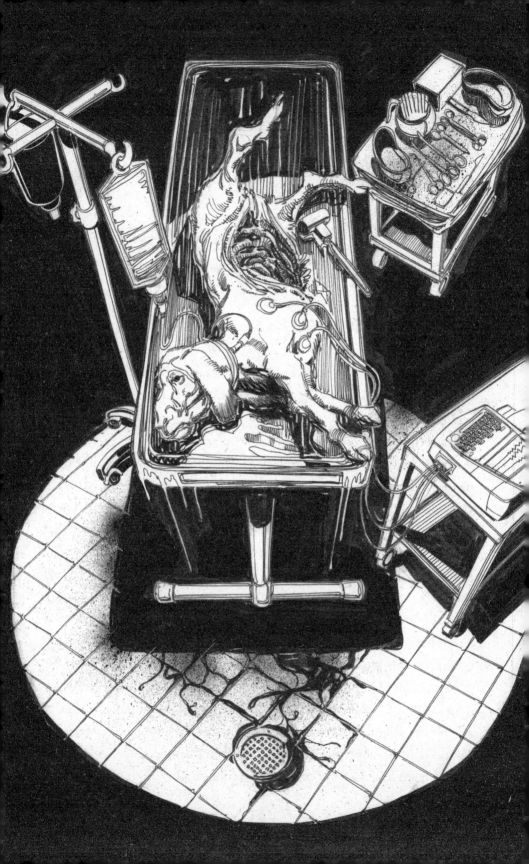

means when it's time to learn about examining a prostate, you're literally bending over in the classroom and shoving your finger up one another's asses. You put on a glove, lube up with some K-Y, and look for the smooth, round nub that feels like the cartilage at the tip of your nose. You've got one finger up your partner's asshole, the other touching your nose to compare textures, and you're palpating for any nodules or unusual stiffness.

The commentary is priceless.

"Relax—your mom loved this last night."

"Jesus, you're tighter than a ten-year-old boy!"

Everybody's second-favorite procedure, urethral catheterizing, aka having a needle of pain threaded up your dick, gets the same treatment. Except when I say needle, picture a catheter the size of a drinking straw.

Sure ain't the way they do it in medical school.

There's also a lot of emphasis on that old-school lab work—counting white blood cells and scanning samples for anomalies under a microscope. Machines can do that work very quickly, but we needed to be prepared to check our teammates for infectious diseases in third-world countries where the only equipment we'd able to count on were a microscope, bell counters, and slides.

You can't practice amputation on a friend, so when it comes to live tissue and trauma medicine, we switch to a different kind of four-legged mammal—the large flock of goats in the climate-controlled barn adjacent to our classrooms and labs. Your collateral duty is feeding, caring for, and cleaning up after the animals, and you wind up learning a lot about your four-legged charges. One thing that stuck out to me was what happens when a sick goat is separated from the flock. Give him a buddy in the pen on the left and a buddy to the right, and once they're in his sight line his condition will start to improve. Sequester him to protect the rest of the herd, and his condition will deteriorate fast. They're social animals, like us, and their survival depends in part on their cohesion with the flock. They bleed just like us and share our basic anatomical structure, too, which is where their bad luck begins.

It looks like the DOD is gradually reducing its reliance on live tissue training, so all you PETA members ready to start letter-writing campaigns can turn your attention back to Sea World. The goats are never in pain, their living conditions are humane, and they've got a bunch of Navy SEALs and Green Berets in raincoats and rubber boots cleaning up their droppings with squeegees and fire hoses. Sure, if the military can find a way to create simulations that are just as effective at teaching combat medicine without the animal bloodshed, I'm all for it. But if you wouldn't sacrifice ten goats to save a human life, you've never held a young marine with an AK-47 round in his gut. Even Shane Hyatt, who kept a picture of his dog in the place in his wallet where the rest of us had semiclothed shots of our wives and girlfriends, would say the same.

The other thing that struck me is that there's always an alpha in the flock, whose job it is to keep the herd in line and kick any troublemakers' asses. If there's one goat who's being a prick, the leader of the pack will come out of nowhere and strike the misbehaving goat with its head. It's interesting, because you might assume that the goat acting like a dick was the alpha, when in fact the leaders are always pretty calm. That's sort of the ideal when it comes to special operators, too. What you want is a dominant personality that's also extremely controlled. It's precise, targeted action you're after, not random bar fights, although we do indulge in our share of those every once in a while. Sometimes they find us.

One likely spot, until it closed, was a bar called Tortilla Flats in San Luis Obispo. Located near our training facility ███████████████ and popular among the SEAL community, the place had earned the nickname "Tortilla Fights." One reason why was the famous MMA fighter Ken Shamrock. His gym, the Lion's Den, was nearby, and rumor was he'd tell his students to test out their skills by picking random fights with SEALs. Thanks to Ken, everyone had a Tortilla Fights story. One night I was standing there at the bar with Eric, who'd continued on into long course with me, when of those Lion's Den fuckers smashed a beer bottle into the left side of my face. Blindsided and close to blacking out, my primary response

was to bleed profusely and lose several teeth. Eric guided me outside the club, holding my nose as I exhaled to assess the damage. Sure enough, my lower left eyelid filled up with air—the prick had fractured my maxillary sinus and lower orbital ridge. Damage to sinus function is bad news for a SEAL, and the doctor I visited on base a few days later said my chances of diving again were slim. Fortunately for my career, my sinuses healed up just fine, and the only permanent damage was some lumpiness on the left side of my face.

What did I do to deserve that friendly kiss on the cheek? The only possible provocation was my T-shirt, a freebie I'd gotten off a Danny Inosanto seminar. But in Ken Shamrock territory, repping a martial arts instructor who'd trained with Bruce Lee was the Tortilla Fights equivalent of flashing a gang sign.

The guy had disappeared into the crowd in the direction of the bathroom, so we went back inside the bar and jumped the first dude we found in the can. Eric threw punches while I held the prick from behind. The only problem was, Eric was shitfaced, so every other punch hit me in the head.

A few months later I smashed in the same side of my face during a helicopter jump. The deployment bag containing my chute, which was hooked on to the end of the static line, landed me with a brutal left hook that punched a few of my remaining teeth straight through my lip.

That sucked.

Never having been a top-of-the-class student, I was pretty surprised when I came out of the medical long course as the honor man, which meant I'd be promoted a full rank. I hadn't ever studied that much in my life. For me that achievement really solidified the extent to which becoming a SEAL helped me tap into potential no one really predicted. The change in rank also meant I'd be eligible for a promotion to a leadership position within my platoon, to LPO (Leading Petty Officer)—the guy in charge of running the boys, making sure their bags are packed, and translating the chief's orders at ground level.

Once my activities took me into the covert realm, my background as a medic became nothing more than a convenient cover. But at the time I could tell you the length of the loop of Henle that extracts water and sodium chloride from urine as it passes through your kidneys, or that atropine (used as an antidote for nerve gas poisoning or for cardiac arrest) reduces parasympathetic response by competing with acetacholyne at the nervous system's synaptical receptor sites.

After the long course, the SEAL medics went on to study paramedic emergency medicine, dive medicine, and orthopedics. You see a lot of shit when you're riding around in an ambulance, and one night while we were out on call in San Antonio during paramedic school, a car in the right lane caught my eye as we pulled up to an intersection. It was dark, past midnight, but the stoplight was shining a reddish glow onto the driver's face. Tears were streaming down her cheeks. When the light turned, her face changed, and she floored it.

I watched her speed ahead through the windshield from my seat in the back of the ambulance. The paramedic sitting in the front seat glanced up from his paperwork.

"Looks like she's in a hurry."

We all had our eyes on the road at the moment when, instead of taking the hard left at the dead end, she plowed straight off the asphalt and onto a field. Her car rolled over several times, headlights and taillights flashing in a discombobulated jumble in the night.

The radio was still playing as I came over to the driver's side. Steam was hissing out of the radiator, but otherwise it was eerily quiet. She wasn't behind the wheel. But there was no hole in the windshield where you'd expect a body to have gone through. The two paramedics scanned the field with their flashlights. I went over to the passenger side. Nothing. But something on the floorboard caught my eye.

She was folded down into the space between the seat and the dash like a pair of pants. Her legs were tucked up into her chest, but her head was flipped completely backwards, resting on her spine. Her lumbar had snapped, leaving her face tilted directly up at me, her eyes wide-open and her cheeks still wet with tears.

I'd gotten close to bodies on board the USS *Cole,* and during the dissection component of our paramedic course, but hadn't come right up to the moment of death up till that point.

You had to wonder what her story was. She happened to be gorgeous, in her early twenties. Her path from the stoplight seemed deliberate, but there are easier and more dependable ways to off yourself than to go skidding out onto a plateau. Could she have just been speeding too fast in the dark, crying too hard to notice the end of the road ahead? Drunk off whatever bender had led to her filling her trunk with a twelve-pack of Miller and peeling down the same street our dispatcher had brought us to? Seemed like I'd never find out.

Two weeks later, a fellow medic and I walked into a Joe's Crab Shack in a different part of town for lunch. While my friend was talking to the hostess, my gaze wandered over to a nearby shelf. It had been repurposed into a little altar for a burnt-out candle and a framed picture. Inside the frame was a face I'd grown intimately acquainted with for a brief but memorable moment in time.

I turned back to the hostess.

"Hey, can I ask who that is?"

It turned out the stranger in the car had been a waitress at that same restaurant.

"She died two weeks ago in a car accident."

That episode gave me this strange sense that I was walking through my life like a character in a movie, showing up in scenes that were connected to one another somehow. I didn't have the script tying it all together, but odds were nobody else did, either.

Once we'd graduated from 18 Delta, an ongoing slate of refresher courses and sustainment training would take us back into hospitals for modified rotations and to Native American reservations where sewing up stab wounds and extracting rotten teeth was the unfortunate norm. But the truest, day-to-day reality of the job itself was the examination of enough herpes-covered, black-and-blue, and just plain ugly Navy SEAL dick to last me many lifetimes.

You'd never imagine dick injuries could be so common until you personally witnessed the aftermath of a penis being crushed to a deep vascular purple between two forty-five-pound plates or seen what one wrong step on a ladder could do to your own testicles. Then there were the STDs, inevitable even in a platoon with just fifteen other guys. I'll never forget the kid who came to me with a herpes breakout that he'd spread all over the place in an attempt at shaving the problem away.

"You married?" I asked.

"Uhhh, yeah," he replied. "What does this mean?"

"Let's talk this through," I said, putting on my best bedside manner.

Sucked to be that guy.

Echo Platoon was particularly susceptible to medical malfunctions. Our long list of injuries and maladies ran from Matt Mills slicing off his thumb with a rotary saw to an outbreak of the superbug MRSA. Methicillin-resistant *Staphylococcus aureus* is usually contracted in hospitals and nursing homes, where the bacteria evolved to survive antiseptic environments. How four of the members of our platoon caught it during a stateside workup or a jungle training block in the Philippines was a mystery to both me and Glen Doherty. Matt, a new SEAL who in typical form had been the first to exhibit symptoms, had scratched the wound on his side and spread the bacteria around his torso and neck. The multiplying ulcers had acquired a dark, necrotic look. The ailment I mistook at first for a spider bite revealed its contagious nature when the men began passing it back and forth as we hopped between Singapore, Guam, and then back to the Philippines. Soon several of the boys were covered in huge, painful ulcerated lesions. To prevent necrosis, the immediate course of treatment was a series of radical debridements. Unfortunately a numbing shot of Lidocaine was no match for the gory process of slicing, squeezing, and spongeing the infection out of the wounds by any means necessary. The poor guys would sit there biting down on towels as Glen and I cleaned the wounds, packed them with gauze, and repeated the process until the infections abated. Just a little while later, "Rico," a Puerto Rican SEAL with the physique of a Greek god, got so fucked up by dengue fever that Glen and I had to immerse him in a bathtub full of ice to bring his temperature down.

Hands down, my favorite medic story of all time involves Mike Ritland, Echo Platoon's intel rep. We were already pretty friendly, but we got *real* close a couple of months before our second deployment together, and my third took us to Kuwait, then on to Iraq.

We'd stopped in Singapore for a couple of weeks during our deployment to train with the Singaporean SEALs, mostly on close-quarters combat and in a simulated GOPLAT environment. Not knowing what was ahead of us in the Middle East, we were making the most of a relatively cushy situation—a peaceful urban environment, decent hotel rooms, real food. Only some guys just don't know when to stop. Due to an extremely overenthusiastic consumption of hotel buffet cheese, Mike hadn't had a bowel movement in a week. A giant piece of compacted fecal matter was stuck in his colon, bloating his stomach out like he was six months pregnant with a baby made of cheese and regret. We tried laxatives, made sure he was hydrated, had him chomp on a bunch of dried fruit. Nothing worked. When he called me up in agony I told him there was only one thing left to try. Then I rallied the rest of the boys and told them to meet me at his hotel room in ten minutes. I prepped a glove and some K-Y, had Mike bend over the bathroom sink with his pants down, and waited for a knock at the door.

"Wanted you to have an audience, Mike," I said as the rest of the platoon sauntered in. By then I'd been promoted to LPO, a level of authority I was definitely abusing at this particular moment.

"Fuck you guys," he said.

Then he just leaned back over the sink.

"Whatever."

He was so damn desperate to get that baseball-size shit out of his ass that he just did not fucking care at that point. I squatted down and started digging around in his rectal canal like an auto mechanic with his hand up a tailpipe, two fingers in knuckle-deep. The thing was hard as a rock, but eventually I was able to break it up with a come-hither motion.

Gotta do what you gotta do. That's the day-to-day life of a medic in any corner of the military. But asses were just a sideline for me. Without a doubt the main focus of my tenure as a medic was the male phallus in all its various shades of glory and disrepair.

There's nothing like quality time to foster intimacy within a platoon. Email access wasn't a given in those days, and we'd sometimes go for weeks without communicating with our families and significant others. Distance multiplied by temptation could be a potent stew, and the steamy cloud of built-up testosterone in our all-male environment pressurized the pot. The lid would blow off at intervals during shore leave, aka liberty or "letting the animals out to play."

Those moments of freedom could create the kind of memories you'd rather forget. Like the time I busted in on my swim buddy at the exact moment when he slipped a dirty submarine to a very surprised lady friend. Call it a rusty churro or an unexpected rear entry, if you need it spelled out. That chick jumped halfway across the room, and somehow he still convinced her to get back into the bed. They were so preoccupied they didn't even notice me.

It was a nice break from all the full-frontal masturbation I've witnessed over the course of my career, to be honest. If you were picturing America's elite fighting forces spending their downtime reading philosophy, sorry to disappoint. Most of the time we've got our noses up in the porn trunk and our hands down our pants. Spanking the meat was such an acceptable way to pass the time and blow off steam that we even traded tips, recommending our favorite lubes and jizz disposal techniques like we were trading casserole recipes.

The hunt for private spots to do the deed was an ongoing concern, and some guys just flat-out gave up. There isn't a whole lot of shade in the blasting-hot sand desert of ███████████████, California, where we practice our land navigation skills from time to time. We'd logged the temperature at 119 degrees by midmorning that particular day, and after forty-eight hours of almost continuous trekking, we were beat. We returned to a desolate base camp, so tired, hungry, and thirsty that our tents looked like a mirage. So did the big, fat, baldheaded SEAL sitting in the middle of our camp on top of a bucket, naked as the day he was born except for his combat boots. There aren't a large number of overweight SEALs, but this guy was a bona fide fat-ass. As we came up from behind we could see his ass practically inhaling the bucket. The sweat was streaming down his back, funneling down his crack to the base of that nasty rust bucket where it formed a salty sweat pool in the sand. He'd been sitting like that long enough that a trail of army ants was feeding off the puddle. And, as you've probably guessed, his right shoulder and elbow were violently shaking. He was just staring out into the desert beating his cock to death, burned bright red and glistening in the boiling sunlight like a bald bulldog covered in mayonnaise.

Some things you can never unsee.

I once woke to bright daylight and a continuous, rhythmic slapping noise during a graded exercise in ████████, another middle-of-nowhere California location where we train. We'd passed out under a tree after jumping out of a helicopter with our Zodiacs, transiting across fourteen

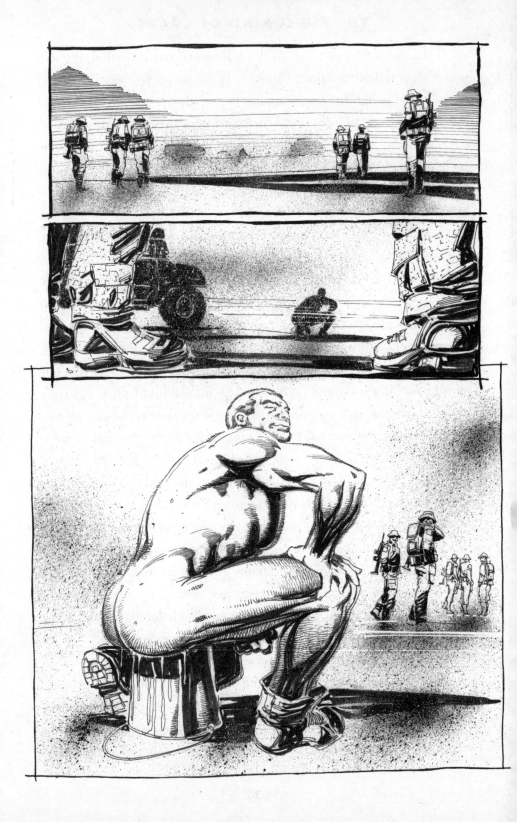

nautical miles of ocean water, and then humping about ten kilometers through the night with our gear and seven days' worth of water and food on our backs. Once we reached high ground overlooking the target, where role players were sitting around a campfire, our job was to collect and send imagery back to the command and control center via satellite. In the meantime we'd rest in shifts during the day.

My lieutenant, Dan, was fast asleep less than a foot away from me. A scan of our surroundings revealed the tree trunk shaking to the beat of the strange noise. I looked up just in time to see our platoon chief, supposedly on overwatch up in the branches, shoot a huge blob of thick, milky goo all over our unlucky lieutenant and his gear. After the deed was done, he shook himself off and tucked away his dick with a self-satisfied grin.

Obviously when the single guys could give their wrists a break and find the real thing, they took the opportunity. But once you've been overseas for long enough, that picture in your wallet or ring on your finger can start to feel a little abstract.

Here's what all the other SEAL books will tell you about our afterhours pursuits: "Things got a little rowdy after those nineteen shots of Bacardi at the Aloha Lounge down in Hawaii, and some of the unattached boys had their fun with the local *wahine*. The women out there were beautiful, especially after twenty-four days of eating snake soup in the forest. But the married men among us hung back at the bar."

That last line is a nice bit of public relations for the SEAL brand, but it isn't strictly accurate. When single guys are scoring all around you and women are hurling themselves at your feet, even the happiest married dudes can break.

I'm not exaggerating about the kinds of opportunities that present themselves on a regular basis, either. Once you become a special operator, even the homeliest guy has some pull. It took me years to realize that, though. For years, I *was* the married guy hanging back at the bar. Which isn't saying I didn't come close.

One night in Bali I was playing babysitter for a bunch of inebriated SEALs at the Sari Club, a tiki-style establishment with thatched huts and palm fronds all over the place. The Indonesian island was a hot spot for Australian and European vacationers, who on this particular occasion included two hot young Danish chicks—a blonde and a brunette, who started chatting me up. Occasionally going off to dance, my new acquaintances kept coming back to the spot where I was nursing a beer to chat with me some more. Ordinarily clueless, this time I was getting the message.

When closing time came around, the brunette asked me back to their hostel a few blocks away. Taking a little stroll didn't feel like an ironclad commitment to whatever was about to happen. If we'd had to get into a car, my conscience would probably have kicked in. But when we walked into the small room with its two single beds, everything felt a whole hell of a lot more real, especially when the blonde came out of the bathroom in nothing but a G-string. When she came over and tried to get in the mix, a wave of guilt washed over me. Making some half-assed apologies, I got out of there in a hurry.

Who knows what they got up to after I left.

On the way back to my hotel I ran into my nuts-to-nose buddy Eric, who'd closed down the bar but still had energy to burn. More than lightly intoxicated, he convinced me to accompany him to a tattoo parlor so he could get inked on his thigh—his flesh being ripped open to reveal lizard scales underneath.

A few years later, the Sari Club would be blown up by a car bomb planted by the militant Southeast Asian Islamist group Jemaah Islamiyah. Another club and the U.S. embassy were hit with smaller bombs. The attack, killing two hundred of the clubs' occupants, was financed by al-Qaeda.

To this day I'm still kicking myself for turning down that threesome.

I was on the Coronado Bridge, on my way to the command for an early morning meeting, when Carrie called with the news that a plane had crashed into the World Trade Center. On base, a group of team members were gathered around a television tuned to CNN, and I rushed onto the quarterdeck just in time to see the second tower hit at 6:03 a.m. PST. By the time the towers came down and a third plane crashed into the Pentagon thirty minutes later, the shape of the world had been fundamentally altered.

There were twelve SEAL platoons deployed around the world at the time of the attack. Within days, several more joined them in the Persian Gulf. And within weeks, another platoon from SEAL Team 3 was on its way to Afghanistan.

After a workup early in the year, the recently renamed Echo Platoon would have its turn in October 2002. No one told us as much, explicitly, but word came down through the rumor mill: Naval Special Warfare was getting its assets into position. There was a high probability that we were going to war with Iraq.

In the months following the attack, we'd all spent time puzzling over its meaning, putting the pieces together. The hole that had been blown into the USS *Cole,* the U.S. embassy truck bombings, the prior attack on the WTC, al-Qaeda, Osama bin Laden, the Taliban, their relationship. In retrospect, these "new" enemies of ours had been coming after us for decades. But how those events were connected to Saddam Hussein and his WMDs was beyond our pay grade. Saddam had been flouting our sanctions and killing off his own people for decades. If suddenly the powers that be had decided to shift their focus to the potential danger presented by Iraq, who were we to question that?

It may sound screwy to civilians, but soldiers train their whole careers for one thing—and it's not growing tomatoes. SEALs train longer and harder for combat than practically anyone else, and our time had come. We were ready.

We were more than ready. We were fucking psyched.

A week after landing in Kuwait, our commander diverted us to the Philippines for a month. The Filipino SEALs were getting ready to confront some Islamic extremists in one of their southwestern provinces. The mission in Iraq was delayed. After that, our platoon was sent to Hawaii and Guam for additional training and rehearsal and some downtime. Every location change involved a massive transport and loading and unloading of gear, which is one of the aspects of being in the military that isn't mentioned in the brochures.

In early February 2003, we were placed on standby in Kuwait, where we began rehearsing the operation to board and secure the Mina al-Bakr GOPLAT, some twenty-five miles offshore.

10
GROUND WARFARE

IRAQ, 2003

THE ALLIED MILITARY ASSAULT BEGAN WITH A SERIES OF AIR STRIKES over Baghdad. Saddam Hussein's location was unknown, but his primary palace was blown to smithereens by day two of the war as ground forces began crossing over into Iraqi territory from the south. As soon as we hit dry land after taking down the GOPLAT during that covert nightime mission, Echo Platoon was ready to join them. But it was another week before we got our orders to pack up our Humvees and head north.

The light-footed precision choreography of our waterborne assault in the Al-Faw peninsula faded into the rearview as we transitioned into ground combat, traveling up Highway 1 toward the cities of An Nasiryah, Baghdad, and Tikrit. Now we were part of the heavy machinery of war, along with the two hundred thousand allied troops moving across Iraq. When we caught up to the front lines, the sight of the combined artillery was awe-inspiring. Swiveling your head in either direction, all you could see was an endless column of armored vehicles stretching out to the horizon, the barrels of their massive guns pointing toward the interior of Iraq. Tactically, forward momentum into the northern cities had always been considered crucial to the assault. But at the last minute, Turkey had reneged on its agreement to let us send in sixteen thousand troops from its territory into the top of Iraq, cutting off a direct path to Baghdad and Tikrit. All we could do now was push on as efficiently as possible from the south.

We were heading to Baghdad when our platoon was diverted to the small city of An Nasiryah, where an Army convoy had made a wrong turn behind enemy lines. A nineteen-year-old supply clerk named Jessica Lynch was lying in an Iraqi hospital with a broken back and crushed legs, a prisoner of war. Eleven soldiers had been killed, and American marines were being ambushed on the front lines.

A portion of the Iraqi military had shed their fatigues when the allied forces rolled into Iraq. Some had gone home to their families—just like their fathers, friends, and brothers had thirteen years earlier, during the Gulf War. Like the soldiers we'd found on board the GOPLAT, they weren't interested in laying down their lives for Saddam. But others had changed into civilian clothes and turned to the guerrilla-style ambush tactics that went on to dominate the war in Iraq over the rest of the decade.

Saddam's batshit-crazy sons, Uday and Qusay, and a few hard-line generals continued to command the loyalty of their troops. The infamously sadistic Uday would probably have enjoyed killing off any deserters, before raping their entire families and feeding them to the lions he kept as pets. His band of stalwarts was hunkered down in the nearby town of Suq-al-Shiyukh. And they were sneaking over from their hideout to a resupply hub and forward operating base on the outskirts of An Nas, to ambush American soldiers in the middle of the night. Shortly after Lynch's capture, Uday's men had laid waste to twenty-nine of our soldiers in a single twenty-four-hour period. On our second day in An Nas, Glen Doherty and I helped the marine medics pull some of their bodies off the front lines. One young marine had been hit in the head with an unexploded rocket-propelled grenade. The entire side of his face and skull was caved in, and as we lifted him onto a stretcher with gunfire in the distance and Cobras whizzing above our heads, our sense of the gravity of the situation was acute. Two weeks earlier we'd been sitting

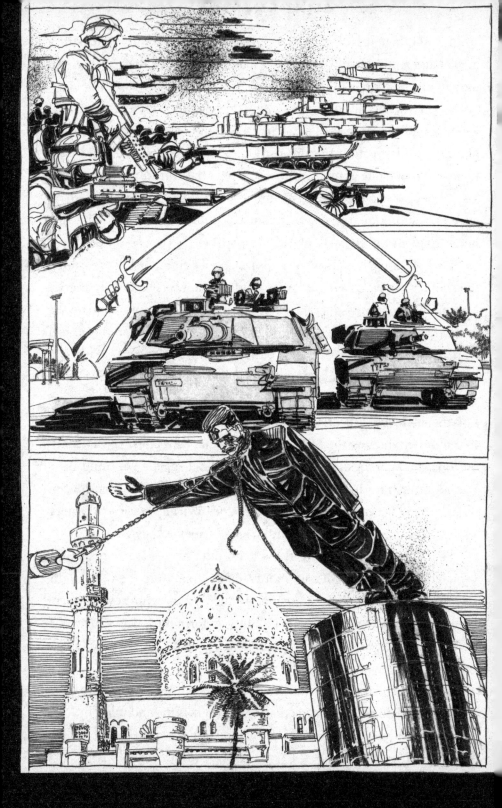

around in our tent city in Kuwait, playing rounds of mini golf with a bucket and a putter. Now these kids, a decade younger than most of the men in our platoon, were being sent home in metal boxes.

When we met back up with our platoon, neither of us mentioned what we'd seen. If the guys were unaware that there were men dying several hundred yards in front of our position, telling them would needlessly fuck with their state of mind. They could hear the gunfire and explosions just as well as we could. There was no need to reemphasize just how close any soldier in an active war zone was to potentially losing his life. Better to focus on the tasks ahead.

Two Marine generals whose names should ring a bell were calling the shots in An Nas: General James Mattis, who was heading up the 1st Marine Division, and General John Kelly, his second in command on the ground. Later that day General Kelly briefed us just a few hundred feet from the front lines, looking each of us in the eye. "There's a small town suburb area full of bad guys, population eighty thousand, forty-five klicks to the southeast," he said. "That's your area of operation. Go over there, find the men who've been killing my marines, and start killing them." In that moment, he saw the SEALs as extra guns, with a few special skills on top. The general's troops needed relief, and maybe we could help. Without much in the way of specific intel regarding their identities or whereabouts, he wanted us to descend on the town and take no prisoners. We were going to ambush the ambushers, whoever they were.

The rules of engagement in the beginning of that war were pretty vague. Later the ROEs got a lot more nailed down, from the rules themselves to the paperwork soldiers had to file and the attorneys who got involved. But at that point we had all the information we needed. We quickly nicknamed the town Suckass and prepared to go face-to-face with the pricks who were killing marines.

Except our commander had a different idea. He got in a helicopter, flew back to Kuwait, and immediately got on comms and told our leadership that it would be too risky for us to comply with General Kelly's orders. The highest-ranking Naval Special Warfare commander in Iraq at the time, he was a supposed hard-ass who'd been commanding officer during my first couple of years at Team 3. He was ultracompetitive when it came to training, the kind of guy who'd do anything to get ahead, from cutting swims short to actually dunking other SEALs to improve his time. But when it came to the battlefield, all that bravado shrank down to the size of a shriveled testicle in fifty-degree ocean water.*

In a pattern that would repeat itself throughout that deployment, we got the word that leadership was pulling the plug on the Suckass mission.

"We're not putting our boys in harm's way."

"There are too many unknowns."

It was the classic "Nobody's dying on my watch" mentality. And it meant we had to stand down on a call for help from a Marine general in the middle of a shitstorm.

Navy SEALs are supposed to be used for targeted, well-planned missions with a beginning, a middle, and an end. The disconnect between our original mission and the current reality was causing some reticence on the part of our commanders. But we were already being deployed in an unusual capacity that had us moving forward with the war. What was the point of wasting our skills when we could have been put to use saving lives and putting down Uday's henchmen? We were an elite fighting force being treated like a bunch of teenage girls out past their curfew.

Eventually we learned not to ask for permission from our direct commanding officers for small, local ops. We'd get the Marines to tell us where the heat was and follow up on their intel. Later on we moved into a task unit headed by a commander who had more of an aggressive spirit. Once he got a taste of the kind of overprotectiveness we were being constrained by, he laid down a new law: "From now on, we're not telling them what we're *going* to do. We're telling them what we *did*."

Back in An Nas, Echo Platoon was diverted to securing roads and

---

* Naval Special Warfare leadership was a shit show, then and now.

bridges for the remaining supply convoys. The troops ferrying munitions and life support from Kuwait into Iraq continued to make a visible target, and the camp was periodically under siege.

We stuck around in the area until the POW situation was resolved. Our peers rolled in for the Jessica Lynch rescue while Echo Platoon looked on from a nearby position. The Iraqi soldiers guarding the hospital had already taken off by the time we showed up, and the operators didn't face any resistance on their way into the building.

———————

About a week later, our platoon got into mid-convoy position in the middle of the night with the goal of a predawn departure for Baghdad. We were continuing our northward march. Or we would be, once we got our act together.

In the time it took for the thousands of marines to rack and stack their vehicles, half the lineup passed out. Long enough for the sun to come up. When I cracked open my eyes to daylight in the rear of the Humvee, I could see our breacher and lead navigator, Shane Hyatt, asleep at the wheel with his nonregulation headgear tipped over his face. Our officer in command (OIC), Dave Janssen, a levelheaded leader with a Tom Selleck mustache, was snoring away beside him. Our comms guy and lead climber, Hank Nicholson, was snoozing in the backseat next to me. Our gunner, nicknamed Dozer for his resemblance to a bulldozer and his tree-trunk legs, would have been manning our Browning .50-cal. machine gun if he hadn't been slumped into the turret. Ahead of us, where the night before there'd been a convoy of fifteen trucks loaded up with marines, there was now nothing but a bunch of tire tracks. Behind us were three Humvees containing the rest of our platoon. And behind them were a dozen other vehicles filled with marines, their occupants all fast asleep.

"Hey, Shane," I called out, "wake up!"

"Oh, *shit*!" he shouted back as he fumbled for his binoculars. "They're fucking gone!"

The front of the convoy had taken off without us, oblivious to the fact that the back half of the caboose had fallen off the rails. We'd been left in the dust, sitting ducks for any member of Uday's forces who might have been looking to rack up an impressive tally of American casualties.

The only thing that diverted Echo Platoon from a trip to the hereafter that morning was timing and luck.

We had an epic boatload of issues with communications and logistics during that deployment. It had been so long since our community had seen sustained action that we were frequently testing equipment or joint operations protocol in the field for the first time. Comms, gear, transportation—in each of these areas we experienced repeated failures. The brand-new ballistic helmets that headquarters had outfitted us with had some serious ergonomic issues. Bulky, heavy, and incorrectly weighted, they wobbled around on top of our heads like clunky salad bowls. Their charm was only enhanced when night-vision goggles were added to the mix. The extra weight of our NODs would drag the helmets forward until they bumped against our foreheads, forcing us to compensate by bolting dive weights to the back. So much for Naval Special Warfare's superior gear and tech.

A few of us opted out of the helmets altogether. Shane, who'd always had issues with authority, wore a ridiculous Australian duster hat that attracted a holy boatload of attention from management. Consequently, as his LPO, I'd taken so much heat over his stupid getup that at one point we'd practically stopped speaking after arguing about it for the hundredth time. Unfortunately for us, Shane felt empowered to wear the hat in perpetuity after having won a bet with Dave, our OIC, during an explosives training session in Arkansas. If Shane managed to set off a complicated timber-cutter charge without a hitch, he could wear the hat whenever he liked. If he didn't, Dave would take a shit in the hat, which Shane would then have to wear for twenty-four hours straight.

My own everyday headgear was a black-and-green checkered *gutra* I'd picked up back in Kuwait City, the same kind of scarf I'd seen around Saudi. Zero ballistic protection, but great for shade and sand. And not nearly as controversial as Shane's Crocodile Dundee crap.

Just as dangerous as our salad-bowl helmets were hearing protection devices that made it impossible to tell which direction gunshots were coming from. But the biggest liability of all had to be our flimsy borrowed Humvees. Our Marine and Army counterparts were outfitted with fortified tanks, but we were cruising around in unarmored Humvees with light-weight plastic doors. Our higher-ups hadn't necessarily been planning on sending us into the fight after the GOPLAT mission, so we'd had to make do with available transport options. At the time the SEAL Team 3 mobility program was dedicated to DPVs—Desert Patrol Vehicles, dune buggies that looked cool but proved to be giant fucking failures. Command hadn't accounted for a new reality in which SEALs would be driving up to a target. We were meant to be a direct action force and were now being used in a conventional, longer-term combat capacity. Fittingly, our military-grade RVs were stocked to the brim with supplies. We were carting around so much shit, down to tents and lawn chairs, fuel tanks and five-gallon jugs of water mounted to the outside of our Humvees in caged racks, that there was barely any room left for the men.

We'd had to laugh when the ███████ guys had rolled up for the Jessica Lynch rescue in their ██████ Humvees and their starched cammies, smelling like Irish Spring after a stay at a Saudi hotel. Some of them had been my mentors during STT, rock-solid operators at the top of their game. But within the community there was always a bit of humor about the privileges their ██████ status afforded them.* They'd done their relatively uneventful rescue, picked up some national exposure, and then gone home to their clean sheets. The rest of us went back to sleeping under our trucks.

---

* For entertainment value, reread redacted portions and replace all redactions with the words "big dick."

Our vulnerability was most obvious when we transited near more densely populated areas. As we moved on from An Nas, we settled into a role that would occupy us for the remainder of our time in Iraq: traveling alongside and sometimes ahead of the troops to provide overwatch and route reconnaissance. We'd sit in the middle of bumper-to-bumper traffic in our fabric Humvees, neck-to-neck with masses of civilians evacuating their cities and towns, wondering if our time was about to be up. We didn't know much about Saddam's Fedayeen, or any of the paramilitary groups or tribal militias operating inside the country at the time. But we'd heard that the bad guys wouldn't necessarily be in uniform. As the supposedly unconventional fighting force, we were now rolling around in camouflage in plastic toy cars, in an environment where the enemy was not nearly as visible. A single shot to a fuel container would have taken any of our vehicles up in flames.

Later on, SEALs in Iraq would be riding around in armored Humvees, mine-resistant ambush-protected vehicles (MRAPs), and tanks. But the level of danger they faced was greater by many magnitudes than what we experienced in the earliest stages of the war. The landscape would only get worse for the troops who came after us, when the insurgency kicked in and the country was littered with roadside IEDs.

To lighten the tension in the air we'd hum the sound track to *Sanford & Son,* a 1970s sitcom about a junk dealer who drove an old, beat-up pickup truck loaded with salvaged crap. The World War II–era frogman armed with nothing but a dive knife had been replaced by a hoarder.

A collateral focus as we transited was the destruction of enemy weapons and ordnance. Heavy-duty rockets, pointed toward Kuwait, had been abandoned or stashed all over Iraq. Smaller caches of RPGs, AK-47s, and grenades were dug into shallow pits in the ground. Toward the end of our deployment we lucked into a massive, twenty-foot-long surface-to-air missile loaded onto a mobile launcher. Blowing that up with several "soap dish" charges, premade sets of C4 explosives about the size of a bar of soap, was just plain fun. The plume of smoke and flame shot about two hundred feet up into the air.

Every few days, we would roll up suspicious men of fighting age and turn them over to the closest conventional unit—particularly if we found any weapons or suspect tattoos. The Iraqi Fedayeen, known for brutally torturing civilians during peacetime, deliberately dressed in civilian clothes to confuse the coalition troops. But they could sometimes be identified by their tattoos—three dots, joined by a crescent moon if the fighter had participated in jihad, or a winged heart with an *F* at its center for aspiring martyrs.

Some of the Marine and Army units started running into Fedayeen launching grenades and firing automatic weapons out the backs of civilian pickup trucks. On a few occasions we took some pop shots from the side of the road and chased down the perpetrators, but for the most part Echo Platoon encountered little resistance. Eventually we caught up to the marines we'd been tailing behind and merged with the 1st Marine Division, a twenty-five-thousand-strong force moving up Highway 1. The convoy wasn't hard to miss. It stretched out for something like thirty miles. Its four brigades had advanced to the southern edge of Tikrit, preparing to take the city at dawn. The line of hundreds of LAVs (light armored vehicles), Humvees, and command/control vehicles was standing down for the night before facing whatever awaited us in Saddam's birthplace, the home of one of his several dozen palaces. Using their vehicles, some of the marines had set up a bumper-to-bumper, acres-wide perimeter at the intersection of the highway and a rural country road.

Through my NODs I could see a field and a small clump of trees off in the near distance.

We pulled up alongside the marines' leadership battalion, who informed us that the area had been secured.

"All right, everybody," I told the guys, "we're inside a secure Marine perimeter, so let's try to get some sleep while we can. Everybody jock down but keep your weapons close."

I took the first watch, scanning the area with my NODs while my guys started loosening their bootlaces and unbuckling their gear. An actual base camp wasn't something we'd be seeing again until we got back to Kuwait. For now, we'd be sleeping on the highway. That was the plan, anyway, until the night unraveled.

No single word can accurately describe the sound explosives make as they detonate. There are actually two sounds: the extremely loud snap or clap that heralds the start of an explosive event as the materials shatter, and the low booming shock wave that comes in underneath as they burn at high velocity.

As the unmistakable snap, boom, and echo of a blast ripped through the empty field, those of us who weren't already on the ground hit the deck.

I looked through my NODs and saw some marines using what turned out to be an 84mm antitank rocket to detonate an Iraqi guard truck. The truck happened to have a shitload of unexploded ammunition on board, so they were doing a good job of turning our camp into a well-lit target. Setting off large explosions in enemy territory in the middle of the night seemed like a pretty bone-headed move. Since most of my guys were on the ground and didn't have their NODs on, they immediately assumed we were coming under attack.

Ghhhh kkhhhhhh khhahhhh khhhhh ghhhhhh.

There wasn't really time for me to set the record straight, because moments after the explosion, all hell broke loose. Several of the marines' LARVs started lighting up the skies with their .50-cal machine guns, and we could see their tracer fire going in the direction of the exploded vehicle. *What the hell?* Why were the marines firing on the Iraqi trucks our aerial attack forces had taken out earlier that day?

The answer came in the form of rounds snapping above our heads. Suddenly we were taking shots to our unarmored Humvees, there was

chaos everywhere, and it was becoming abundantly clear that the marines hadn't, in fact, cleared the area inside their perimeter before we collectively let down our guard.

"Contact, contact, contact!" I called out. "Everybody get ready to fight!"

Sympathetic detonations due to the marines having exploded the Iraqi truck weren't the only noises around. There was also a barrage of enemy fire, and it was raining down on our position from the field to our left.

With the fast-twitch muscle memory response that accompanies a reaction to live fire, the guys grabbed their weapons and got into prone positions. Everything from that point on seemed to happen simultaneously. As the men formed a 360-degree perimeter with guns pointed in all directions, I scanned the landscape in the direction of the fire and pretty quickly spotted three or four Iraqis with AK-47s in ski masks and trench coats, crouched down beside a bush at the corner of the intersection. Clearly they thought they'd struck gold by creeping up on a full division of marines with their guard down. What they didn't know was that at least some of us had full visibility on their asses through our night-vision goggles.

In the middle of the ambush, Matt Mills, still a "new guy" in that he'd earned his trident just a year and a half earlier, started calling out for my help from behind one of our Humvees. The Rhodesian chest harness we used to store our magazines had crisscrossing straps across the back, and in pulling it over his body armor he'd gotten stuck with one arm half in and the other out. Even with bullets still flying all around us, we couldn't help laughing as I helped him cram his arm through.

"Tango, tango, tango," I called out to Hank and Rico, the guys closest to me, as I raised my head to look out over the hood of the vehicle. "Do you see the targets at your twelve o'clock?"

Reaction time may have been a split second delayed, given that this was our very first ambush. Adding to the overall atmosphere of complete and utter fucking confusion was the fact that the gunshots seemed to be coming from an area in between us and some marines a hundred yards away—making the potential for taking friendly fire high. So once we got the bad guys in our sights we didn't immediately open up on them.

The same couldn't be said for our friends across the way, who immediately started shooting their weapons in the direction of the gunfire. A good portion of the bullets whizzing by our ears seemed to be coming from the marines we were supposed to be protecting. But there was no time to attempt to clarify the situation on comms.

"You see 'em?"

"Yeah."

"Well, then smoke those motherfuckers!" I called out.

By then two of the bad guys had disappeared into the darkness, and the operators within range had started opening up on the remaining target. I took a knee and joined Hank and Rico as soon as I looped back around from untangling Matt.

We had the upper hand in terms of visibility, and with several of us firing multiple shots at the target's torso, we had no problem hitting our mark.

We shot the AK right out of the ambusher's hands, and later even saw the bullet holes through the pistol grip and the forward hand grip—along with a few in the hand that had been holding the weapon.

The guy took off running after he dropped his gun. He didn't make it far, but once we caught up with him he wouldn't go down for a while. When he finally did fall to the ground we counted eleven bullet holes in his torso and right arm.

An officer who'd joined us to fire some shots tried to take credit for the kill, claiming his were the decisive rounds. Establishing a forensic timeline in an ambush situation with multiple shooters was pointless, not to mention egotistical. In any case, the "green-tip" 556 bullets we were using in our M4s at the time flew so fast they'd zip right through bad guys without them even noticing they'd been shot. This one even refused to quit breathing.

We approached the target with caution, in case he'd been holding on to a grenade. Shane was tasked with administering the security round.

A shift in our ROEs would eventually make that shot illegal, but it was standard operating procedure at the time. I stuck around to watch the target get his head blown off.

Under his trench coat he was wearing an Old West–style gun belt, like he'd come prepared for a shoot-out. Only thing was, his secondary weapon was a plastic toy pistol, just for show. Guess funds were limited in the cave he'd crawled out of.

Unfortunately his AK was real and it was absolutely loaded, and so were the guns his friends had deployed. Before they disappeared into the darkness, they'd managed to wound a couple of marines who'd stumbled upon them in the field. I rushed back over to our vehicles to join Glen in tending to them. One had been shot in the leg. The other in the chest, by a round that partially penetrated his thoracic cavity.

Glen put a tourniquet on the first marine's leg while I created an occlusive dressing around the second marine's chest wound. Once we got them stabilized as best we could, their commander had them medevaced out. We never found out their names, but I later heard that the soldier with the leg wound didn't make it. The other marine had been partially protected by an ammo magazine and a paperback book in his flak jacket. That book and extra piece of ammunition may have saved his life.

Meanwhile our OIC had been on comms trying to get a line out to someone on their end.

"Cease fire, cease fire, don't shoot. American soldiers are in your line of fire."

Communicating with the Marines and the Army had been a painful proposition from day one of our operations in Iraq. Compatibility between the various systems was always an issue, whether it was UHF versus VHF signals or encryption that didn't match up. Either they didn't hear us or we'd dialed in on a line to Copenhagen, because we never got through to the Marines that night.

Glen ended up busting out into the field to deliver the cease-fire message in person. When our platoon went out to clear the area and look for the enemy combatants who'd run away, we found a little observation nest within the tree line, some thirty feet from the spot where a portion of the marine convoy had pulled over.

Greg Mathieson, an NBC cameraman who'd snuck into Iraq ahead of the war and had posted up with the Marines for the night, actually caught video of the truck blowing up and gave an account of how things appeared from the other side of the perimeter. He and his crew had set up their satellite dish right by the stand of trees the shooters had been hiding in, and at the moment when the shit hit the fan they were lending their sat phones to a few marines who hadn't been able to call home in weeks. Then, as he recounted in an interview in a military journal: "SEAL Team 3 came in behind this guy and took him out in the darkness. We didn't even know [they were] there. The Marines didn't know it, either. They just showed up out of nowhere. One Marine told me, 'Yeah, that's how these guys are. They show up out of nowhere and they disappear into the night. We don't know how they get here, or how they get out.'"

Whatever fancy extraction plan they thought we had in store was just a figment of Navy SEAL myth, at least in this particular case. We'd be rolling into Tikrit at dawn just like everybody else. Despite the harrowing surprise ambush we'd just faced, there were still a few hours of shut-eye to be had. So on this night, like all the others, we all crawled right the fuck back up underneath our Humvees and tried to get ready for whatever the next day had in store.

It's tough to find time to sleep during a war that's in its infancy. At the outset we were always on the move. No fenced-off camps to sleep in, no built-up forward operating bases decked out with gyms and seventy-two-inch TVs like you heard about once war in Iraq became a long-term reality. The comforts of home were whatever could fit in your Humvee.

In the middle of the night I dreamt that a faceless army of Fedayeen in trench coats was creeping over a wall and slicing our throats open, one by one, as we slept. I woke with a surge of adrenaline and banged my head on the bottom of the Humvee.

That's the story of my first combat kill, which isn't even mine to claim. It was a group effort—despite what some lying dirtbag officer might say. Realistically, unless a sniper is involved, most combat kills are group efforts. Technically we'd all just softened him up for Shane, who delivered the final shot.

The scumbag who busted our collective cherry was a foreign fighter, probably out of Syria, who'd come to Iraq for the express purpose of killing Americans. A Fedayeen in a long black trench coat with a balaclava in his pocket—and now a corpse immortalized in a framed photo my daughter grew up seeing every day on the wall in my office.*

SEALs kill people. Everybody knows that. It's part of our job description. This just happened to be a collective first for most of our platoon, aside from the snipers.

A bad guy pointing a weapon at you isn't some abstract moral quandary that keeps you up at night. He might have kids, a brother, a sister, a mother, a father who'll mourn his death, and you'll feel a split second of compassion if you dwell on the repercussions that spiral out from his death. But in the moment, shooting a bad guy pointing a weapon at you poses no more of an issue than shooting a paper target. If it did, we'd have to take a good hard look at our training.

Better them than me or my buddies. And better overseas than in our own backyards here in America. Those were the thoughts that always ran through my mind.

The next day Echo Platoon moved into Tikrit from the east with the Marines' 2nd Battalion, covered by a squadron of Cobra attack birds from above. We were expecting a bloodbath, and we'd manned up accordingly.

* Within a couple of years of Operation Iraqi Freedom, taking pictures with deceased enemy combatants would become a punishable and even court-martial-worthy offense.

What we found instead were empty streets and a deserted palace. The dead quiet gave us a creeping feeling that the previous night's ambush wouldn't be our last. But the assault proved to be bloodless.

The brand-new palace had already been looted, and the world's most wanted dictator had never gotten the chance to move in. His primary palaces in Baghdad had either been blasted into dust by Air Force pilots or turned into operations posts for allied forces. Saddam was already in hiding in the underground hovel where he'd later be found about forty klicks away. Most civilians had hit the road.

The cavernous building was covered with a layer of marble, but you could tell that everything underneath had been put together on the cheap. If any furniture had ever passed through the palace's massive, mosaic-tiled doors, it was gone by the time we showed up. There was a movie theater with a big red curtain but no seats, and more than a few broken windows. So in the end we spent hours clearing an empty palace and then set up our lawn chairs on the front porch.

With the exception of our snipers, who went out to provide coverage for the Marines as they continued to clear the city, the rest of us spent the next three days dicking around on the palace grounds. I used my sat phone to call Carrie for the first time in weeks, told her through her gulping tears that despite what she'd been seeing on the nightly news we were safe and sound. Journalists had been embedded within the troops in the hundreds, giving our loved ones an alarmingly vivid window onto the experience of combat. After I was done I passed my phone down the line.

Once we'd taken turns pissing in Saddam's gold and marble toilet seats and taking water-bottle sponge baths in his showers, the boys and I took some time out for a photo op with our M4s, M60s, and sniper rifles. My trusty *gutra* was wrapped around my head, and for a patriotic touch I'd draped Old Glory over my shoulders.

The flag can be a soldier's last resort signal for help, and in a pinch it might even prevent one of your own bombs from being dropped on your head. Mine went with me everywhere I operated, for twenty years, usually tucked between my body armor and my heart. Later on it would be hidden within concealed compartments in the special luggage I traveled with.

We stayed in the Tikrit area for several days after leaving the palace, then drove all the way back down Highway 1 the way we'd come.

———————

After six weeks in Iraq, we did a handover to a SEAL Team 5 platoon back in Kuwait. Our tents had already been taken over by incoming personnel, and the camp was buzzing with new activity.

At the postdeployment debriefing the next day, Shane joined me in reaming out our leaders in front of the entire team.

"Anybody got anything for the leadership?" they asked after they'd gone through their administrative bullshit.

We sure did. I kept mine short and professional.

"The opportunity to serve our country during active combat is the pinnacle of any soldier's career," I remember saying. "You stole that from us.

"And it might have been our only shot."

Shane went on forever when he finally got his turn. Give that guy the floor and you'll never hear the end of him.

We showered for the first time in more than a month, passed out for two days, then hopped into C-17s and slept the whole way back to San Diego.

When we got onto the tarmac, the relief we should have felt at being back on home ground was delayed by another round of administrative bullshit—a line of vans hauling x-ray machines, U.S. customs agents insisting on scanning all of our gear. Implicitly accusing us of smuggling illegal war trophies wasn't exactly a morale builder. We had a ton of gear, we were jet-lagged and exhausted after six weeks of sleeping with one eye open under our rigs, the process was taking forever, and we were all anxious to get over to the area where they'd corralled the families. Eventually Glen used a bit of his natural charm to distract one of the chicks manning the machines, and I started shoving our gear around the scanners. Another problem solved with a little bit of teamwork.

Despite the demoralizing welcome committee, it was good to be home. Beej had stayed on the straight and narrow, graduating from high school and closing out his first year of college in Indiana. With an empty house and a monthlong break ahead, Carrie and I had the chance for what felt like a fresh start.

Returning stateside from any deployment is like cracking the glass on a black-and-white photo. Even the burritos from the gut trucks that show up on base right at the end of your morning workouts taste great after six months of MREs, and every Home Depot or Walmart has a new significance. You're back in the land of plenty, where the thin piece of plastic you're carrying around in your wallet is the only thing that stands between you and the fulfillment of your every want and need. Carrie and I would typically get a small group together for fish tacos at the house to celebrate, but my list of homecoming rituals boiled down to a solid cup of coffee and a jumbo pack of Kit Kats.

We'd been back only for a week or so when President George W. Bush stood on the deck of the USS *Abraham Lincoln* off the coast of San Diego and declared the end of major combat operations in Iraq, three weeks after the fall of Baghdad. The victory rang a little hollow for those of us who'd felt the tug of an inept command's leash in Iraq. For all we knew this was going to be our only chance to use the skills we'd spent the past decade busting our asses acquiring. What none of us realized back then was that we'd have plenty of opportunities to do so over the next ten years and beyond.

We all found out later that the bureaucrats who'd sold the president

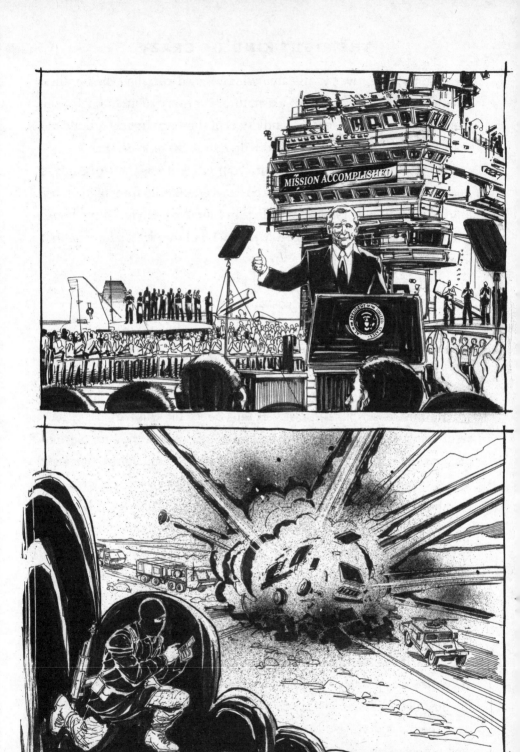

on the notion that we could stabilize Iraq with a lean fighting force had severely underestimated two factors: the chaos that would follow the fall of Saddam's dictatorial regime, and the size of the insurgency that would rise up in its place. Given our quick victory during Operation Desert Storm in 1990, we had all the reason in the world to believe that the band of pussies our military had encountered back then would fold in no time at all. What was really needed in Iraq, it's clear in hindsight, was a sizable peacekeeping force to suppress the insurgency and maintain order.

As for the missing WMDs that made the world question the validity of the whole enterprise . . . We had to ask ourselves why, anytime we rolled up Iraqi soldiers, they'd be carrying a gas mask and autoinjectors of epinephrine and the anti–nerve agent atropine. When questioned about why, they'd inevitably reply with just one word: "Saddam." History had given them plenty of reasons to believe that their leader would be capable of turning his arsenal against his own forces.

Any way you look at it, angels weren't losing their wings when a dictator who'd mass murdered his political opponents and gassed a hundred thousand Kurds was executed by an Iraqi tribunal, five days after Christmas in 2006.

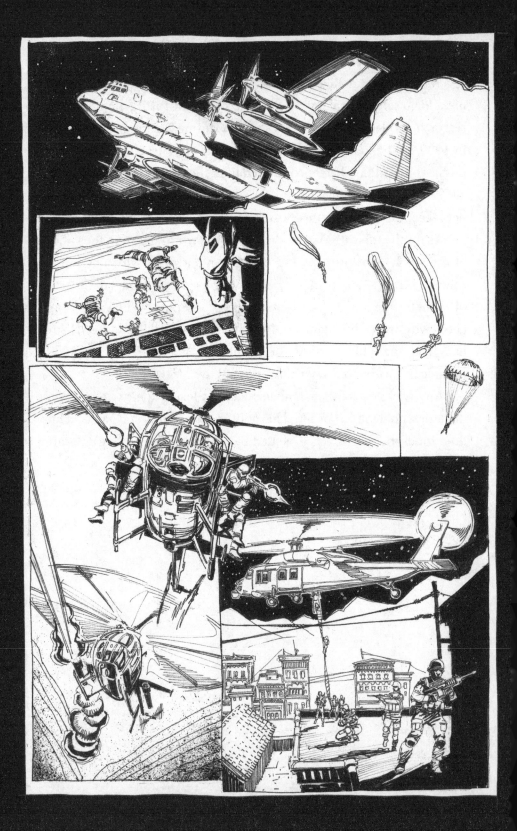

PART II

11

SQUIRREL WORLD

SAN DIEGO, LOS ANGELES, 2003-2004

SOME TIME AFTER ECHO PLATOON HAD GOTTEN BACK FROM IRAQ, THE former command master chief who'd helped out with Beej reached out to see if I wanted to get screened for a sensitive program they were building out. At the outset, he was pretty short on details. But with memories of being hamstrung in Iraq still fresh in my mind, I jumped at the chance to try something new.

We'd kicked off the war in Iraq with the largest coordinated assault Naval Special Warfare had ever undertaken and had blown up plenty of ballistic missiles, IEDs, and a few bad guys along the way. We'd scouted routes and bridges ahead of the Marine convoy and sometimes behind enemy lines, which gave us an unusual vantage point on the type of conventional warfare that, up until then, Navy SEALs usually only parachuted, helicoptered, or swam into and out of. Hell, taking ground was something no division of the United States military had done on that scale since Vietnam. But the powers that be hadn't really known what to do with the SEALs in the early stages of the Iraq War—and my platoon had been held back by a couple of ladder climbers whose primary concern was covering their asses.

At the screening at one of our government-issue beige brick headquarters buildings in Coronado, there were forty or so other SEALs standing in the hallway in their fatigues. A half mile up the road from the BUD/S compound where we'd earned our tridents, that particular command was the epicenter of the SEAL community on both coasts. "Dozer," Echo Platoon's gunner and ordnance specialist, had gotten the call, too. The rest of the guys looked familiar.

We waited our turn before being pulled into a windowless conference room for rounds of individual testing and background questions. The former master chief was there, along with two or three other higher-ups I'd encountered before. But the admiral heading up Naval Special Warfare at the time could have been sitting in the room, for all I knew. The rest of the men sitting around the table were dressed in civilian clothes and didn't waste any time introducing themselves. Instead they proceeded to grill us one-on-one. There were some standard interview questions, then some riddles and math problems, trick-fuck questions that went on for a while. They had me turn around in my chair and draw the contents and cardinal directions of everything in the room. The long table where the interviewers were sitting, a smaller side table off to the right, the flat screen on the wall, the American flag in the background. They were testing us on situational awareness, vigilance, and memory.

We learned later that the program would involve a training pipeline designed to give special operators a new set of skills. Led by the master chief, it would include a few other higher-ups from the head shed, plus a SEAL reservist turned Drug Enforcement Administration agent and a case officer from the CIA—a short chain of command reporting directly to the admiral. Our job was figuring out Naval Special Warfare's role in the holy trinity Donald Rumsfeld had made famous at the time: "Find, Fix, Finish."

SEALs had always been trained to do the finish: kill or capture. But we were tasked with bringing more attention to the first part of the equation, creating an early reconnaissance and advance force operations capability that could travel alone. What it boiled down to was that the command wanted to get ahead of the war on terrorism.

As the decade wore on, the military and intelligence establishment's growing appetite for surgical, targeted drone strikes only reinforced the need for solid tracking information, gathered from parts of the world where our intelligence agencies didn't necessarily have the human resources. What they were looking for at the screening were a couple of experienced special operators to handle the training piece of the puzzle.

██
██
██
██
██
██
██
██
██
██

████████████.* The idea was to get someone like the guy at the beginning of the movie *Black Hawk Down* who's weaving in and out of a Mogadishu market, running undercover surveillance in a pair of Oakleys and a T-shirt before being picked up by a helicopter on a remote beach. The real person that scene was based on would later become a friend. But back then I knew nothing about him or the world he moved through.

A couple of weeks later I got word that they'd selected both me and Dozer, the two guys with combat action ribbons on our chest from our recent deployment, to build the training pipeline for this sensitive new program. All the other SEALs in that hallway were experienced, ranked E6 and above. But we had something that hadn't been seen in the halls of

* Another ridiculous redaction of unclassified information.

that particular command since Vietnam and Korea: combat experience, mine as a battlefield leader.

Being a medic probably helped in my case. That's always a great story to tell if you need to explain your presence in a questionable spot. The fact that Dozer got picked was no surprise: his other nickname was Data, after the *Star Trek* character with a computer for a brain and a chip to mimic human emotions. Like his animatronic namesake, Dozer could recite the contents of obscure military manuals word-for-word.

I didn't know it at the time, but that day was the last time I'd wear my cammies again, outside of official events. The next ten years would take me out of the huddle of combat and into duties that would go far beyond training other SEALs.

It was still dark out when I left for a monthlong trip for training in late October. As my flight took off over San Diego Bay, the sunrise stained the sky with a crazy wash of color.

The guy who would teach my courses was a crusty old professional with a silver mustache who told what sounded like dubious stories about his supersecret government work. But you never know. The company actually had a past protecting national secrets, and most of the students in that particular course were straight out of D.C. Everybody's named "Bob"—the classic cover name for a certain generation.

We started with the basics.

███████████████████████████████████

███████████████████████████████████

███████████████████████████████████

███████████████████████████████████

███████████████████████████████████

███████████████████████████████████

███████████████████████████████████

[redacted]*

We didn't do much beyond get the lay of the land on that first day in training. But the date, October 26, is seared into my memory because of what was going on two thousand miles away. While I was dozing away on the San Diego runway, Carrie, three months pregnant with our daughter, was driving home into what turned out to be a massive fire that charred a million acres and burned thousands of houses down to the ground. The night before, she'd woken up in the middle of the night smelling smoke. We'd both gone back to sleep when I told her I couldn't smell anything. But she *had* smelled smoke with her bionic pregnancy senses, it turned out. She'd smelled it miles away, before the winds really started kicking in and turned a lost hunter's signal fire into an inferno. The sunrise I'd admired that morning on the runway was the result of a fast-moving wildfire, being blown directly into the area by the Santa

* Well, these are starting to get ugly. Sorry about that. Go grab a cold one and let the alcohol fill in the blanks.

Ana winds. The smoke particles in the air had choked off the sun's blue and violet rays, leaving behind vivid streaks of orange and red.

That night I flipped on the TV in my hotel room, and right there on the national news was a camera crew filming from the bare dirt lawn of my brand-new backyard in Scripps Ranch. Almost every one of our immediate neighbors just beyond our cul-de-sac, many of them marines commuting to the Miramar air base, lost their homes. The fact that we hadn't even put in landscaping yet wound up protecting us from the flames.

I was ready to turn right around, but Carrie had made her way to a friend's place and told me to stay put. By day three, the fires in my immediate neighborhood were contained and I was able to turn my full attention back to the course.

Four weeks of the kind of detail work we'd be focusing on isn't for everyone. But if you've got the right set of personality traits, the work has its own satisfactions—kind of like putting together a challenging puzzle and getting that final piece to stick.

Having the curtain pulled back was a little like gaining access to the Batcave. And I didn't mind putting the skills into practice.

During the day, we'd review new techniques in the classroom. After sundown, we'd practice. It's a typical military way to train. Learn a new skill, demonstrate it under stress.

I didn't have much information about how these skills were going to be deployed. But it wasn't too difficult to imagine a range of scenarios.

The material may have been everyday business to the Bob, Dick, and Harry contingent, but the three of us had been hooked from the jump.

* Did I mention that the reviewer who butchered these pages never worked as a security professional (and apparently never checked in with Special Security Officers to identify what information was actually classified)? The fate of any veteran's book is largely a matter of luck. In my this case, everything was left to the interpretation of some old geezer locked up in an office filled with dusty manuscripts and the stench of administrative decay. Cheers!

After the course, I carried on with my independent studies, all with an eye to bringing the coursework home to the SEAL community. Apparently all I can say is that it was a fucking blast.

But while it would always be my first love, the ultimate goal held obvious appeal to the intelligence community, and, by extension, to the emerging mission of the Department of Defense. Not for the first time and not for the last, my new line of work allowed me to tap into some of the thrill-seeking behaviors I'd exhibited as a teenager and apply them to the greater good.

When I came home, our neighborhood was a charred and blackened mess. We moved back in as soon as the streets were open, but the place was a ghost town, with demolition crews tearing down drywall all over the place.

We'd both been more than a little surprised at the prospect of impending parenthood. We had talked about having kids over our seven years of marriage, but our timing never matched up. One of us would get the itch, the other would get cold feet, and a few months later we'd trade places. What we'd been through with Beej wasn't anything we were looking to repeat. Neither of us was in too much of a hurry to confront the topic, and my left-nut situation left us with a bunch of doubt about our odds.

The crushed nut was also the main reason we never bothered with protection. We figured I was basically shooting blanks. So getting home from putting some SEALs through a night dive to find a sonogram Carrie had left on my pillow was a bit of a shock.

"Congratulations, you're going to be a dad!"

The stress of nearly losing our home early on in the pregnancy hadn't been ideal, but dealing with some tenant-related crap was the final straw. We were six weeks from our due date when Carrie's water broke. She got into a heated argument with a flaky couple who were renting the old house we'd had before Scripps Ranch, and now she was going into early labor in the middle of the night.

We rushed to the hospital in a hurry, scared out of our minds. But once we got there everything slowed to a crawl. Thirty-six hours until Carrie was ready to go, then a long battle of the wills—Carrie, the ob-gyn, and a whole team of nurses against one tiny baby girl.

Tension has a way of making me go extra goofy, so Carrie's memories of the final stages of labor include her husband helpfully whispering "Don't poop on the table" into her ear. Who says medic training doesn't come in handy in the delivery room?

When she finally showed up, the newest member of our family just quietly looked around like she was taking the temperature of the place.

That same day, Hank Nicholson, Echo Platoon's lead climber, married his longtime girlfriend in a quickie courthouse ceremony. The two of them stopped by the hospital to see us on their way home, and there were smiles and hugs all around.

Like all new parents, we had that moment of disbelief when we pulled away from the curb.

"This thing come with an operating manual?"

Aside from a bit of jaundice, our little girl was perfectly healthy. She freaked everyone out by refusing to cry for a bit, which was just a preview of the fact that she turned out to be the easiest baby of all time and basically the best kid ever.

12
LITTLE
GREEN BOAT

DJIBOUTI, 2005

THE LITTLE GREEN BOAT WAS FLYING A SUSPICIOUS NUMBER OF FLAGS, and its name had clearly been painted over more than a few times. Most vessels are required to display the flag of their nation of origin, together with the courtesy flag of the country they're passing through. The owners of this particular ship were either working on their flag collection or deliberately trying to conceal the provenance of their craft.

Local intelligence had other good reasons to believe the boat belonged to a very bad guy, and they wanted their suspicions confirmed.

I'd been going around marketing our new capabilities. I'd brought a helper along with me from the command, a West Coast SEAL who'd been temporarily removed from operations after some kind of personal issue. Keith was a good guy, but he was going into this totally blind. On the other hand, neither of us really had any idea what the fuck we were doing. There's no other way to explain the fact that we packed and hauled a grand total of seventeen suitcases full of crap onto a commercial flight through Kenya.

██

██

██

██

███████████████████████████████.*

We looked like a couple of terrorists who'd watched one too many episodes of *Inspector Gadget*. And we'd leashed together our luggage into two straight lines that we dragged behind us like a couple of numb-nuts. Somehow we managed to make it through the twenty-two hours of travel, but we were tripping over our own feet the entire time, our suitcase chain toppling over at every curb. It was a downright ridiculous way to transport operational gear, particularly for a couple of special operators who were supposed to be inconspicuous types.

Every single person we crossed gave us a second look, and the Army guys who picked us up from the airport in several vans had a chuckle at our expense when they saw our load.

"Looks like you guys forgot the kitchen sink."

In our excitement at being able to deploy in this new capacity, we might have gone a little overboard. Our final destination was the East African republic of Djibouti, a poverty-stricken country with limited resources. Djibouti was a stable democracy in an unstable region. It was also a busy center for maritime trade—and, due to its location along the Gulf of Aden and the Red Sea, a key transit point to the Persian Gulf states. Capitalizing on the only thing they had going in the period following 9/11, its rulers had begun renting out space for military bases to a host of power players. The United States had established a naval expeditionary base there at Camp Lemonier, a space formerly occupied by the French Foreign Legion.

* Comparing the redactions in this book to those in other Pentagon-reviewed books, it's becoming apparent that the military doesn't have a fucking clue as to what's already been released or redacted.

The base had turned into a goat-infested junk heap in the years since it had been taken over by the Djibouti armed forces, but the boys from the Naval Construction Battalion had gotten to work cleaning the place up in a hurry. We'd be staying in one of the preengineered steel buildings the military uses for semipermanent installations.

Our main contact put a large unused warehouse at our disposal—big enough for us to set up shop, and with plenty of room for all of our shit.

Our initial recon had revealed that there was no safe place for two Caucasian males to hole up on the harbor. Anytime we so much as let up on the gas pedal a flock of little kids would mob our vehicle, hounding us to let them dust our car with their oily rags. Even if we'd managed to avoid them, pulling over to the side of the road would risk attracting the attention of squatters. You never knew who might be paying a little too much attention to your whereabouts and reporting back to the local police for a fee. Even in civilian clothes, two white guys with military bearing were bound to attract attention on the streets of Djibouti.

Our first job came down to a bit of soldering and basic electronics, some of which I'd picked up from a technical surveillance school in Florida known for its old-school methodologies. A lot of the instinct for wiring came from those Saturday afternoons with my dad, the two of us retrofitting the Oldsmobile's stereo system to keep up with changing technology.

As time went on I'd sometimes wonder what other skill sets I might have inherited from him.

Driving past crumbling colonial buildings, garbage-strewn alleys, and a few camels and goats, we made our way toward the shops on a busy main street. We weren't about to have a single bottle of glue shipped all the way over from the command, and we tended to keep our distance from our neighbors on base. Duct tape, it turned out, was global. So were superglue and electrical wire. The products at one of the all-purpose hardware and grocery stores still known as *supermarchés* in the former French colony were dusty and off-brand, but they did the trick.

We stuck pretty close to base throughout that first trip. Later on, returning on my own, I did a bit more exploring. There was a small hotel with a courtyard surrounded by palm trees and jasmine, where the French owners served up a legit steak frites. We all knew to steer clear of the Sheraton just outside the base. Discussing sensitive information in any of the rooms was a bad idea, since the Germans used the hotel as an extension of their barracks. Which meant the French, who host the German and Spanish forces on their naval base a few miles away from ours, were highly likely to be listening. Business as usual in Djibouti.

Civilians may have been shocked to hear that we were listening in on our allies during that dustup with Angela Merkel's phone back in 2013. But for members of the military and intelligence community, the only surprising thing about that piece of news was the fact that it got out to the general public. Because here's the truth: every country with the capability to do so is listening to any potentially actionable chatter it can pick up. On every continent, at every hour of the day. Friends, foes, and acquaintances, too. So if wired hotel rooms and intra-European espionage sound like plot points out of an episode of *Homeland,* you're probably not paying enough attention to the news—or maybe you're not reading between the lines.

* The redacted panel (opposite page) did not contain instructions on how to build a bomb. (*That* material was covered on page *166* of my first book, *100 Deadly Skills,* which was reviewed by the Pentagon and published with only slight modifications.) Another random act of censorship by the Department of Defense.

The NSA is nowhere near the top of the heap, by the way. That honor goes to the Israelis, whose history and location have given them ample reason to be on guard. They spy on their allies (the United States included) more than some of our enemies do.

———————

After the glue expedition we were ready for a dry run on the streets near the base. We needed to know if dust kicked up by other vehicles, bumps in the road or sudden stops, or unexpected third-party interactions would somehow compromise our gig. Kids swarming our vehicle with their dirty rags anytime we went into town were the likeliest concern. Luckily they didn't tend to hang around the harbor.

We headed out for a first pass at midday. As predicted, the level of scrutiny from the two locals manning the kiosk at the entrance was negligible.

"Hello, American! What brings you here today?"

We flashed them our pearly whites and our embassy badges, but we could have shown them a page from a children's book, for all they cared.

"Afternoon! We're just heading over to the store to buy some *siddiqi*."

The word *siddiqi* means "friend" in Arabic, but in common usage it also stands for booze. Our early intel had revealed the presence of a duty-free shop in the harbor, an obvious destination for a couple of non-Muslims in town on business. Djibouti wasn't dry, but with access to alcohol limited in any majority-Muslim country, duty-free shops always draw Westerners.

Overpriced? You bet, and the beer was laced with formaldehyde.

"Aaaah, you buy me some, too!"

And that was it. Thirty seconds of small talk, and we were in. Pretty much the standard around the world—a smile goes a long way. We pulled up to the store, bought a couple of bottles of liquor and a pack of cigarettes, and circled back to base via an alternate route.

As we got to know the rhythms of the place, we saw that the level of awareness at the gate tended to plummet around lunchtime. It wasn't just the harbor. The majority of the adult males in Djibouti checked out after the daily flights from Ethiopia delivered their late morning shipments of khat, a bitter green leaf with stimulant properties. By around one in the afternoon, the shipments had been distributed to all the corner khat stands. By two, you'd walk into stores in town and find the doors wide-open. No one manning the register, no one home upstairs. Everybody was too busy chewing the national drug, with these baseball-size gobs lodged in their cheeks. It takes about an hour of chewing for the effects to accumulate. Most men would put in three or four, intermittently spitting up green goo. They'd be on their ride until nightfall, when they'd wander around the streets like zombies. Red eyes, a huge gob of khat in each cheek, and a cigarette in between.

Tried the stuff once, didn't feel a thing. Probably didn't give it long enough, but it tasted like dirt and left your whole mouth a baby-shit green.

According to the intel, there were thirty-three known ships in Osama bin Laden's fleet. One of them was a small green craft with a white superstructure built on top. The names didn't match up. But there was no mistaking her characteristics.

That was as far as the job was supposed to go. In theory, we'd accomplished our mission. But the boat's owner was our great white whale—the number one priority of the DOD, the CIA, the FBI, and the NSA. We hadn't signed on for a game of catch-and-release. We were here to fuck with bad guys. And we'd found evidence that the world's most wanted terrorist had a boat parked 150 nautical miles from the harbor where his henchmen had blown a hole into the side of the USS *Cole*. He was widely thought to be hiding somewhere in Pakistan, but you never knew where a piece of intelligence might lead.

I'd come full circle from those street tricks in Bangkok. The fifteen-year-old dork magician in me was pretty proud of his new trick, and the results of the new intel were encouraging.

You never know which aspects of your high school résumé are going to come in handy later on in life.

───────────

The boats parked beside the target ship were dark, and nothing seemed out of the ordinary. No deck hands or pedestrian traffic in sight.

Once I reached the pier, I walked up to the target ship and climbed right up its portside loading ramp like I'd done it a thousand times before.

*

Every once in a while I'd stop to scan my surroundings and listen for any odd sounds. Getting caught at this point in the op would leave me with limited options. In the covert world, pulling your gun is beyond a worst-case scenario—it's a sign that you've completely fucked up and utterly failed. If I got caught, pulling out the SIG P239 I had tucked in my waistline would have compromised the operation and thrown all our hard work into the toilet. So my working plan was to punch whoever it was in the face and sprint into the darkness.**

All that remained now was getting my ass out of there.

I left the same way I came, keeping my pace nice and even.

Not bad for my first op.

It was easier back then, before there were cameras on every corner tracking your every little movement. Defeating them would take even more ingenuity and a few additional tools.

We were cogs in the machinery of the United States government, and we'd completed our task.

A few days later, we packed up our seventeen suitcases full of crap and wound our way back to San Diego. Flying commercial meant we didn't have to wait around for the next available military flight. But it came with the disadvantage of hustling our gear through airport security.

* What a waste of black ink.

** To sum up the lesson here: Never get caught. But always have a backup plan. Even if it's a dumb one.

We got a taste of the potential scrutiny that could entail when we were forced to recheck all seventeen pieces of our luggage through customs at the Nairobi airport. Once the ordeal was behind us, we got on the plane and immediately passed out.

We sat on the tarmac for thirty minutes before we were finally roused from our slumber by a couple of flight attendants tugging at our sleeves. It took us a minute to realize that the sounds we'd been hearing in our half sleep were their heavily accented voices, repeatedly calling our names over the intercom. Apparently they'd been at it for a while, which meant every passenger on that plane shot us death rays as we were escorted off the flight. The atmosphere on the tarmac wasn't any better. Four Kenyan soldiers in fatigues were hovering over our open suitcases under the wing of the 747. The suitcase they seemed particularly focused on was the one we'd filled with our semiautomatic weapons.

"This luggage belong to you?"

The soldier who appeared to be in charge pointed one hand toward the suitcase in question. His other hand didn't stray too far from his weapon.

I'd had the officially stamped letter of approval from the U.S. embassy out of my pocket before we reached the tarmac, and Keith and I made a show of closing our cases while they passed it back and forth.

It was another full hour of wrangling and phone calls to the embassy under the baking heat of the Kenyan sun before we were able to board. Maintaining positive contact with your weapons is paramount in any situation. The last thing we'd want would be for them to confiscate our gear. The whole time we could see the passengers staring daggers at us through the windows.

"Don't think we're going to be making any friends on the flight home," Keith said as we reboarded, both of us completely drenched in sweat.

Chalk it up to a learning experience. We weren't exactly selling the clandestine nature of our work by traveling with that amount of operational gear, and most of the shit we brought was available in town anyway. Our seventeen suitcases weren't getting codified into the secret squirrel manual anytime soon. But the overall results for our first substantial solo expedition in this new capacity were pretty damn good. It wasn't your everyday op.

A year or so later, I was in an unrelated meeting at a government agency on the East Coast when I happened to recognize a still photo being projected onto a screen.

"Hey," I whispered to a friend. "You're never gonna believe this."

A lot of the time in my new line of work, you'd be jumped into a complex situation and briefed only on what you needed to know to get the job done. More often than not, I was collecting information with little clue about the endgame. So it was pretty cool to have this collection of pixels come back around to me.

Back home, word started traveling around the community about the type of stuff I was involved with, rumors, mostly.

"Dude, I heard about that shit you did in China," a friend said as he accosted me in the halls of the command. I gave him the brush-off, not confirming or denying. But I never went to China. Whatever my fellow SEALs were hearing about my activities, 50 percent or more had to be inaccurate. And that suited me just fine. If I occasionally missed the camaraderie of being on a team, the work itself was such a natural match for my skills and tendencies that any regrets were fleeting. In a funny way it was almost like I'd been rehearsing for tasks like these my whole life. Wreaking havoc around a Saudi Arabian compound after dark or swiping thousands of dollars' worth of jewelry from my classmates' parents may not have contributed to the greater good. But those early activities did tap into an aptitude for deception and a tolerance for risk that would prove more and more useful as I continued down my new chosen career path.

13
BACK TO SCHOOL

D.C., LOS ANGELES, 2005

I TOOK THE LESSONS LEARNED IN DJIBOUTI AND WORKED THEM STRAIGHT back into the course that Dozer and I were building. Clearly some operations would require a logistics team to prep the groundwork, enabling a two- or four-man team to travel light. But in many other cases, we'd be better off working with available resources.

The bulk of that material would be covered during the five-week technical section of our course.*

* Let's be real—the Pentagon completely fucked this chapter. Ironically, most of the course work they didn't want me to describe was never classified to begin with.

Dozer would handle the collection piece of the puzzle. Finding subject matter experts to teach the technical blocks fell to me. Our task was vague at first, and the higher-ups gave us a long leash. Giving SEALs a new training pipeline to execute as we saw fit was pretty well in line with the bottom-up culture of our command structure.

We knew surveillance would be front and center. The events of September 11, 2001, had shown the military and intelligence community how easy it was to fail to connect the dots on intelligence data. We had eyes and ears in the sky, signals pinging from satellites twenty thousand miles from the planet we call home. But confirming that data with eyes and ears attached to an actual human asset now had a renewed sense of value to our national interest. We were going to need more bodies in the field, watching at all times.

Over the course of a decade in which the threat of cold war had receded and modern intelligence gathering had become more reliant on data and tech, the intelligence community had gotten a reputation for being bureaucratic, risk averse, and increasingly isolated. But intelligence and operations hadn't always been so segregated. A precursor to the Central Intelligence Agency, the Office of Strategic Services (OSS) had been established during World War II to coordinate unconventional espionage among the military and executive branches. After the major intelligence failures of 9/11, that boots-on-the-ground approach started to look a lot more appealing to all of the agencies. The OSS existed for only four years, and there's debate over how much the agency really accomplished—along with how many of the legendary tales of its exploits were true. But fiction or not, the trove of OSS stories was an inspiration to me.

As we began building the course, I got smart on the OSS era's Jedburgh teams, the three-man coalitions that parachuted behind enemy lines. Flying into Nazi-occupied villages in the middle of the night, the Allied

French, American, and British teams disguised themselves as villagers and set up the resistance from the inside.

Once they were on the ground, they trained civilians to execute sabotage operations against the Nazis and fed the information they collected back to their bosses.

It was a ridiculously badass example of military units being deployed for unconventional, intelligence-based operations. And it gave me a blueprint for thinking about the kinds of skills we needed to cultivate.

The Jedburgh teams traveled light, both for convenience's sake and to avoid detection. No Humvees filled to the brim with lawn chairs. A radio was their most prized possession, and their training pipeline was designed for small teams working behind enemy lines, with minimal resources.

They were also working in a low-vis capacity, and learning on the fly. If they parachuted into France, the French member of the team would train the British and American guys on how to blend in and avoid giving away their cultural identity. A bunch of SEALs would have a harder time as white guys generally working in not-so-white environments, but that kind of cultural awareness was a place to start.

Like the Jedburgh teams, our guys were going to need to become well-rounded, flexible operatives who could both collect information and act on it.

None of this was being taught by the United States military. Especially at the beginning, I contracted most of the coursework through private companies.

I would spend the next ten years of my career building and refining the course, which went by different names over its lifetime. The content shifted and evolved to keep pace with existing technology and lessons learned on the ground, but the coursework followed a basic structure. We typically got the ball rolling with concealed weapons training.

* Note to the Pentagon: Blacking out entire pages is just fucking lazy.

To round things out, a two-week-long full mission profile would test the men on their ability to put everything they'd learned into action. The assessment wove the skills into a detailed story line, with a cast of characters designated to role-play as targets.

Our students were operating in a three-dimensional world, with enemies around every corner, so we had countersurveillance on hand to bust anyone who wasn't following protocol.

We held the last phase in Los Angeles back then. Between the mountains, the highways, the ocean, and the pockets of urban chaos, the city and its outskirts had the topography for a well-rounded test. We raced cars in the desert an hour outside Palm Springs and ran surveillance ops on city streets, and our bad-guy role-playing network was staffed by friends from the teams and support folks from the command. A beach vacation that involved messing with a bunch of spec ops guys wasn't too hard a sell.

That's real life. Bad guys take walks, they eat meals, they have full-time jobs. They do things that have no relevance to plots to bomb American embassies or facilitate the spread of radical ideologies. They do things that normal people do, and that's the job—sifting through the bad guy's mundane daily habits to find the off-kilter tell. Our training took this all into account.

When you start down the path of this line of work, there's no glory in it. In all likelihood, you're not getting any awards. For the most part, my career became a black hole after Iraq. More often than not, the missions I went on would never be publicized—not even inside the community. Most of my trips weren't even documented in my personnel jacket, the military's official record of your deployments. And my rank never got bumped again. There was no classifiable system in place by which to rate my activities, which you need in order to qualify for rank assessments and commendations.

So you don't want the guy who needs to go around pounding his chest and downing beers with his buddies after every mission, or who wants some kind of official recognition for his actions. In these discreet scenarios, ego and recklessness will get you killed.

We were looking for self-starters, guys who were motivated but also subtle. That combination of qualities doesn't always go hand in hand. At one of the training exercises, an overly aggressive student wound up in handcuffs because he'd made the decision to jump from rooftop to rooftop. Aerial shortcuts are handy and look impressive, but every resident of every house on the block must have called 911 when they heard the loud thuds on their roofs. One resident took a more direct approach. When she saw a full-grown man drop down from her roof and into her backyard, she opened her back door, got him in her sights, and called out to her husband, "Honey, grab the gun!"

The student took off through the side gate and found the cops waiting for him on the street.

That led to a new rule—no jumping from house to house. This was a quiet upscale neighborhood in a major American metropolis, not Ramadi. Some of these very experienced SEALs had been kicking in doors for so long, they'd forgotten how to use a doorknob. Teaching them to rein in their wartime instincts to groom them for low-visibility work in noncombat areas sometimes begged the obvious.

For the first few years, before the course became more established, our student body was a bit of a grab bag. Eventually the course started attracting the highest-caliber operators. But we found similar challenges across the board.

Holding our exercise in an urban environment gave us the opportunity to simulate some of the more chaotic conditions that operators might encounter in crowded urban centers abroad, and we purposely cruised through shadier neighborhoods to throw the guys off. At the time, East Los Angeles was overrun by a network of gangs headed up by an outfit called Mara Salvatrucha, or MS-13, a criminal organization with ties to Central America and a reputation for ruthlessness and retribution. One of our operators had the misfortune of running into several of them during a training session. Our friends wasted no time getting up in his face and questioning his presence on their turf. A ripped white guy in civilian clothes walking alone through their neighborhood had to be a cop.

Before they could find out the answer, he'd beaten the shit out of all three of them and stripped them of their weapons. By the time the rest of the team rolled up they were already "subdued," which is just a fancy word for unconscious. We handed the dirtbags over to the LAPD and went on our merry way.

One of my favorite moves as a notional bad guy was a disappearing act I pulled in the Hollywood Hills, where a spiderweb of steep, narrow roads makes it difficult for a vehicular tail to operate without detection, and a number of dead spots create an ideal environment for a loss of comms. At some point in their careers these SEALs would be operating overseas in places with little to no cellular coverage. In the event that comms failed, they needed to be able to figure out what to do.

Best of all, the location offered an extra twist that I took full advantage of as the bad guy: the possibility of ditching your car, disappearing onto a trail, and then hopping on a rented horse and riding off into the sunset.

That still makes me laugh.

A horse was one possibility they definitely hadn't seen coming.

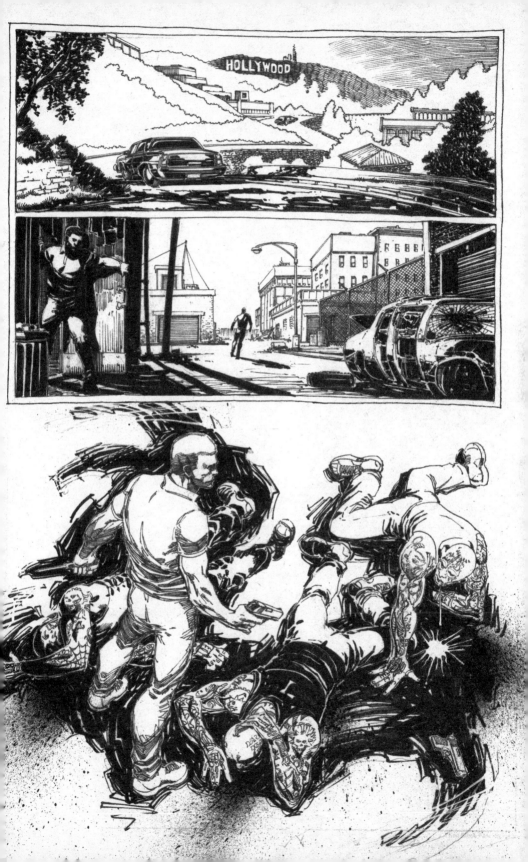

14
MIXED SIGNALS

SAN DIEGO, MOUNT VERNON, 2005

ALL THE SEAL TEAMS STARTED GETTING CLOSER TO THE INTELLIGENCE community after 9/11, but my work put me in regular contact with a wide assortment of players from that realm. In building the training program, Dozer and I cultivated relationships within some dozen or more of the agencies, military units, and defense companies that touched on intelligence gathering. We even headed overseas to interview our counterparts at her majesty's SAS (Special Air Service) and SRR (Special Reconnaissance Regiment). The Brits were already conducting the type of training and operations we were just starting to get our heads around. Their experiences dealing with the IRA and other well-organized agents of disruption provided a real-world template for us to emulate and, in my opinion, eventually surpass.

.*

By then we'd expanded the course beyond its original mission, to serve across the U.S. Special Operations Command—better known as SOCOM. Word had traveled back from the Rangers, Marines, and Green Berets who'd started taking the course by special request. Eventually we were certified as a joint endeavor of the special operations community.

With the course on a quarterly schedule, my contact and I spoke regularly over the phone, San Diego to D.C., to coordinate logistics. She had a great reputation professionally and a girl-next-door vibe. She didn't have anything particularly special going on in the looks department. But she'd been one of the few people in D.C. to lead female surveillance teams, and most important, she behaved like one of the guys. The special operations community is one corner of the military that's still almost exclusively male. All combat jobs are now open to women, but so far none have been able to make it through BUD/S. After ten years of training and operating in a pile of jism-crusted socks, being reintroduced to the coed workforce was an unexpected bonus of my distance from the teams.

I wasn't spending much time at home during this period. Between the course and my new deployment schedule, trips were often thrown

* More bullshit censorship of material that was never classified to begin with.

together on a moment's notice. When I was in town, it could be difficult for me and Carrie to get our lives in sync. Typical military-couple issues, and the kind that build up over time. Carrie had her own stuff going on, an independent life and a career in health and fitness that she'd carved out in my absence. The nature of my job meant I could divulge even less information about my work and my whereabouts. More mystery, more distance. It was easier to talk to someone who understood the lifestyle, and over the months my contact became something like a friend. A friend who liked to flirt, with a mind almost as filthy as mine. When you put a bunch of special operators and female intelligence agents together in a professional environment, boundaries are going to be pushed. Suddenly every work-related conversation took on a double meaning.

I need you to be more aggressive in the follow.

Oh yeah. I want you to parallel my guys. And feel free to penetrate as much as you want.

The innuendo wasn't subtle, and the combination of friendship and perverted banter went on for long enough to create confusion. Before long we were confiding in each other about the challenges in our relationships, and going into pretty explicit detail about our circumstances (or lack thereof) between the sheets. Things went too far, and one day she told me she loved me.

Call me clueless, but I was totally taken by surprise. That really wasn't the path I was going down. To me, the fact that we were both married meant our flirtation was basically safe.

"Hey, I'm not looking to leave my wife," I told her.

I'd assumed we were on the same page about that. But on her end of the picture, there was a guy lying on the couch with a dip of Copenhagen drooling out the side of his mouth every night, the remnants of a twelve-pack of Heineken strewn all over the living-room floor.

She didn't have much to lose.

We hadn't even kissed, but she'd built the thing up in her mind.

"Where did you think this was going?"

Suddenly I was this manipulative asshole who'd led her on and rejected her. Maybe she just wanted to blow up her own marriage, with mine as a welcome casualty. Either way, she threw a shit-filled grenade into my family life.

Despite spending most of his time in a drunken haze, her husband had begun to harbor a sneaking suspicion that something was going on. She told him the same version of the truth that had been playing out in her mind, and he called Carrie one afternoon and told her we'd been having an affair. According to him, every business trip I'd been taking was a pretext for me to bang his wife in hotel rooms all over town.

"Where do you think the two of them are right now?"

He knew my entire itinerary, and used that knowledge to time his call so I'd be stuck on a flight back from a meeting at SOCOM when Carrie picked up the phone. I came home to an extremely angry and confused wife who'd filled up several notebook pages documenting his call.

Carrie, who hadn't completely bought his story, told him to have his wife call and face the music. A few days later, she did. Because I'd given her way too much information about the issues in my sex life, she was able to describe specifics about my anatomy that only a woman who'd been with me could know.

There was no denying that I'd had intimate conversations that shouldn't have taken place.

"How does she know that your dick curves to the left?"

That's a question you never want to hear from your spouse.

Carrie never fully believed my side of the story, but we managed to reach a stalemate. My friend's husband's response wasn't quite so measured. That batshit lunatic had already tried to run his wife off the road once, but now he lost it completely. According to the version of events she relayed in another late-night call, he choked her, ass-banged her, and then got himself a one-way ticket to San Diego.

"He's probably coming to kill you," she told me after finding a letter he'd written to her detailing his plans. Then she called the cops.

A threat to a DOD member is actually a federal issue. So our little problem spiraled from local law enforcement in San Diego and D.C. to the agency her husband worked for and the NCIS, four agencies suddenly activated because of our bullshit.

Our state of siege lasted several days. At one point Carrie managed to get him on the phone to try to talk him down. The Alexandria Police Department finally found him passed out in some motel room, so drunk he hadn't even made his flight.

Carrie and I managed to stay married for seven long years after that, but the trust was broken for good.

There was definitely no one to blame for that piece of the fallout but me.

Nobody was pressing charges, so the whole thing died down without any professional repercussions. But a bureaucratic shuffle soon after that gave me some additional professional distance. Marketing the new special operations capabilities we'd been building to the intelligence community had yielded an interesting professional development for me and Dozer.

We'd already broadened our student body to Rangers and Green Berets. Now we'd been presented with the opportunity to embed a school-house directly inside one of the D.C. area agencies. SEALs are an attention-getting line item on any government budget, so the powers that be were all too happy to green-light a program spearheaded by a couple of experienced naval special operators.

Through a former FBI agent I found a nice rental in Mount Vernon, Virginia, a tree-lined historic neighborhood near the George Washington estate. Leaving the Southern California climate behind had its downsides, and Carrie wasn't pleased about relocating to the area where our *Fatal Attraction* duo happened to live, especially with a three-year-old in tow.

But the professional upsides—a permanent home for the program, better visibility throughout the intelligence community, a streamlined network of in-house contracts—were solid.

Another upside for me was my new daily commute, which inspired a bit of frogman creativity. Why spend twenty-five minutes sitting in traffic on the bridge to Maryland when a scenic route across the Potomac was there for the taking? A little bit of East Coast weather wasn't going to stand in my way, so I created an improvised amphibious commuting system setup involving a kayak, a metal rucksack frame, and a set of tow wheels. Every morning I would hitch my kayak's stern onto the collapsible wheels, hook the bow of the boat onto that empty rucksack frame, strap the frame on my back—and then run the two miles to the river with the kayak trailing behind me. On the banks of the Potomac, I'd unhook my boat, paddle several miles across, then hitch the kayak back onto my rucksack and hightail it the remaining two miles to work.

I parked the contraption in a shady bit of grass by the parking lot.

At the end of the day I'd do it all over again.

The evening commute sucked. The summers sucked more. In the winter I'd have to break through ice to get my rig in and out of the water. And on the other side those fuckers at the security gate *always* made me show my ID.

Really? How many other guys were showing up to work dripping with sweat, strapped to a fucking kayak?

A couple of techs working with me at the schoolhouse actually did buy all the gear to try out the routine for themselves.

"Screw this," they said after throwing in the towel on their first attempt. "You're insane."

The looks I got from other runners and drivers on the road were priceless. But my growing distance from any routine associated with the teams meant my physical conditioning was up to me. Hands down, it was the best commute of my life. Every morning, my car pool was just me and the bald eagles soaring in the sky.

Soon after I landed in D.C., I reached out to an operator named R.J.. He'd been a founding father for all kinds of crazy solo ops the rest of the SEAL community would never hear about. We'd gotten to be friendly over the years, and I'd had him come over to speak to the students a few times. He'd told some illuminating stories about his experiences in the field and shared a few tips on how to avoid getting fucked by some tiny overlooked detail: the dry-cleaning tag with your name on it, some old crumpled-up movie stub in your pants pocket.

With two hundred pounds of muscle, a six-foot-three-inch frame, and a classic frogman mustache, the guy certainly didn't look like the poster boy for discreet operations. He was the icon of a Naval Special Warfare operator—the kind of guy who'd haul out a longboard just before a hurricane to test his personal limits. But he was also the smartest SEAL I'd ever met, fluent in several languages, well versed in politics, economics, history, and science. Any disadvantage posed by his hulking stature was outweighed by his intelligence and the breadth of his experience. The two of us didn't interface often, but when we did I'd hang on to his every word. When he called me up and asked me to join him for a meeting at the Pentagon, I was more than happy to tag along. R.J. had been out there doing his own thing for so long that he'd become the ultimate spec ops solo operation salesman.

He didn't brief me much beforehand. All he told me was that he wanted me to do a "show-and-tell" on some tracking and collection devices. "Bring the cool shit" was pretty much all he said.

The briefings were already under way when I walked into my assigned slot to find a room full of suits, with a couple of congressmen and senators in the mix.

Jesus. I was glad I'd remembered to put on deodorant.

The amount of leeway R.J. had to pitch his schemes directly to the upper echelons of power in and around D.C. was downright nuts.

My toys weren't anything you couldn't get on the consumer market, if you knew where to look. Tiny cameras used for medical procedures, audio and tracking devices . . . but they seemed to make a good impression.

R.J. was pitching them on a streamlined special operations side mission. Pursuing PIFWC (Persons Indicted for War Crimes) in the Balkans had been a priority for the allied coalition working to bring justice to the region in the decade following the Bosnian War. The International Criminal Tribunal would eventually apprehend every last one of the generals, commanders, soldiers, and police officers on its most-wanted list. But after 9/11 the DOD was reallocating resources to more urgent concerns.

With a couple of Predator drones and some operators with advanced reconnaissance training, R.J. argued, the mission could continue with a considerably smaller footprint.

"Using advanced surveillance capabilities and some overhead support, a couple of men could do the work of an entire platoon."

The idea was for the two of us to give it a test run as a proof of concept. All we needed was a green light. That, and a few million dollars to rustle up the Predator.

The initial reception seemed to be strong, and R.J. followed up with some encouraging news. But the thing never got off the ground.

R.J. never stopped thinking big, though. Personal hero of mine, and definitely someone worth idolizing. Still does contract work to this day after finally retiring a few years back.

Despite my being tied up with the schoolhouse, short-term operational trips continued to take me overseas. ████████████████ ██ ██ ██ ██ ██ ████████████████████████████ Though I didn't know it at the time, those deployments were building up to the most important mission of my career.

15
A DANISH RABBIT STEW

SOMALIA, YEMEN, 2005-2006

A FAILED STATE WHERE ANARCHY HAS BEEN THE NORM FOR DECADES, Somalia consistently ranks as one of the world's most dangerous hot spots. It's the kind of high-threat area where journalists are routinely kidnapped for ransom and/or killed, and any passing white guy who isn't a known quantity needs some sort of an alibi. Usually along with a hefty security contingent.

My first trip to the country took me to a small city where the airport was just a dirt runway with a couple of half-finished terminals crumbling nearby, and my taxi was an escort made up of three or four armed "technicals." The term is short for "technical assistance grant," after a standard line item that United Nations and nongovernmental employees in the region used on their budgets to write off their security escorts. Pickup trucks with anywhere from three to eight armed men inside and a rusty Russian bullet launcher mounted into the flatbed. . . . Before most of the NGOs checked out of town, a multivehicle security caravan was a necessity for any foreigners traveling inside Somalia.

It had been a dozen years since the events that inspired *Black Hawk Down*, but footage of the bodies of dead U.S. soldiers dragged through the streets of Mogadishu by cheering mobs wasn't something the American public or the Department of Defense would forget anytime soon. The U.S. State Department had shut down its embassy when Somalia descended into civil war in 1991, and the Battle of Mogadishu two years later had left the U.S. military with a permanent lack of appetite for putting boots on the ground in any part of the world where our interests were peripheral.

On their end, the Somalis had fielded losses in the hundreds during what they called "the Day of the Rangers." For some of them, Mogadishu had been the opening shot in an ongoing war with the United States.

But now our intelligence agencies had a renewed interest in the area. Since the overthrow of the country's dictatorial president, Somalia had been run by whichever militants or warlords had the biggest guns. Roving bands of armed men answered to the most powerful warlord in their particular stretch of turf, and half the time the government that was supposed to be running the country was in exile. That lawlessness, along with a wide, unguarded coastline, made Somalia a safe haven and point of transit for bad actors of all stripes. Recently the country had been harboring dens of violent and increasingly ambitious pirates along its shores. The busy shipping lanes in the Gulf of Aden and the Indian Ocean were crawling with targets. On land, extremism was festering in the chaos engulfing the country. Chased out of Afghanistan and Iraq, al-Qaeda had been joining up with the recently formed militant group al-Shabaab to build training camps and drum up support inside Somalia. They didn't have any recruitment problems, given the large population of unemployed young men.

My job, on paper at least, was to spend three months training a local security force on the basics of surveillance and intelligence gathering. The training would work out in everybody's favor if we could help the Somalis fight terrorism and piracy within their own borders.

Minimally educated and ranging in age from early twenties all the way into their sixties, my students had clearly been drafted off the street sometime in the not-so-distant past. Our classroom was a balcony under the blasting equatorial sun with a whiteboard leaned against a wall, and their salary couldn't have been more than a hundred dollars a month. While I sketched and an interpreter translated, they would nod along with dazed looks of incomprehension on their faces, like they'd never seen a diagram in their lives.

Maybe they hadn't.

Teaching them to use the flip phones I'd purchased in-country took an entire day. Things are different now that Africa is crawling with cheap Chinese telecom, but back then none of the locals had had much exposure to cell phones.

I had a hard time getting across the notion of perspective. Basic sketching is a fundamental piece of intelligence gathering, and a land warfare skill Navy SEALs are taught for use in target reconnaissance. If your tech fails, at least you'll be able to draw a picture. But my explanation of the difference between overhead and perspective sketching drew a balcony's worth of blank looks. Like many members of traditionally tribal or nomadic societies, Somalis tend to think of themselves in terms of their familial or clan social structures rather than as individuals. So I improvised.

"Tell them to try drawing the picture from the goat's point of view," I said to the interpreter. "What does the goat see?"

They scribbled the scene on sheets of paper and showed me the results.

"Great. Now draw the picture from the bird's point of view."

"Aaaaaaaah!"

The lightbulb went off, and that goat-bird dichotomy was permanently enshrined in training manuals back home.

You didn't see Caucasians on foot in most parts of Somalia, and my bosses would have preferred me to stay safely ensconced in our little balcony classroom when I wasn't in my hotel.

But we would have attracted attention no matter what. More than once as we ran our routes, passing Somali men would catch my eye and slowly draw a thumb across their throats.

The overt threats of decapitation didn't exactly make me feel welcome, but I'd made contingency plans of my own. A Heckler & Koch MP7 submachine gun tucked into my pack was my constant companion. Compact and lightweight, the weapon was quiet, recoil-free, and just plain cool. For extra insurance I'd tucked a selection of frag grenades alongside the gun. Random explosions on city streets wouldn't be sanctioned by any embassy on earth. But if shit went sideways, I wasn't going down without a fight. Allowing myself to be taken hostage and potentially risk the lives of fellow SEALs who'd have to come rescue my ass? No fucking way. I'd be taking out entire city blocks in order to avoid that possibility. Commandeering vehicles, boats, and/or planes—whatever I had to do to get the fuck out of Somalia and closer to the extraction team who'd be heading my way from a neighboring country.

That was the unofficial plan, at least.

On paper, I'd mitigated the risk factor by having a local fixer accompany me on my surveillance jaunts, ducking into little shops or ratty cafes with my inept tails behind me. Everywhere we went, he introduced me as a Danish wildlife researcher. What could be more neutral than an animal lover from a country known more for saunas and sausages than for projecting military power overseas? Anti-American sentiment still rang strong in Somalia, and our support of an Ethiopian invasion in December 2006 didn't help.

What neither of us realized was that a Danish cartoonist by the name of Kurt Westergaard had just lit the entire Islamic world on fire with a little drawing of a prophet in a bomb-shaped turban. When the Danish newspaper *Jyllands-Posten* published Westergaard's infamous

Muhammad cartoon in September 2005, they broke a cardinal rule against corporeal representation of the Prophet. Representing the messenger as a terrorist obviously added insult to injury.

I was just settling in for an evening of jerking off to thoughts of Jessica Biel in my crappy hotel room when I got a pretty agitated call from my fixer.

"Get your things together right away, I meet you out back."

"Huh?" It took me a second to piece together his broken English.

"We don't have time. A lot of people, they coming your way."

"What the fuck?"

I hadn't done anything particularly worthy of assassination by mob on that specific day, as far as I knew.

"Hurry up. They're on their way now, and they are coming to kill you."

I immediately started packing up my shit while keeping an eye out on the street. He hadn't been exaggerating. Just as he rolled up I saw a mob of hundreds of people, pretty much the entire town, approaching the hotel on foot. They were armed with anything and everything you could possibly pick up from an open-air black market—machetes, Kalashnikovs, RPGs, your average arsenal of Russian pistols. And they didn't look very happy.

Operating inside my little training bubble, I had no idea what the hell was going on in the world. But I had a pretty strong intuition that I was about to get my head sliced off at the neck. I whipped around the side of the building and slid into my keeper's tinted SUV with seconds to spare. The contract pilots we'd staged in a neighboring city met us at the airfield to do the extraction in under an hour. The official military "quick" reaction force would have taken longer.

Eventually that cartoon led to the 2006 Danish embassy attacks in Damascus, Beirut, and Tehran and the violent protests that drew hundreds of thousands across the Middle East. We had to pull back on operations for a while after that first round of rioting and bombings. Westergaard would spend the next decade in hiding, nearly losing his life in a 2010 home invasion by an ax-wielding Somalian fanatic.

––––––––––

That little episode gave me a visceral understanding of the way a lack of melatonin could mess with your ground game. Operating as a white guy in that part of the world wasn't ideal. On repeat trips I began to experiment with ways of making myself a little less visible during reconnaissance gigs.

██████████████████████████████████████
██████████████████████████████████████
██████████████████████████████████████
██████████████████████████████████████
██████████████████████████████████████
██████████████████████████████████████
██████████████████████████████████████
██████████████████████████████████████
██████████████████████████████████████
██████████████████████████████████████
██████████████████████████████████████
██████████████████████████████████████
██████████████████████████████████████
████████████████████████.*

   With the support of my small chain of command, that became my version of a low-signature op. Not exactly what my SEAL forefathers had in mind, but they couldn't have envisioned the types of scenarios

* The redacted material has never been classified by either the Department of Defense or the intelligence community. The redacted material has never been classified by either the Department of Defense or the intelligence community. The redacted material has never been classified by either the Department of Defense or the intelligence community.

we were currently confronting. The mission wasn't necessarily about creeping up on our enemies in the middle of the night. And the endgame wasn't a piece of land or a shipping lane or an oil field or the spread of democracy, but the sanctity of ordinary Americans' uneventful daily lives. We didn't want to be at war. Our fat asses just wanted to watch the Super Bowl in peace with a giant bag of Cheetos by our sides. So we'd made it our business to interrupt the threats against our nation before they could become a bloody reality.

The thing about unstable nations is that they have a way of attracting not only extremists, but also foreign actors looking to exert influence. We weren't the only ones in North Africa and the Middle East with a complex set of goals and ambitions. From our allies to our sworn enemies, any nation with a robust intelligence service had skin in the game and operatives in the field. And whatever your goals were, you could be sure as shit there'd be somebody out there doing their best to foil them. There were many potential reasons for an operative on the ground to step outside the tactical playbook in order to reduce his visibility. Assassination attempts by members of al-Qaeda who'd been tipped off to our whereabouts by foreign intelligence officers weren't unheard-of. But covert warfare was more common, and it was fought through the delivery of weapons and ammunition to the homegrown armies that festered throughout Yemen, Somalia, and North Africa. Iran, to take the most obvious example, had a history of fomenting rebellion and attempted coups on the government of President Ali Abdullah Saleh, with whom the United States had established a strategic alliance.

I'd return to Yemen and Somalia again and again—toward the end of the decade almost exclusively in pursuit of a high-value individual. He was a senior al-Qaeda recruiter, a radical imam, and a dual American-Yemeni citizen. We'd nicknamed him "Triple-A," and over the years he'd become our second-most-wanted target. But for a while he was just being watched.

Long before I joined the hunt to find him or even knew his name, Triple-A and I had some overlap much closer to home. During my early

THE RIGHT KIND OF CRAZY

years as a SEAL, he preached at a mosque in San Diego. And in that mosque—just fifteen miles from the house Carrie and I were living in at the time—two of the hijackers who crashed a plane into the Pentagon on September 11 attended some of his sermons. I might have stood behind the evil little shit at the grocery store at some point, for all I knew.

The U.S. authorities weren't able to make a direct link after 9/11, partly because he didn't start radicalizing (at least publicly) until later. But they did discover something interesting while trying to make their case. The imam had a secret life that involved regular visits to prostitutes. So much for the upstanding moral code he advertised to his followers. No to watching television. Yes to whores. Cool philosophy, *habibi.*

Hookers aren't great for the reputation of religious leaders. Law enforcement could use the intel to draft him as an informant or discredit him to the Muslim world. So when one of his favorite escort services tipped him off to a recent visit from an agent working the case, he panicked about his little secret getting out and fled the United States, first to the United Kingdom and then to Yemen.

———

Semi-related business frequently took me over to Hargeisa, the capital of the supposedly autonomous region of Somaliland in the northwest part of Somalia (a distinction nobody else recognized. The local director of intelligence was a shifty, slippery type the Americans had nicknamed "Insane Hussein." British intelligence was still thick in the area more than forty years after Somaliland had ceased to be a protectorate of the United Kingdom, and the erratic, unpredictable Hussein was constantly trying to play his international friends against one another to cage resources.

"The British gave me Range Rovers. What are *you* going to do for me?"

Dressed in seventies swag and riding around in his shiny four-by-four, the guy had such delusions of grandeur you'd have thought he was heading up MI6.

He definitely wasn't.

When he sent his goons out to follow me, it didn't take long to notice. Everywhere I went, a beat-up Toyota was tailing me from a totally observable distance. The four Somalis stuffed inside were another dead giveaway—Insane Hussein didn't have the resources to set up a proper surveillance team with multiple cars swapping in and out. The other easy tell was the fact that every time I'd get out of my car, they'd immediately get out of theirs.

The whole thing was a joke. His agents would follow me right out of meetings we'd have in his office and back to the dingy hotel room where I holed up on a stained mattress. Hargeisa didn't have much to offer in terms of entertainment, and my only company was a roomful of giant rats. So who could blame me for deciding to have a little fun? Not too different from the way we'd toy with our students' expectations during training. Just a little bit more diabolical in its intent.

I added a little routine to my daily travels, and milked the act for all it was worth. Anytime I spotted my tail, I'd drive to wherever I was going and take a deliberate glance at my watch. Stalling for a few minutes before getting out of the car, I'd look up at the sky, like I was expecting something. Then I'd take another look at my watch. *Hmmm, must be late.*

Another look back up at the sky. Another check on the time, and then I'd finally exit the vehicle.

Within half a day I'd trained the intelligence agents of Hargeisa to run through the same routine.

Looking back in my rearview mirror, I'd see four heads craning out of the busted-up vehicle and frantically swiveling around to scan the sky at every stop. After 9/11, aerial surveillance had become so common in global hot spots that locals assumed every American came with their own private Predator. The first drone strikes against al-Qaeda targets in the region wouldn't take place until the following year, but that clown car full of intelligence experts thought I'd made a special appointment to have them blasted into the ground.

Another memorable Insane Hussein situation had us caught between a rock and a hard place when a high-level asset got rolled up by local security on a trip back into the country. To the Somali police, he was a terrorist. He wasn't. But Insane Hussein wouldn't take the hint. When my friends got to the end of the line with their discreet attempts at diplomacy, I was asked to come up with some creative ways to get our man out, without tipping our cards.

I was more than happy to get to work planning a good old-fashioned prison raid. Prisoners escape from Somali and Yemenese jails on a fairly regular basis (many of the suspects in the USS *Cole* bombing had mysteriously vanished from their cells), so we knew the prison wasn't likely to be an African Alcatraz. The more interesting part was getting our source out of the country. Given Somalia's ample coastline, I took the opportunity to go full frogman on the situation.

In a series of trips over a two-month period, I buried three Zodiac boats by the shore in the vicinity of the jail. Deflated, the combat rubber raiding crafts we typically use for insertions folded down to the size of fifty-gallon drums. Using the full scuba tanks I'd buried along with them, a small special operations or paramilitary unit could have them inflated and ready to go within minutes. Once they were out on open waters, a submarine would ferry everyone to safety.

After burying and camouflaging the components, I noted the satellite coordinates and photographed nearby landmarks. If the plan ever came to fruition, the odds were pretty good that I'd be long gone by then. The more likely scenario was that it would get filed away in some special cabinet for good ideas axed by administrative caution.

It really wasn't any of my business.

But years later the subject came up over coffee in D.C. with one of the officers I'd been helping.

"Remember that extraction plan you put together for us down in Somaliland?" he asked. It would be nice to say we were hunched over a couple of black coffees like every hardboiled law enforcement professional ever in the history of TV. In reality we were probably chatting over a couple of grande mochas with an extra pump of chocolate and whipped cream on top.

I shook my head.

"Well, that all worked out."

He didn't tell me anything else, and I knew better than to ask. We both took sips of our manly drinks and moved on.

Secret squirrel business has its own particular code of conduct. It can also have a familiar cast of characters. One night in Somalia I ran into a former SEAL who'd crossed over to the dark side, not as a freelancer like me but as a full-fledged "blue badger," a permanent employee with blue-badge security clearance and a modest paycheck to match. We had spaghetti under the stars in the courtyard of the hotel, just outside the city. Predictably he tried to recruit me, but I'd never been interested in acquiring anything other than the green security badge meant for soldiers on loan. Besides, I had the best of both the military and intelligence worlds in my current gig, without the endless paperwork. Being a freelancer suited me just fine.

Another time I was rounding a corner in Sana'a, the capital of Yemen, when I almost bumped straight into Glen, my friend from SEAL Team 3. He'd moved into contract work after leaving the Navy in 2005, but we'd stayed close.

Like many of the guys on our team, Glen had been ambivalent about continuing on in the service after we got back from Iraq. After spending some time in group medical, he'd done some odd jobs as a medic for wealthy finance types. They'd pay to have him come along on their adventure trips so he could stitch them up anytime they cut themselves on a reef. Fun while it lasted, but no long-term potential. Now he was back to doing high-risk security work for three times what the military would pay. Not all that much, since the military is notoriously cheap, even if this particular security company was at the top of the heap. In some ways the work could offer the upsides of military work without the

commitment or constraints on your time. But if things went south, the job would entail the same amount of risk—without fully armed birds and AC-130s on the other end of your radio to pluck you out of harm's way.

In the moment we pretended to be strangers. He was unmistakably an outsider, a buff white guy dressed in a polo shirt and khakis clearly providing protection detail for embassy employees in the area. We both knew better than to give anybody watching a reason to believe we had anything to do with each other. A couple of days later we managed to meet up discreetly at a cafe nearby. Owned by an American couple who lived above the shop, it was widely known as a safe place to talk. The walled-in courtyard was surrounded by cameras, and there were some fucked-up antennas on top of the building. Whatever that couple was doing in the country, it didn't seem to be exclusively related to hospitality.

Glen and I would fly together from time to time after I got my pilot's license around 1998. Spend enough time jumping out of airplanes, and some guys develop an itch to grab the controls. He'd been working toward a commercial pilot's license, and we'd taken turns flying a rented Cessna over the mountains to the east of San Diego a couple of times.

We made plans to do it again before too long.

On my next trip to Yemen, or maybe the trip after that, a new employee showed up while I was doing some work for the embassy. When I walked into his office to brief him on a tagging-and-tracking job, I was greeted by a pair of bright, crystal blue eyes that looked weirdly familiar. An old-timer with the look of a guy who'd spent too long sitting on his ass raking in his senior executive pay, he'd clearly volunteered for an Africa assignment just to get out from underneath his desk. We didn't piece it together until our third meeting—he'd moved to Saudi in 1982, just like my family, and we'd met on the plane over from Texas. Crazy that a stranger's features would make such an impression on me as a kid, but we'd all spent hours together at customs while the Saudis ransacked our luggage.

Funny enough, his name actually *was* Bob.

I had to wonder if Bob and the agency he worked for had something to do with the reason my dad had moved us to the Middle East. How all those habits of his stacked up is something I'm still trying to unravel.

I did manage to get him talking some, soon after my return from BUD/S. We'd had time for only one story that particular night, and after I shipped off to 18 Delta we never got to continue our talk. My mom had to fill in the rest with the patchy stories she'd been told, which started up soon after the two of them met.

My dad had been spending summers working for the family business, building houses with his father while working toward his college degree. One of those houses was just down the street from my grandfather's, for a neighbor named Bob Denson.

Another Bob, and a squirrelly one, but with a flashy sense of style and a Texas swagger. Never seen without his cowboy boots or hat, Denson was a private eye with his own security and investigations firm, and he was connected in Dallas law enforcement circles. In 1963 he'd been the lead investigator for the defense on the trial of Jack Ruby, the nightclub owner who'd gunned down Lee Harvey Oswald on his way into county jail for the assassination of President John F. Kennedy. Even though they were on opposite sides of the aisle, Denson had a special connection with the Dallas County attorney general who led the prosecution, Henry Wade. Five years after the Ruby case, the two of them secretly optioned the rights to the trial story (along with fifteen boxes of files from the district attorney's office) to a Hollywood producer. The movie never got made, but the whole thing raised some eyebrows.

A few years after that, Attorney General Wade would lose his most famous case in a 1973 trial against a certain "Jane Roe."

Denson's investigation gigs ran the gamut from high to low, from big trials to run-of-the-mill infidelity claims. A smart kid with a photographic memory, a friendly face, and some heft could be useful in his line of work. My dad's barrel chest had stuck around after his football career bit the dust, and Bob asked him if he'd like to make a little extra money on the side. That sounded a lot better than stocking shelves at the Howdy Doody, so my dad accepted the offer and started working some light surveillance gigs for Bob. Denson became a friend, maybe a mentor. The two of them would go deer hunting together some weekends. At least that's what Bruce told my mom they were up to. He never mentioned the surveillance, only that he was "doing something for Bob."

We came along for the ride once.

I was only four or five, but the episode stuck around in my memory bank. My mom didn't know what her husband was up to, and she didn't trust or like Denson much. One night as my dad was getting ready to go out, she grabbed my hand and told me to keep quiet.

"Where are we going?"

"Shhhhh, we're just going to play a little game. Stay quiet for Mommy and then you can have a lollipop."

We snuck out of the duplex ahead of my dad and climbed into the back of the old pickup truck he was driving at the time.

"Lie down, we're going for a ride."

As my mom remembers it, Dad drove around to different spots, parked for a while, took some notes in a little black book, then drove on to another spot.

When he'd come back from those nights away, they'd have a bunch more cash on hand. The jobs kept on coming for years, a couple of times a month, until we left for Saudi.

The story my dad told me that night after BUD/S must have happened over one of those long "hunting" weekends. A high-up exec at Texaco had gotten himself abducted by a group of guerrilla fighters while working down in Colombia in the early 1980s, a time when active U.S. oil exploration in the region created a lively trade in foreign ransoms.

Bob Denson was hired to get him back safely, and he'd brought my dad and a few other men along to help with a propaganda mission.

"Basically it boiled down to us dropping flyers all over the village where the VP was being held," Dad told me.

"There didn't turn out to be much to it."

The idea was to send the villagers a message, and the message was pretty straightforward—"Release the Texaco official, or you and your families will be killed."

Apparently it worked. The Colombians released the hostage without claiming their ransom, and the Americans came home after a short, uneventful trip.

"Hey, how come you never told me any of this before?"

"Well, there's more to it—but we'll have to save that for another night."

The two of us took a trip to the shooting range a few days later, taking turns on a semiautomatic rifle I'd bought myself as a graduation present. I'd just gotten through an advanced firearms training course, yet still the guy completely crushed me. The dude had a level of aptitude on a weapon he didn't regularly handle that went far beyond anything you'd expect of the tinkering, middle-aged dad down the street—or the mechanical engineering professor in your freshman classroom.

The story my mom told me after his death helped explain that. It also helped explain why he'd never mentioned anything associated with his days of working for Bob Denson, aside from the one night after BUD/S.

While my dad was still in college, early on in their marriage, something went wrong during a surveillance gig. Either that, or Bob Denson hired my dad to kill someone in the late 1970s.

My mom's memory of the events is blurry, probably because it's something she'd rather forget. But she does remember that my dad had been acting nervous for weeks.

Finally he broke down and told her that he'd shot someone. The man was in a wheelchair, paralyzed from the waist down, and my dad was going to have to appear in front of a grand jury, maybe go to jail. My mom was terrified, of course, and Bruce still wasn't telling her much about what was going on. The two of them went out to buy a suit, and she remembers combing my dad's long hair for his court appearance. Bob Denson was in the background, coaching Dad and possibly pulling strings. I'm guessing Denson's good friend Henry Wade may have been involved as well, because nothing ever came of the case.

One day a few years later my parents were shopping at the local department store when my dad turned white as a ghost and rushed back out to the street, dragging my mom behind him. He'd seen the man he'd shot inside.

These pieced-together stories jangled around in my brain for years before I finally took some time to look into them, after I got out of the military. Maybe I could figure out how much truth there was to the wheelchair story my mom had told me, I thought. A few phone calls and some online digging turned into a foot chase. But the trail went cold pretty quickly. The Denton County police station didn't have on-site records going back to the 1970s, so they sent me to the county courthouse. Down in the courthouse basement, there was no record of my dad ever having been arrested. Subpoenas were stored separately, at the Dallas County courthouse. Only at the courthouse, there was no record of my dad having been called to trial in any case.

That was sort of the end of the line on the paperwork front. My dad had been cleared of criminal wrongdoing and wiped from any records I could find. Maybe the sight of that man in the wheelchair was the reason he moved our family eight thousand miles away. Or maybe he was up to something else altogether in Saudi. Seems like I'll never find out the real reason he carried a semiautomatic pistol everywhere he went or crushed me at the shooting range.

16

*

EAST COAST, VARIOUS

A LITTLE WAYS INTO MY PLACEMENT IN D.C., A FELLOW SEAL NAMED
Ted pulled me into a Special Mission Unit reporting directly to ████
████████████████████████ Command. The more tenured of the
two of us, he was a seasoned operator, a professional down to his core,
and one of the nicest guys you could hope to meet. His subdued style
sometimes got him overlooked. But he was one of the unit's founding
fathers, with serious smarts and a sense of caution that was a good balance
to my tendency to gamble. Our professional relationship would outlast
both of our Navy careers.

The unit moved at light speed and didn't micromanage, an outgrowth
of the culture of the team it was attached to. Every operator on that team
had free rein to become the expert in whatever they wanted to be, by
whatever means necessary, whether that meant training in combatives
with the best jiujitsu fighters in Brazil or taking a year to climb the
world's tallest mountains. For me it was a dream job, with an affiliation

* The contents of this chapter title represented a clear and imminent threat to
national security. This chapter title has been dealt with accordingly.

with a team I'd hoped to join my entire career. The SMU had a specific need for an advanced program with a streamlined capacity, the first of several we'd stand up within the unit.

██

██

██.

The program ended up being just the first of several programs we'd stand up within that SMU. Unfortunately the transition would involve a second move for my family, to the East Coast location where the Special Mission Unit was based—and just a little over a year after we'd settled outside D.C. I'd sold Carrie on the first change of address as an extended shore leave that would give us time and space to reconnect. But I'd wound up traveling just as much, sometimes for shorter stops and sometimes for back-to-back three-month trips. Now we were taking off again, just as she'd been preparing to launch a business of her own. Moving again so soon, with a young daughter in tow and our marriage at a low point, was probably the kiss of death for our relationship. But when the military calls, especially at that level, you answer the phone and pack your bags.

Like anyone interested in clandestine operational tactics, I'd read the book *The Master of Disguise* by Tony Mendez soon after it came out. A retired CIA officer, Mendez famously smuggled a group of Americans to safety in the wake of the Iranian hostage crisis by passing them off as Canadian filmmakers (an episode that became the basis for the movie *Argo*). That book informed my thinking in terms of what was possible within government channels, and once we got the go-ahead from our commanding officer, Ted and I started putting together the pieces.

A friend of mine out in San Diego, Stu Segall, had made his fortune on low-budget Hollywood productions like *Silk Stalkings.* A self-made businessman with a career arc that included a stint producing hard-core

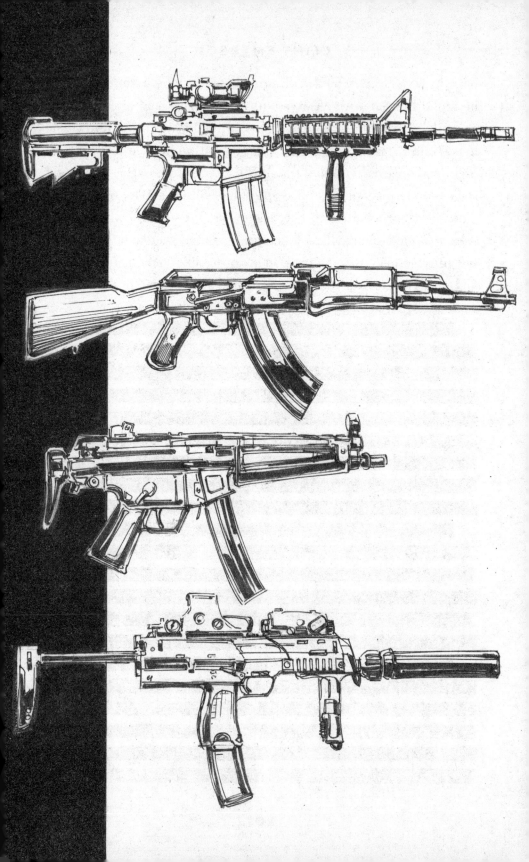

porn, he was the guy who'd made Ron Jeremy famous. In the early 2000s he found himself with an excess of studio space, and after a chance encounter with some DEA agents he got the idea of using it to create hyperrealistic tactical training facilities for the military. I'd used his facilities for a concealed-weapons training block a few times. He had a sound stage semipermanently set up as an Afghan village, and for our training block he'd put together an overseas restaurant scenario where actors were walking around with AK-47s slug over their shoulders. Idiots with big guns were all over the place in countries like Yemen and Somalia, and we needed to override some of our students' combat training so they could safely navigate through those environments.

.*

For a more permanent solution, we looked closer to home.

The West Coast trips were good opportunities to reconnect with some of the boys from SEAL Team 3. Glen Doherty was based out in Encinitas, a beach town just north of San Diego, and on one of my visits, we met halfway between Los Angeles and San Diego for lunch. Glen was still working the overseas rotations, and still conflicted about the gig. He'd been back to Iraq several times, a depressing assignment that highlighted the intractability of the Middle Eastern conflict.

We spent some time talking about our love lives, a subject the two of us had logged many hours on in the past. Glen was divorced by then, on the other side of a relationship that still left him pretty tortured. Part of him wanted to settle down and start a family, but he also had this wanderlust that wasn't so much about women as it was about the unfulfilled ambitions he carted around. In recent years he'd started emailing

---

* Let's try a joke:
   What's black and white and red all over, and can't go through revolving doors?
   A nun with a spear stuck in her head.

a small group of us these missives about where he was in life, what he was thinking about. He'd title them "Glen v.1," "Glen v.2," "Glen v.3," like he was working through the glitches in his own operating system.

He was preparing for a trip to Libya, which he told me would be his last.

My own relationship issues provided plenty of grist for the mill. As far as Carrie was concerned, this all solidified my reputation as a two-faced liar, and the move definitely hadn't improved things between us.

My long-term plan had always been to put in the full twenty years of service that entitles members of the military to their retirement pay. But every job has its ups and downs, and like anyone faced with the prospect of renewing a contract (in our case, every four years), I'd sometimes play with the idea of trying on other possibilities on a brisker schedule. At one of these moments I happened to be seated next to a woman who worked for a pharmaceutical company on a plane ride back from D.C. We got to talking about her work. She was plugging Big Pharma as a path to riches and success, and she was chatty, going on about how my background as a medic would make me a natural at sales, and how much she loved the lifestyle and her brand-new convertible Thunderbird.

I forgot her name as soon as we stepped off the plane. So when she texted me her number I'd put her down in my phone as "T Bird."

We exchanged a couple of texts after that. I saw her as a potential business contact, back pocket insurance in case I ever did get itchy feet. But you can already see where this is going.

When I'd leave town on assignment, my cell phone didn't come with me. Carrie had the password and was in charge of contacting me through Navy channels if anything important came through. I didn't have anything to hide. But when a text from a contact listed as "T Bird" came through with nothing but the cryptic acronym "IMU," it sure didn't look that way. To Carrie, *IMU* could stand for only one thing: "I miss you." So she called the number to get confirmation on her suspicions.

My professional acquaintance picked up the phone and immediately started gushing.

"Oh my gosh, Clint, I never thought you would call!"

T Bird had been using the professional angle as a pretext for pursuing me as a romantic prospect.

When Carrie informed her that she was my wife and asked to know who the fuck *she* was speaking to, T Bird got a little spicy.

"Maybe you should ask your husband."

That didn't go over too well. The voice mail from a woman offering me a private tour of a small Hawaiian island didn't either.

The trail of evidence was stacking up against me. Things got to the point where there was nothing I could say to convince Carrie that a line hadn't been crossed. And the reality was that while I hadn't technically hooked up with any of these women, I was constantly pushing the envelope, testing the edge. For Carrie every trip I went on was just an excuse, in her mind, for me to meet up with female agents for down-and-dirty trysts. Her suspicions became so consuming that she even considered hiring a private investigator, but talked herself out of it. If I did want to hide something, she reasoned, I had the perfect skill set.

She had a point. . . . When your husband teaches the course, there are probably better uses for your money than hiring a two-bit private dick.

17

PIRATES
AND BIG FISH

SOMALIA, YEMEN, 2011

"THE PIRATE, THE PIRATE!"

My local contacts were gesturing toward a Somali man in his early fifties on the side of the road. Short salt-and-pepper beard, bloodshot eyes, oversize sport coat and slacks, untucked button-down shirt. Scuffed-up European business clothing three sizes too big and a few decades behind the curve, the alternative to the traditional *thawb*. He didn't look familiar to me, and I wasn't in Somalia to hunt down pirates, at least on that particular trip. But you can't round a corner in certain parts of the world without running into a bad guy. We hadn't made it far enough for me to set down my bags. The U.S. authorities had circulated Mohammad Saaili Shibin's photograph to anybody we were remotely friendly with in and around the area, and my local police escorts had recognized the man. Apparently the guy shuffling by the side of the road had been the lead negotiator for the bad guys during the deadly hijacking of the *Quest*, a month and a half earlier.

The American missionaries on board the fifty-eight-foot yacht had been sailing the world passing out Bibles when the *Quest* ran into trouble off the coast of Oman. They were supposed to stick to the well-traveled shipping lanes, and for some unknown reason they'd veered off course.

When they did, nineteen pirates in a lightweight skiff took the opportunity to board their ship. Onshore, Mohammad Saaili Shibin was stalking the hostages online to determine their potential worth. As he made his calls to members of their families, the Navy positioned a destroyer between the yacht and the shore. If the pirates transferred their catch to land, we would officially lose control of the situation. They'd be able to squirrel away the hostages for weeks or months while haggling over a multimillion-dollar ransom.

Not too many people know the details of what went down on board that yacht, but from what I heard some infighting broke out as the pirates began to panic. The situation disintegrated when the pirates fired an RPG at the destroyer. Before the spec ops team dispatched with the Navy contingent could board, the pirates had killed and/or mortally wounded all four passengers on board the *Quest*. Two pirates on board were killed immediately by the spec ops team as they boarded, two others were found dead on the scene, and another thirteen who were on board or on a skiff nearby were arrested and brought to shore.

The thirteen who'd been arrested were small-time criminals. It was their bosses we were after. The feds were determined to make a dent in the network of moneymen, launderers, and negotiators who were netting the Somalian economy hundreds of millions of dollars a year. Now that we'd lost American lives in the fight, they smelled blood in the water.

To say that the oceans around Somalia were extremely dangerous at the time would be a major understatement. Increasingly the busy shipping lanes around the Horn of Africa, a critical byway for global trade, had become a harrowing gauntlet for any vessel passing through. At the least the trip was probably going to cost you a couple of million dollars. At the exact moment my plane had touched the ground, more than fifty vessels and eight hundred hostages were being held in the area.

Think about that for a minute. Anytime ISIS takes a Western hostage, it's sure to make headlines. But bands of heavily armed criminals were hijacking fishing boats, yachts, and huge commercial containerships on a weekly basis, and it had become business as usual. Pirating was a thriving industry that was costing the international business community and insurance companies billions in lost revenues. International naval task forces were ramping up their efforts to restore order, but the pirates had become more aggressive in response. By 2013 the situation would be somewhat under control. But it was a shit show for a good long while.

The American authorities had been tracking Shibin all over East Africa since the murder on the *Quest* in February. And now we'd seen their man walking down the side of the road. I hung back in the rear vehicle while we reeled in our surprise catch of the day. Shibin was a top priority for the feds, but some on-the-ground diplomacy would have to take place before he could be extradited to the United States. No need to complicate the situation by throwing a random white guy into the mix before then. This was strictly local for the moment, and it wasn't my gig anyway.

I'd flown in for an operation not unlike the assignment that had brought me to the harbor in Djibouti for my first gig. This time I was traveling much lighter. My ultimate destination was the harbor, a busy, transient port that was a resupply center for midsize commercial boats— and a convenient point of transit for bad guys moving to and from Yemen, or any of the countries bordering the Persian Gulf.

I waited in an empty office while Shibin was interrogated by local officials down the hall. They requested my assistance with one aspect of the arrest. In order to maintain our uneasy geopolitical alliance, the handoff to American authorities would need to be cleared with several local clan leaders. That would take some time. After the initial interrogation, Shibin would be released for about forty-eight hours while the clan elders debated his fate, and we needed to make sure he wouldn't disappear on us before they came to an agreement.

*

While the politics played themselves out. Once the clan elders had given their approval, the feds took over on the logistics of the extradition. Pirating wasn't an act of war, so the investigations wouldn't fall under military jurisdiction. It was only the luck of the draw that had put me in his orbit to begin with, so I was happy to hang back in the shadows.

Shibin was sentenced to twelve life sentences in an American prison, the highest-ranking pirate we'd ever managed to capture and prosecute.

The gig I was actually there to do went off without a hitch.

———

Somalia had existed as a unified republic only since 1990. Ever since, its southern half—a Soviet-backed Marxist state for a while, in an interesting turn of events—had fought for secession. The whole time, the Yemenese Shia minority, led by a faction called the Houthis, had been battling the Sunni government with the support of Iran. The attack on the *Cole* had shown us in no uncertain terms that al-Qaeda had found a foothold within the chaotic state. Now the contagious forces of the Arab Spring had begun to roll through the country. Protests had begun peacefully, just outside the university in the capital city of Sana'a, but devolved into open street combat after the president's forces fired on the protesters. The only constant in Yemen was chaos, and any U.S. military or intelligence personnel in the region prepared for that as best we could.

* In this redacted passage, we revealed the United States' nuclear codes and gave away our best pirate-fighting tricks.

Traveling between the embassy and my hotel, I'd alternate between a handful of routes to avoid setting myself up for an ambush. Thirteen U.S. embassy guards and nearby civilians had been killed in 2008, when six members of the Yemeni branch of al-Qaeda drove two car bombs and a bunch of heavy weapons through the embassy gates in Sana'a. Ever since, any security personnel in the region had been on heightened alert.

On this particular day there was a surge of activity on the streets as I drove away from the embassy. But I wasn't aware of that until I turned a corner and found myself smack in the middle of a mob of hundreds of riled-up Yemenis. From one block to the next, the streets were suddenly flooded with a thick mass of people, mostly men of fighting age.

A look at the line of cars in my rearview mirror told me I was boxed in, with no choice but to continue bumping along.

Before long the temperature changed.

My lily-white mug had begun attracting attention.

A group of young hotheads surrounded my SUV, trying the locks. When they figured out I wasn't dumb enough to leave the doors open, they started banging on my windows.

I tried to deescalate the situation, but my little monosyllabic outbursts didn't have much of an effect.

"Hey!"

"Stop that!"

I raised my empty hands to try to show them I wasn't looking for a fight. But when a mob gathers momentum, it has a force of its own.

My options were limited. I couldn't back up, and I couldn't drive forward. I'd been in-country for only a day and hadn't had time to charge or activate the phone I'd picked up at the embassy. There was a pistol tucked into my holster, of course, but pulling out a weapon would have escalated the situation fast.

What was I going to do—mow down the entire crowd?

I was completely outmanned, and definitely outgunned. There were Yemenese soldiers in the crowd, but also many civilians carrying arms.

Now the half-dozen young men were rocking the car back and forth with their combined body weight. My tires were catching air and my five-thousand-pound ride was feeling like a tin can on wheels. Out of options, I pulled out my embassy badge to try to convey what I hoped would be a neutral kind of authority. Maybe one of them had a relative who cleaned toilets there. You never know.

Wrong call. My badge and now known association with the embassy only pissed them off more.

"American, American!" they shouted out to the crowd.

All these guys needed was additional provocation beyond the color of my skin, and now they had it.

The commotion around my vehicle increased.

Plowing through the crowd would have gotten several civilians caught under my axles like a bunch of zombies. Which would definitely have pissed off their friends, then left me stuck in place to deal with the repercussions.

The irony of the situation didn't escape me.

All the shit I'd done, and *this* was how I was going to die?

Getting caught in the middle of a violent protest is destabilizing. It's not like combat, where the targets are more clearly defined. You're swimming in an undistinguished wave of civilians. There were women and children in that crowd. There were regular people who were sick and tired of a corrupt, nonfunctioning government that shot up civilians for no good reason. There were also some bad apples, criminals, terrorists, and young men in search of a cause. The latter was probably the group I'd just run into.

Luckily there were also a few peacekeepers. After a few more minutes of trying to pacify my immediate neighbors, I spotted a Yemenese soldier trying to hold the crowd back from my car. For a moment our eyes made contact, and I took a calculated risk.

Rubbing my thumb against my fingertips to make the international sign for cold, hard cash, I waved him over.

He got the message.

Pushing people aside with the muzzle of his AK-47, he started making his way toward me.

I let him in and hit the lock.

"Hey. Thank you. Will you help me get out of here?"

He nodded in response. And once I gestured for him to point his weapon through the windshield, he aimed his gun straight at the crowd.

For a minute I started feeling a little sorry about all the shit I'd talked about Yemenese soldiers while on board the *Cole*. Thanks to this one it seemed like I actually had a shot at getting out of there alive.

Like magic, the seas parted, and we started bumping along.

As soon as I had enough clearance, I floored the gas.

Within just a few blocks, the streets were dead, with no one in sight. A half mile in Yemen was the difference between life or death that day. I pulled into the first gas station we passed and gave the soldier his money, and he jumped into a cab.

After that I made sure never to go anywhere on assignment without a full tank of gas, a fully charged cell phone battery, and a thick wad of cash.

Luckily I had that last part taken care of, or you wouldn't be holding this book in your hands today.

By June of that year the president of Yemen would be wounded by a rocket launched at the royal palace and the country would be thrown into full-scale civil war.

18

WE GOT HIM

YEMEN, 2011

I'D BEEN BACK IN VIRGINIA A COUPLE OF WEEKS WHEN MY PHONE STARTED blowing up.

The news found me around the same time it reached the rest of the world. A few hours after the fact, when the rumors and alerts started bouncing around online. A couple of hours before Barack Obama made his announcement on the night of May 1, 2011: "Tonight I can report to the American people and to the world that the United States has conducted an operation that killed Osama bin Laden, the leader of al-Qaeda, and a terrorist who's responsible for the murder of thousands of innocent men, women, and children."

The headlines the next morning were a little less restrained. "Vengeance at Last!" "Rot in Hell!"—and my personal favorite, "We Got the Bastard!" The number one target of the Department of Defense had been taken down. A team of SEALs had landed two helicopters in Pakistan and stormed the rat fuck's compound. Osama bin Laden was dead, the stash of porn on his hard drives buried in a CIA file that would probably never see the light of day. In keeping with Islamic tradition, the head of al-Qaeda was consigned to a watery grave somewhere in the Arabian Sea within twenty-four hours of the raid.

I had no way of knowing whether the operation I'd done back in Djibouti ever led to actionable information about OBL's whereabouts. I was just one small cog in a very big wheel made up of hundreds of intelligence officers, soldiers, sources, diplomats, and every technology that could be brought to bear.

Four months later I'd play a role in hunting down another high-profile al-Qaeda target—the HVI that a multiagency task force had been watching for years. His name was Anwar al-Awlaki—"Triple-A" for short. A radical imam with a talent for turning young Westernized Muslims into ticking time bombs, he was a dual U.S.-Yemeni citizen. But the privileges of citizenship have their limits, as he would come to find out.

Preaching and lecturing in English, he'd eased listeners in with content on the life of the Prophet before getting them hooked on the harder stuff. He didn't have an accent, and he was technologically fluent. Despite the bushy beard and turban, he wasn't some wizened character out of *1,001 Arabian Nights.* Born, partly raised, and educated in the good old U.S. of A., he liked deep-sea fishing and self-help books and was only a couple of years older than me. Somewhere along the way he'd turned from an increasingly devout college kid into a terrorist. After he left the United States his views radicalized fast. By 2010 he had cofounded al-Qaeda's English-language magazine, *Inspire,* and was calling for jihad against the United States. By then he'd also transitioned to active participation in the planning of terror plots, forming an external operations cell inside al-Qaeda in the Arabian Peninsula (AQAP). Created by the coming together of Saudi and Yemeni militants in 2009, AQAP was the only division of al-Qaeda focused directly on Western targets.

One of the attacks al-Awlaki directly orchestrated involved a pair of briefs.

The "underwear bomber" who packed his skivvies with explosives before boarding a Detroit-bound Northwest Airlines flight on Christmas Day of 2009 was the son of a prominent banker. A college student from the mostly English-speaking country of Nigeria, he'd discovered the imam's lectures in a bookstore in London, eventually traveling to Yemen to receive more direct inspiration—and instruction. Al-Awlaki had been instrumental in designing the attack. Only a last-minute hardware failure and the quick reactions of the passengers on board that flight prevented al-Qaeda from pulling off what would have been their deadliest hit since 9/11. Instead the underwear bomber badly burned his cock and balls and got four consecutive life sentences in a federal supermax. With that kind of sentence, he should have burned his butthole shut.

A couple of months earlier al-Awlaki had exchanged communications with a U.S. Army major who went on to shoot up his military base in Fort Hood, killing thirteen soldiers and support staff and wounding many others.

A year later he'd help orchestrate a plot to bomb two American cargo planes by smuggling explosive materials inside the ink cartridges of printers shipped via FedEx and UPS. That plot also came very close to making the headlines.

These new pieces of direct evidence were the reason he'd made it onto President Barack Obama's secret kill-or-capture list. With Osama bin Laden out of the picture, al-Awlaki's name was close to the top of the list.

For a liberal president, Obama turned out to be pretty decent at killing terrorists.

Unfortunately the target proved to be very good at hiding. Like any high-profile terrorist with crosshairs on his back, he holed up in shifting hideouts and safe houses far from the cities where our surveillance teams could blend into the surrounding density. Once he became an active target in 2010, he went offline, communicating sporadically via encrypted emails or notes sent out through strings of couriers.

While we waited for him to make a move, we went after the low-hanging fruit that might help lead us his way.

Triple-A was smart, and either he knew that certain members of his inner circle were likely to be compromised, or he had them double-dealing.

Either way, he'd feed them bits and pieces of misinformation to camouflage his movements. Nine times out of ten, we'd hear he was going to turn up in some city or town and show up to find nothing.

We'd already missed him twice, in drone strikes I hadn't been involved with. We'd come close in May, just four days after the Bin Laden raid. According to the account given in the book *Objective Troy*, by the journalist Scott Shane, the team running the op had tracked al-Awlaki to one of his village hideaways. They waited until he was in transit on a dirt road to take the shot, in order to minimize the potential for collateral damage. The first several missiles didn't hit the mark. As a cloud cover blocked the view from above, the imam and his entourage were hustled into an al-Qaeda vehicle and driven away. Some of the al-Qaeda members, in an act of martyrdom, swapped into his car and continued to drive. Moments later they were bombed to smithereens.

We'd gotten the right car, but the target had gotten away.

Somehow, this time, we'd have to ensure that the car and the target were in the same place at the same time when we struck.

———

By 2011 my position within the Special Mission Unit had been expanded. On one of my trips to Yemen, I brought along a young member of the unit to join me. The techs had been recruited as support staff for the SMU in a similar capacity to SVD teams, and I was always looking for ways to get them some experience. This particular kid was a whiz but his skills had never been tested outside a classroom or a training scenario. His first real-world lesson would involve some tips on the art of appropriation.

In Sana'a, Triple-A's driver always parked his car outside a twenty-four-hour convenience store. The positioning seemed intentional. A few hundred rials to the shopkeeper would have his car watched through the night. So during our installation we'd have the cover of darkness working to our advantage, but we had to assume there were eyes on us. The trick would be ensuring that there wasn't much to see.

The plan we drew up involved a van. With just a few modifications and a little bit of black magic, it would be good to go.

After a couple of practice runs we were ready to roll.

"Hey, guys, you're good to go."

After getting the all-clear from our guy on overwatch, the tech lit a cigarette and leaned back in the driver's seat.

"Roger."

So far, all the shopkeeper had seen was a van with a couple of males in the front. It would take a *very* high level of vigilance for the shopkeeper to do anything but assume he'd missed the moment when I'd exited the vehicle and entered one of the other shops on the street. A streetlight shining over our cars at an angle did a nice job of keeping the area between the vehicles in shadow. The shadow that log-rolled between the two cars for a split second at ground level wouldn't have been visible from his seated position even if he had been looking.

Nothing to see but an empty van with local plates.

Our man on overwatch would occasionally interject with reports from the street.

"You've got a guy on a motorcycle approaching."

Click.

"Two guys on foot."

Click.

I tuned out the background noise and got to work.

██████████████████████████████████████

███████████████████████████████████████

██████████████████████████████████████

██████████████████████████████████████

████████████████████████

███████████████████████████████████████

███

███

███*

We sat in the front seats for a breath or two, taking a beat to see whether our activity had ruffled any feathers before backing out and pulling away.

Like a standard-issue magic act, the whole thing relied on a couple of cheap tricks, and the bias of the human brain toward previously observed patterns.

Abracadabra, motherfuckers.

Those Army turds were pretty pissed when they saw the van show up in the after-action reports. Since we'd usually put it back where we'd found it by morning, they'd never even noticed it was gone.

Over the next twenty-four hours we watched as the car rolled through a cycle of movements. Nothing out of the ordinary. The driver didn't seem to be heading out of town.

Then, at exactly the twenty-four-hour mark of our operation, everything fell apart.

Fuck.

In search of clues, I drove to the spot where the device had gone black. The coordinates led me to the middle of a random road, which knocked

* Oh well. Really cool operations . . .

** Using really cool gear . . .

out option number two. I didn't see any particularly big bumps or signs of technological components on the asphalt. That left us with the possibility that I had royally fucked up. Which didn't sit too well with any of us.

███

███

███

██████████████████████████████.* The only other thing I could think of was some sort of administrative flub coming from the top.

If you put the odds on the last hypothesis, you guessed correctly.

The contractor our Special Mission Unit was working with hadn't paid the fucking bill.

When some bean counter in a remote office got an email notification about minutes starting to accumulate, he must have asked his nearest higher-up, who didn't have any documentation on file. When they didn't find immediate answers, they promptly shut us down.

A month of planning . . . down the drain.

We went back to waiting for the driver to come back into town. The hunt for Anwar al-Awlaki would have to be postponed.

███

███

███

███

███

███

███

Nerves can be an issue in the type of scenario I just described, but if you're doing things right, you're not worried about getting caught. Worry, if anything, is what will get you in trouble, tripping up your perception

---

* To do really bad things to really bad people.

so that every dog bark turns into a code red, every shoe in your field of vision is attached to the foot that's going to burn you.

My training, combined with my natural inclination toward risky behavior, made the job an airtight compartment with no room for anxiety. Over time, though, the nature of my activities did begin to wear on me in my civilian life.

Shit has to come out somehow, and it tended to bubble up during transitions.

Going straight from a war-torn African country to my daughter's third birthday party and a house full of squealing toddlers turned out to be too much, as I found out during one homecoming. But there were lots of times when I'd have to go decompress in a coffee shop for a few hours.

I'd see my close friends in town, but I was less interested in group dinners or social events. Cities and crowds tended to irritate me. On the other hand, a dark, quiet house could make my pulse race, too. Walking in after nightfall would have me clearing my safe, suburban home like we'd just rolled into Baghdad.

"Idiot," I'd mutter to myself in the middle of a room-to-room check after a night out eating pizza with my family.

Some of the habits I'd accumulated when working overseas would follow me back to the States—like the checklist I'd work through in hotel rooms to make sure no one had fucked with my shit. At some point, sleeping with a gun tucked under my pillow or mattress became routine, even in my own bed. Carrying a handgun everywhere I went, even for a quick trip to the store, was my norm. Over the years I'd accumulated a double-digit collection of forty-odd personal handguns and rifles. High, but not abnormal for an operator.

But I probably took things to the next level by strategically staging that gun collection throughout our home. In every room, there were one or more guns hidden within easy reach in case an intruder came by. Not to mention a few baseball bats and fixed-blade knives for good measure.

Any member of the military who has deployed to dangerous environments has been trained to make vigilance an automatic professional habit. After you've spent time in places where that vigilance is warranted, letting your guard down can seem like a dumb idea. In my case, first-hand experience of countersurveillance from foreign governments gave me the sense that anything was possible on home ground. There were times when I was vividly aware of being watched while going about my business overseas. Directly or indirectly, I'd been messing with a lot of bad people. The world I moved through had already proven to be very small. Who knew when you might run into somebody you'd unknowingly pissed off. . . .

A good night's sleep became more and more elusive over the years.

19
HOMECOMINGS

VIRGINIA, 2011

THE BOEING CH-47 CHINOOK HELICOPTER WITH THE CALL SIGN EXTOR-tion 17 had taken off from Kabul after midnight on the morning of August 6. The helicopter was carrying a strike force to a location in Afghanistan's Tangi Valley. On the ground, a senior Taliban leader was amassing fighters for a counterstrike against the Rangers who'd fired on them earlier that night.

The transport helicopter was only twenty miles away from Kabul. But as it neared the landing zone, Taliban fighters emerged from the top of a building and started firing shoulder-mounted RPGs. One of their rounds went straight into the Chinook's rear rotor blade.

None of the thirty-eight people on board would make it out alive.

Seventeen of the dead were Navy SEALs, making it the deadliest day in Naval Special Warfare's history since the Normandy landings and the gravest attack on American forces during the Afghanistan war.

Anyone who was in the area came into the East Coast command, and all nonessential operations ground to a halt. They'd turned a huge conference room into our crisis management center, and we started working through the somber tasks ahead.

"SEALs don't die." It's one of the sayings we'd repeat as we cleared kill houses. The irony behind our tongue-in-cheek mantra wasn't lost on us.

Death was a possibility we'd all signed up for. But being such a small force, any loss affected the whole. And this was a huge rip through the big blue tent above our heads. The Navy had known huge simultaneous losses in the wars of previous eras, when battleships were sunk with hundreds of sailors on board. But for the tight-knit modern-day Naval Special Warfare community, losses were counted in single increments. With seventeen of our own gone with the launch of a single shot, this was the deadliest day we'd known.

They were setting up tables, one for each man we'd lost. I'd known every one of those men in some capacity and had spent time with many of them overseas just a few months earlier. Some were friends of a dozen years or more.

My gut sank each time I spotted one of their names.

"Mills."

I'd known who the likely losses were since walking in the door of the command. But seeing Matt reduced to the five letters of his last name on a plaque was something else.

Navy officers were already on their way to notify his next of kin: the mother of his one-year-old son, whom he'd married just four months earlier. But his ex-wife, and the two kids they'd had together, were lost in the administrative churn. They'd be watching the news. I was on the next flight out of Norfolk in my dress blues, with a couple of Navy officers in tow.

Matt had been on his first deployment with the teams when he came over to Echo Platoon as we headed to Iraq, but he'd been married with a baby boy before enlisting. We'd stayed in touch after I started to separate from the teams. After Carrie and I moved to Virginia, he and I would sometimes meet up at a boxing club where command had a contract to do some sparring in the mornings. A seasoned and accomplished operator by then, the trip that July marked his tenth tour in Afghanistan.

There's more weight to the duty of notifying next of kin than a person could ever imagine. She was weeping when she opened the door, and I knew that every word out of my mouth would follow a script she'd already been rehearsing in her head. We skipped most of the talking and replaced our lines with silent hugs.

Who gets the flag, where the life insurance policy goes, who needs to be flown out to which event. . . . The Navy looks only at what's on paper when it comes to next of kin, so I was determined to make sure his ex-wife and her kids didn't fall through the cracks. When a military transport plane brought the remains of the soldiers home to Dover Air Force Base, the Navy flew Matt's ex and the kids out from Oklahoma. Only they missed their flight in Dallas the night before, then boarded an early morning plane to Philadelphia, then got stuck on the tarmac in bad weather. Some FBI contacts relayed the message to the TSA, and somehow they got that plane off the ground. But it wasn't soon enough. One by one, the coffins draped in Stars and Stripes were slowly lifted off the plane by two lines of pallbearers. The president and vice president of the United States, the secretary of defense, and a half-dozen other top brass from the government raised their right arms in solemn salute as the procession passed. The boys of Extortion 17 had their final homecoming with a crowd silently standing at attention.

The minute their flight landed, Pennsylvania state troopers raced them to the state line, where their Delaware counterparts took over. When the escort came blazing through, I led them to a back room inside the hangar.

Before I could brief them on what to expect, the door opened and President Obama walked in.

I'd put in a word with a BUD/S classmate on the White House counterterrorism advisory team. While the special operations community generally liked Obama because he kept us so busy, he'd made a lot of enemies in military circles by stripping the Pentagon's budgets down to practically nothing. But on that day he took twenty minutes out of his schedule to sit down with a widow and her two children and let them cry on his shoulder.

Back on base, we began to sort through the men's personal effects, the items sent over from Afghanistan and the gear from their lockers a few buildings over. Any electronic devices needed to be scanned for internal communications or data. My techs and I spent what felt like months working through the many thousands of gigabytes of data, our breath catching in our throats anytime we'd run into photos of kids, girl-friends, parents, wives. For a while after that it was just one memorial service after another in Virginia and Arlington.

I avoided most of them.

I went to Matt's, but only on the last-minute insistence of a mutual friend. I didn't want some canned memorial service muddying my memories of our friendship. What I wanted to remember him for was the last time we were bullshitting together at the command. Or that moment when he got himself tangled up in his gear in the middle of the ambush outside Tikrit, the two of us laughing our heads off while bullets whizzed by our heads. That was Matt. Not some graveside speech about how noble he was.

Toward the end of the summer we finally caught a break in our hunt for our HVI, with a tip that turned out to be accurate. We located al-Awlaki near the northern border of Yemen. This time we'd taken steps to ensure that we'd know the target was inside the vehicle in advance of a strike, using technology that went far beyond what we used previously. President Obama was looking for his 100 percent positive ID, and he got it, with confirmation delivered straight to the White House Situation Room within seconds of the strike. On September 30, 2011, weeks after I'd last been in the country, an unmanned aerial vehicle banished Triple-A from the world of the living.

How did we do it, and what part did I play? The agency that drove the operation isn't in any rush to declassify the details, and I'm not too interested in giving terrorists a lesson in exactly how we go about hunting them, either. There are whole books about the hunt for al-Awlaki and tons of information online about aspects that didn't involve me. Do any amount of reading and you'll also find lots of backlash against the authorization of a targeted killing of a U.S. citizen without putting him on trial.

But it turns out you lose a few privileges when you're directly implicated in attempts to assassinate large groups of American citizens. Al-Awlaki had become a threat to the nation, and killing him was legally determined to be an act of collective self-defense.

It had been a long road to an abrupt finale.

Unfortunately radical Islam loves a martyr. The finale didn't stick.

The folks making the decisions probably had some sense of the risk factors involved when they added his name to the top of their list. The imam's jihadist calls had been catchy before his death. It was always possible that obliterating him might only enhance his appeal to a population of young Muslims already pissed about U.S. military presence in the Middle East. The real unknown was how far his message would travel on the information highway.

In the years following his death, we found out. Since that day in September of 2011, al-Awlaki's influence has been linked to attacks in San Bernardino, Orlando, and Chattanooga—and to a shocking act of domestic terrorism in Boston in the spring of 2013. The Boston Marathon bombing took place more than a year after his death, but the two young Chechen immigrants who perpetrated it lifted their bomb-making instructions straight from the Web pages of *Inspire* magazine. There's also evidence to suggest that, before he was blasted into oblivion, al-Awlaki provided some financial assistance to the animals who ended up storming the offices of the satirical Parisian newspaper *Charlie Hebdo* in 2015.

YouTube finally scrubbed his videos two years ago, but with his calls to action permanently wedged into the darkest corners of the Internet, it looks like dipshits all over the world will still be influenced by that little bearded prick for years to come.

20

FRIENDS, AND ENEMIES

VIRGINIA, 2012

THE WORST TWO MONTHS OF MY PROFESSIONAL LIFE KICKED OFF WITH a phone call in early September.

"Hey, Clint—I've got some bad news."

The voice on the other end of the line was my ops chief, a friend named Dave who'd been the honor man in my BUD/S class. And he was telling me in no uncertain terms not to show up for work that day.

"I don't have any idea what's going on—*but you need to turn around and go home.*"

I cut across three lanes of traffic and made Dave repeat what he'd just said.

"Base police have got your picture up at all the checkpoints. And it looks like they're planning on detaining you if you come into work."

What the living fuck.

My face had been plastered all over base.

All of a sudden my workplace was treating me like a wanted man.

And I had *no* idea why.

Neither did Dave.

"Right now I don't know anything more than you do," Dave went on. "But I'm going to find out what is going on—and then I will call you back."

"Are you . . . fucking with me right now?"

"Dude, I'm completely serious. Do *not* come into work today. I will call you when I know more."

Click.

I turned around and went home.

That call back turned into complete silence over the better part of a week.

From one minute to the next, I'd been exiled from the teams and turned into some kind of criminal.

What the fuck had I done?

I immediately started working my network for answers, but none of the enlisted SEALs knew a thing. Without any clues and with zero communication of any kind from my leadership, my imagination ran wild. The whole thing was a complete fucking mystery. And any answers lay beyond those checkpoints I'd been told to stay away from.

The only thing I could think of was a rumor a friend had passed along a few weeks earlier.

An operator on his team allegedly had some quantity of gold bullion bars tucked away somewhere. And the guy, who'd recently been involved in a high-profile mission, was sniffing around for someone to quietly sell it on his behalf.

"If he wants this to stay under wraps," I'd wondered out loud, "why would he come outside his circle of trust?"

My buddy had just cocked his head. The answer was obvious.

If the rumor was true, the operator had nabbed the gold on target. He was looking for an outsider to broker the deal because he didn't want to share the spoils with his friends. What was strange was that you had a guy going to such great lengths to venture outside his crew. Crookedness tends to run in cliques, a small circle of trust that will protect its own. Then again, this particular operator, someone I knew only slightly, had a reputation for being a self-serving prick.

Given the timing, the person involved, and the fact that he was reaching outside his circle, there was only one conclusion to draw: that gold bullion, if it even existed at all, had been lifted directly out of a compound in Pakistan.

Not just any compound. It was difficult to imagine that the gold had belonged to anyone *other* than Osama bin Laden.

But all I'd done was listen to a rumor.

I hadn't even passed it along.

It didn't make much sense. But sitting in my house with the walls closing in around me, that was the only thing I could possibly come up with.

No call from Dave the next day.

I mentally backtracked through every one of my recent deployments in search of some evidence that I'd broken the law, called a few more guys, obsessively checked my email, reviewed my paperwork.

Nothing.

It didn't seem like that week could get any shittier, but two days later my phone rang again.

Another friend, someone I knew from an early deployment.

"Did you hear?"

My first thought was that he had some information about whatever was going on with me.

But he was calling to tell me something much worse.

Our mutual friend Glen Doherty had been killed the day before, on September 11.

A week and a half earlier, Glen had deployed to Tripoli for another round of contract security work. As he touched in Libya from a flight through D.C., multiple militias were battling for control. Muammar el-Qaddafi had been toppled in October of the prior year with assistance from a NATO coalition. Qaddafi had been a brutal ruler and a vocal supporter of terrorism. But in the vacuum of power left by his sudden dismissal, his massive arsenals of heavy weaponry and chemicals were being raided and sold to the highest bidders. Glen had been in Libya four months earlier, hunting down weapons caches and protecting officers with a paired-down team of former special operators.

Now he was back in time for the anniversary of 9/11. The date tends to prompt heightened security at foreign embassies in Muslim-majority countries. But the State Department's special mission compound in Benghazi was understaffed, with unarmed Libyan security guards manning the front gate. When more than a dozen heavily armed gunmen parked their pickup trucks outside and asked to be let in, they complied. By the time Glen, three other contractors, and two Army Special Operations Forces operators flew over from Tripoli, more than thirty militants had already set fire to the compound. The U.S. ambassador and a member of his staff would die inside the compound from smoke inhalation.

Glen's six-man quick-reaction team was escorted to a second diplomatic building, also under attack.

Ty Woods, another former member of SEAL Team 3 and a friend of Glen's, was one of the contractors already stationed in Benghazi. He was a medic, too, ahead of me in the teams by a couple of years. I knew him only slightly, as a smart, personable guy.

Ty was up on the roof, and Glen raced up there to provide backup. The militants were launching attacks from several locations. He'd been up there for only a few minutes when militants began descending on a nearby position in droves. Mortar shells started dropping, followed by a barrage of small-arms fire. The first shell missed the men. The second one didn't. Glen polished off two militants through his scope before grabbing his med kit. Ty was lying motionless at the other end of the roof. The second shell had likely taken his life. As he ran toward his friend, a third explosion would take Glen's, too.

He was forty-two years old when his life was cut short on the deployment he'd planned to make his last. That's retiring age in spec ops years. But forty-two is young, in civilian time. Glen had a whole life outside the military to live. And anyone who knew him understood how fully he would have lived it.

I wasn't able to make it to his hometown funeral a week later.

I'd been told to stick around in Virginia, on unofficial house arrest.

I wasn't at the Encinitas memorial where his surf buddies scattered some of his ashes on a paddle out, either, or the Rocky Mountain service in Utah where his ski family spread some of the rest on his favorite black diamond run.

Larger-than-life Glen was my friend, not this theoretical Glen who was gone and never coming back. At least that's what I told myself. Processing his absence, in public or in private, wasn't something I'd be ready to do for a while.

All I could do in the moment was sit on my fucking hands with a gaping hole in the pit of my stomach.

I kept on trying to call my friends. A few of them didn't call back.

Another week of house arrest went by before I finally heard from Dave.

"I don't have an update for you, but you should be hearing from leadership soon."

More of the same.

Nothing to report. Except this time he'd need me to meet him somewhere off base so I could turn over my access badges.

I'd still been given *absolutely* no reason for my forced exile—and now it was starting to look permanent.

Another set of increasingly serious repercussions, without a single answer or even a hint as to what I'd done to deserve them. I'd spent two weeks staring at a brick wall I was getting dangerously close to bashing my head against.

"I'm sure everything is going to blow over," Dave said as I handed him my credentials in a fucking parking lot.

He also mentioned that the commanding officer was pissed off about a bunch of guys—not just me.

That's when I called Louis Freeh. The former director of the FBI had served as a federal judge before moving into risk management. But he had a past as a high-stakes attorney with a special interest in dropping the hammer on large corporations and institutions. And more important, he was someone I'd gotten to know and trust during my time in Washington.

The DOD is a Goliath, and as the individual soldier I was an ant. All they had to do to squash me was roll the giant wheels of their machinery right over me. You realize how few rights you have within the military when you find yourself in a situation like mine. But Louis trusted me when I told him I hadn't done anything that could warrant this treatment. We didn't even know what the Special Mission Unit thought they had on me, but he was all set to march me straight over to *60 Minutes*.

I wasn't ready to torch my entire career if there was still a chance of saving it, but the guy's aggressive take on the situation gave me some comfort.

He had some familiarity with the players, since just a couple of months earlier I'd introduced him to the same captain who was now stabbing me in the back.

My connections across the Beltway had gotten me drafted into weekly meetings with something called the CIG—the Commanders' Initiative Group. The only enlisted man at the table, I was being put to use toward Naval Special Warfare's goal of increased communication with the neighboring agencies. But that seat at the big boys' table had been ripped right out from under me, along with the keys to the front door.

Word traveled fast around the community about the group of guys being blackballed by the command, and an arctic chill passed through both my neighborhood and my social circles. Suddenly the guy across the street was turning his back when he saw me. And my phone wasn't ringing off the hook, either.

There was nothing to do but sit in my house in a mounting paranoid rage. Daily calls with Louis Freeh were the only thing that kept me off the ledge. As much a counselor as he was a lawyer, he'd tell me stories about tricky cases from his past to calm me down.

"Whatever it is, it won't be anything we can't handle."

More than anything he was a friend—at a time when everybody else had decided to close rank. Yeah. Everyone in my immediate command turned their backs while Clint was enemy number one. And no one would tell me a thing.

Another two weeks passed before the NSW officer who'd be investigating the situation got in touch. By that point I'd been out for a full fucking month with not a single clue about what was going on.

The officer had been put in charge of looking into any guys engaging in "extracurricular activities," he told me over the phone.

"What the fuck does that mean?"

My fuse was beyond short. It was frayed down to the wire, and I wasn't going out of my way to hide the thick current of resentment that was boiling in my veins. Whatever was going on, it was fucked beyond belief.

"Come into work and we'll sit down and talk."

After a month away from the command, I finally drove back onto base. Eighteen years in the Navy, and they had me check in at the visitor building like I was there to deliver a motherfucking pizza. The investigating officer came out to meet me, and I followed him into a small, windowless room where he had me start by taking an oath. Minus the Bible, the jury, and any semblance of a lack of prejudice, I was basically in court.

On his desk was a fat three-ring binder. Looked like they'd done their opposition research.

As the officer flipped it open, I saw some familiar logos on the first page. One was for a line of travel security products I'd started working on. The other was for a security company I hoped to start when I got out of the military. I'd submitted my retirement papers at the end of the summer, giving the Navy two years' notice of my intention to call it a wrap.

It looked like a simple misunderstanding.

Putting in my twenty and then making something of my own had always been my game plan. In anticipation of the transition I'd started testing a line of travel products for the civilian market. I didn't know anything about product design outside of the hacks I'd developed over the years in dark corners of the world. One thing I *did* know was that my future career was going to involve working for myself, and I'd published a few blog posts on a popular spec ops website to lay the groundwork.

My name was totally unknown outside of the community. And with retirement in my sights, I was trying to get a little online traction for the nonexistent company I'd incorporated, for the sole purpose of getting a head start.

There's paperwork you need to fill out for any nonmilitary income you generate, requesting permission to take on freelance work. Like a good soldier, I'd done the due diligence and had the papers signed by five of my higher-ups. My company wasn't generating any income, but I wanted to make sure to tick all the right boxes.

It was easy enough to explain.

The form was tucked somewhere in that binder, I assumed, so my paper trail should have had me covered.

But in early September the command had been turned upside down by the publication of a book called *No Easy Day,* originally released under the pseudonym Mark Owen.

A SEAL who claimed to have fired the bullets that killed Osama bin Laden after the point man's first shot, "Mark" had royally fucked up by failing to put his book through an internal review, leaking details of the operation that were later deemed to be compromising. There were a whole host of consequences spiraling out from his failure to follow protocol.

The Joint Chiefs of Staff had called up the commander of our unit and railed him for letting an operator write a book about a classified operation. And that commander had gone fucking nuts.

Suddenly, anyone who'd published a book, an article, or a fucking pamphlet got on a blacklist of about twenty dudes. Any connection to Mark Owen, who was also under review for having convinced a bunch of his friends to consult on a hyperrealistic video game, was another nail in the cross. And any publication that hadn't been through the review process was getting a thorough second look.

At that point, having your book reviewed by the Department of Defense wasn't mandatory for current or former service members. But if you accidentally (or intentionally) revealed information that the DOD deemed classified and you hadn't had your shit vetted, you would be liable for violating the professional nondisclosure agreements you signed throughout your career. Naval Special Warfare had gotten caught with its pants down when details of its most high-profile recent mission were laid out for all the world to see. And now they were going into overdrive to compensate.

Completely unrelated to my future plans, a couple of years prior I'd self-published a book as a teaching tool. My philosophy on the habits that would help operators stay safe overseas had evolved over time. In order to make the content stick I'd broken down some of the concepts onto paper, eventually getting the results bound into a book. The thing cost only a few bucks apiece to print. So I swallowed the costs and handed it out to our students for free.

The book had nothing to do with my military service, life as a special operator, or any ops I'd been a part of. The content was general information about the psychology of blending into foreign environments, and all of my immediate leaders knew about it. Some of them even handed the book out to *their* families and friends. There was no reason to think I'd need to put it through a review, particularly back then when the atmosphere was much more lax.

But *No Easy Day* had changed everything.

I came out of that interview with my head spinning. At least now I had some idea of what was going on, but the investigating officer still had me escorted off base. Which didn't do much to decrease my anxiety.

"Just a formality."

Umm, okay. So that's what this whole thing was?

I phoned Louis on my way home to give him the debrief. The focus was these "extracurricular activities," but I'd filed the paperwork months ago. So why was I being targeted?

"You're saying they *gave* you permission? And they have the form you filled out?"

I assumed as much. What the hell else was that binder for?

"Call them back and make sure."

Lo and behold, the head shed had conveniently "forgotten" to include the form in their fat stack of research.

Another two-week period of silence only increased my paranoia. I hadn't done anything wrong, but the process of being investigated had me questioning my own version of events. Could I have fucked up without realizing it? Most of my handful of blog posts had been about personal and travel security. But a couple focused on trends in terrorist activity or highlighted interesting news stories. Maybe all of a sudden it looked like a SEAL was broadcasting internal operations in public blog posts? Since very few people at the command really knew what the fuck I'd been up to, that hypothesis wouldn't have seemed so far-fetched. But I'd gotten my information over the Internet, just like everyone else.

I even started wondering if my phone was being tapped.

The past several weeks had given me a window onto the many ways the military could fuck with their employees. And my familiarity with the government's capabilities only amplified my potential list of fucked-up possibilities. What would prevent them from using those capabilities against me?

A month and a half into the ordeal, my immediate commanding officer got in touch for the first time. His signature had been right on that paperwork—along with my command master chief's, my executive officer's, and my department head's. But all of a sudden his bosses were coming down on him for something he'd given Clint permission to do.

So he sent me a letter ordering me to sell my company.

Just a formality, right?

Fuck you.

"You did the right thing," he told me when we finally spoke. "But I'm going to need you to divest yourself of the company and send me the proof."

He also directly attributed the issue to *No Easy Day.*

There was one last thing: they were going to need me to show up to a Trident Board, where I would have the opportunity to defend myself in front of a panel of master chiefs.

"It's ultimately to your benefit, to make sure we can clear you for good."

The only thing that prevented me from walking at that point was the specter of losing all my retirement benefits. So I sold the company to Louis for fifty cents.

In the room full of master chiefs I'd known and worked with for years, it immediately became clear that neither the form nor the company nor the self-published travel book was the issue.

The real issue was Mark Owen.

The investigation was a targeted witch hunt, and every single question centered on our previous points of contact.

I did know Mark, though not very well. And I didn't have the best impression of the guy.

We'd had a single unproductive meeting about my cybersecurity products about a year back. My first design was a metal-cloth-lined cell phone pouch that would eliminate the threat of identity or patent theft for business travelers abroad. Since he had connections in the business world I was hoping he would hook me up. He didn't.

But in a random coincidence, I'd bought a house off him when we'd moved from D.C. to Virginia, before we'd ever met.

Carrie and I had seen about thirty homes that day. His stood out for being immaculate and in great condition. His wife was handling the sale. Finding out that the house had belonged to another SEAL was the clincher.

"So you bought [Mark Owen's] house."

I stared down the master chief who was asking the question.

"Yeah, Walter. You *sold* him that house."

What a fucking joke.

That particular master chief was the person who'd built the house, lived in it, and then sold it to Mark Owen before I ever came on the scene. Virginia was a small world, and SEALs liked to keep things in the family. It wasn't that crazy for a house to have been owned by three SEALs in a row—and the men in that room knew it.

Those three months of prolonged stress weighed on me more than any operation I'd ever been a part of.

Despite my big ideas and my independent streak, I'd always managed to work inside the system. And here I was getting hammered by a command that was known just as much for its excellence as for its own foibles. Just inside that room full of master chiefs, I could have called out eight of the ten men for indiscretions ranging from DUIs to travel claim fraud.

But again, it wasn't about the alleged infractions.

"Long live the brotherhood."

Until brotherhood made things inconvenient for a few guys at the top. Hang out inside a fence line full of sharks, and eventually you're going to get bitten.

A few hours later my master chief called me and told me I'd get to keep my trident.

Uh, thanks.*

In the end, Mark Owen was forced to turn over millions of dollars' worth of book earnings, and every one of the guys on the command's blacklist was punished in some way. A few of them had their tridents pulled for a year and were forced to sweep the quarterdeck each day. They'd gone from seasoned, respected operators to janitors at the command.

Based on my experience, an association with the author of *No Easy Day* was probably their most damning infraction.

My commanding officer stood up in the middle of quarters one morning and blurted out his lame-ass version of an apology.

"By the way, whatever you heard about Clint, he's good to go."

"The system failed Clint."

Okay, thanks.

Where were you three months ago?

The whole experience made for a special prelude to retirement. It was a shitty note to end a career on, that's for sure. Since there was no fucking way I was going to serve out my remaining time in the Navy working under a bunch of backstabbing hypocrites, I requested a transfer to a nondeploying command.

I'm still working through my feelings about the whole thing, in case you couldn't tell.

---

* That was the moment when I decided that I was going to write a few books once I'd officially retired.

21
BRAIN TISSUE

MARYLAND, 2013

LEAVING THE NAVY WASN'T A DECISION I TOOK LIGHTLY. NOT EVEN AFTER my command stabbed me in every single orifice and hung me out to bleed.

Nothing on this planet could have been a better fit for my skill set than being a SEAL. The trident was the fulfillment of every dream I'd ever had. But for all the adventure and the sense of purpose Naval Special Warfare had given me, the military took away a lot of freedoms. My most recent experience only confirmed how far its reach could extend on a bad day. But even on the good days, I'd never wanted to spend my whole life on the inside. I'd missed a good ten years of my daughter's childhood. Retiring after twenty years would have me out at forty-one, with hopefully at least half of my life and an even bigger chunk of hers still ahead of me.

Plenty of time to bank some cash and fill my garage with shiny new toys. After the way the command had treated me on my way out, succeeding on my own terms felt like a nonnegotiable outcome—and maybe even a bit like a score I had to settle.

The personality type that leads to success in the teams can be an asset in the business world, and as a SEAL working in a unique capacity I'd always been given the freedom to think beyond standard military parameters. But transitioning to life on the other side is still a wake-up call for even the most well-adjusted guys. A category that didn't exactly define my current state of mind.

My reality check started the year before I got out, when I began looking into a small host of medical mystery issues I'd been sweeping under the rug. A pattern of anxiety that had started percolating around the time my squirrel career kicked in, and which had only been amplified in recent months . . . Crushing migraines going back to my first deployment. And dreams that messed with my sleep patterns for years before I thought to bring them up at a doctor's appointment.

The dreams started around the time the frequency of my deployments went through the roof, but I ignored them until it was time to get my medical files cleaned up. The settings, blurred-out versions of a clandestine working environment, would change a little each time. But the general idea was always the same: A tech op in the middle of the night, in a faceless warehouse or on a random street overseas. My hands were busy, welding small pieces of surveillance equipment together or sanding down chunks of wood, contact joining bundles of red and yellow wires. And then I'd feel it, the way you do in a dream. You don't hear or see the monster stirring under the bed. Suddenly you know.

Someone was coming, from behind a door. Someone who'd seen me. I was about to be rolled up. Only I'd never see the ending. I'd wake up with my heart thumping so hard against my rib cage that I thought cardiac arrest would be next. There was so much adrenaline surging through my veins that it would take me another three hours just to get back to sleep.

None of my symptoms were surprising for an operator, and I got off easy in practically every single respect. The bracelet some of my friends and I wore, with the names of the men we'd known and lost, was reminder enough of that. But together my cluster of issues pointed to the potential for a mild form of traumatic brain injury, or TBI. The combination was enough to get me admitted to a four-week intensive outpatient program at the National Intrepid Center of Excellence in Bethesda, Maryland.

Before anyone in the NFL was ready to listen, one of the center's founding doctors had been sounding alarms over the risk of repeated concussions in football players. Now he was part of a team dedicated to diagnosing the "invisible injury" that affects a large percentage of vets.

You'll hear a million horror stories about the U.S. Department of Veterans Affairs, but NICoE, run by the Department of Defense and geared toward active-duty members of the military with nonacute symptoms, doesn't fuck around. At check-in, I was assigned a team of a dozen doctors and specialists. Not just brain doctors like you'd expect—I'd be seeing audiologists, psychologists, physical therapists, and sleep specialists to address the full spectrum of my issues. They put me through an MRI machine that digitally sliced my brain into forty thousand segments and spit out a three-dimensional model, and hooked me up to electrodes as I slept. Every day, from morning until midafternoon, we attended group sessions and an individualized schedule of appointments tailored to our needs. It was a full month of focus on the particulars of my physical and mental health. And at that moment it was exactly what I needed.

A hundred and twenty appointments and four weeks later, my half-inch-thick medical file was swollen to six times its original size. Despite regular annuals and the extensive dive physicals we ran through every five years, two decades in the Navy had left me with a laundry list of undiagnosed health issues. There were hearing deficiencies in both ears, which I'd suspected but hadn't paid any attention to. Sleep apnea. A bundle-branch block on the right side of my heart—usually the result of hypertension, heart attacks, or embolisms, if you weren't born that way, which I wasn't. And the kicker: seven scars on the lower portion of my brain.

That was definitely a "holy shit" moment. I'd walked in the door basically healthy, at least in my mind, and come out on the other side with all kinds of problems.

My short- and long-term memory had both been compromised by repeated wear and tear, and my brain function dropped off a cliff after four to six hours of activity. My heart's right ventricle was contracting with a delay, because it only received a referred electrical signal from a clump of bundle-branch tissue on the left side of my heart. I was holding my breath for minute-long increments while I slept because my brain was failing to send the proper signals to my lungs. And the anxiety and nightmares I'd been trying to suppress were consistent with a diagnosis of low-grade PTSD—although they don't tell you as much at the time, because apparently the diagnosis can be triggering.

The scars left behind by the undiagnosed injuries in the brain were probably caused by years of proximity to explosives and gunfire and lots of trips over big waves in small boats. Due to the repetitive concussive motions associated with our training, SEALs have some of the highest rates of non-combat-related TBI. One likely reason is the amount of time we spend out on the water with a crapload of gear on our heads. Small, fast boats like RHIBs and MK5s tend to crash right through the waves, and as they skid along, they send our brains rattling up into our skulls. The helmet and night-vision goggles we're often wearing add an extra load to our head and neck, and the helmet itself gives our skull a good beatdown. Our frequent parachute jumps create similar issues—the hard opening, at the moment when the chute deploys, violently jerks our brains around inside our skulls.

There's also the way our particular community tends to ignore non-essential guidelines. To protect our ears and brains from overpressure, we're supposed to only fire half a dozen rounds of .50-cal per day, and two blasts from a shoulder-fired rocket. We'd routinely fire off twice that amount as we trained, sometimes just for the fun of it.

They say a SEAL ages five years for every year he deploys, and at NICoE I definitely saw the truth in that. But would I do it all over again?

In a fucking heartbeat.

My hearing turned out to be especially weak in the upper frequencies. That means the female voice, especially over the phone, can be particularly hard for me to decipher. Couldn't have made that diagnosis up if I'd tried.

Once we moved from diagnosis to treatment, I started receiving shots of Botox to the head, neck, and shoulders, along with acupuncture and a mild electroshock-type therapy. I even got hearing aids (which I immediately chucked into the junk drawer in my kitchen), a handicapped parking pass, and a special license plate. One thing I've noticed is that Texas cops are a lot more sympathetic about speeding tickets when they find out the asshole they just pulled over has a disabled veteran ID.

The thing about brain injuries is that, unless they're acute and involve bleeding, they can't really be reversed. The only thing to do is learn to manage the symptoms through lifestyle adjustments and a mixture of alternative techniques.

That's how I wound up in a room full of special operators banging on bongos under the instruction of a very earnest music therapist.

Supposedly the act of repetitive drumming merges the benefits of sound therapy and meditation to reduce the symptoms of anxiety.

Maybe there is something to that. But a lot of the time in those group sessions I'd just default to my patented method for getting through long meetings—picturing everyone naked. You probably do it sometimes on the subway, on the street, at a restaurant. I do it pretty much everywhere, in those in-between times when regular people think about what they're having for dinner.

Man, woman, tall, short, athletic, obese, anywhere in between. It's not sexual, it's not intentional, but if we've met, there's a pretty good chance I've mentally undressed you. That doesn't have anything to do with the scars on my brain, as far as I know. Just a random habit of my naturally overactive synapses and my fucked-up DNA.

While waiting for a slot to open up at NICoE, Navy medical sent me to a shrink to kick off my exit process. Up till then I had been one of those operators sitting in the squad room slamming PTSD claims as they rolled in. "Here comes another future customer of the United States military's benefits fund."

It's ironic that I took such a dim view of trauma when I grew around family members who, looking back, definitely suffered from PTSD.

Before we moved to Saudi, I'd spend chunks of the summers with my grandpa while he built homes around Dallas, sleeping in an RV on his work sites. He would scare the crap out of me when he'd wake me up screaming about the World War II memories permanently stuck in his dreams. He'd been a member of the Army's famous 101st Airborne Division and had fought the Japanese for five years straight in New Guinea and the Philippines. There was a mini fridge at the foot of the bottom bunk, and every night he'd kick the living shit out of it while reliving his deployments.

In the morning he'd wonder why his feet hurt so much.

"God damn, my foot hurts!"

Then there was my uncle Drew, who'd served in Vietnam with the Army's "Easy Company," an infantry regiment whose World War II predecessors were the subject of the Steven Spielberg HBO miniseries *Band of Brothers*. He might have had a few other postings as well. When he came back from Vietnam, Drew never unpacked his suitcase. It wasn't until twenty years later that his son Todd found it up in Uncle Drew's attic. Inside were a pair of shower shoes, two sets of tiger-striped camouflage uniforms, and a black beret. It looked like Uncle Drew had been a member of Vietnam's covert Tiger teams.

The only story Drew ever told me about his service came from his time as a sergeant, about a helicopter insertion into a very hot landing zone.

The men jumped and managed to hit the ground, but seconds later the helicopter's skid got caught on a tree stump. The helo flipped upside down. The radioman was chopped in half by the rotor blades, and several other members of Uncle Drew's platoon were instantly killed. Uncle Drew saw a finger with a wedding ring on it lying on the ground, and he tucked the ring into his pocket to bring to the widow back home.

He couldn't get two sentences into that story without breaking down in tears.

But still, I didn't connect the dots.

It's not like I hadn't witnessed addiction and emotional issues within the teams. I saw them on a firsthand basis starting back with my first deployment, when my platoon was holed up in a Bahrain hotel on a break between maritime ops in the Gulf. At checkout time, our task unit chief was nowhere to be found, and somehow being the new guy got me deputized to go bang on his door. What I discovered in his room wasn't pretty. As the chief slowly inched open the door you could hear bottles clicking together on the floor.

"Hey," he said, looking at me through the crack like he wasn't quite sure who I was. "Hey, chief," I answered back uncertainly. "Uh, you know we're taking off, right?"

He shuffled away without answering, so I nudged open the door a little wider. The room was pitch-dark. All the lights were off, and the curtains were duct-taped to the wall. He was wrapped in a towel, sweating profusely.

He'd been hiding a secret only a few men in the platoon knew about: a history of alcoholism and depression, with possible bipolar tendencies. The task unit commander usually instructed hotel staff to empty out his minibar, but he'd mistakenly assumed Bahrain was one of the Middle Eastern countries where booze was prohibited.

That fall, back in Coronado, things took a turn for the worse. On Christmas Day, despondent over a custody situation and suffering from a postmania low, the chief hung himself from a doorknob in the barracks.

Brutal, and completely fucking heartbreaking for his family.

But his problems predated the Navy. Though the stresses and excesses of military life might have made his issues worse, they didn't stem from combat.

Operators tend to get a little jaded when we know there are guys out there abusing the system for a chance to take home 100 percent of their salary for the rest of their lives. I'd seen one officer scam his way out of the command with a spinal injury he'd picked up off-road racing between deployments. But the shrink I saw just before NICoE helped me open up my perspective on PTSD, and even start to wonder whether I might have some myself.

She focused mainly on the nightmares, using a technique called "dream scripting" that worked through the power of suggestion.

"Let's try changing the end of the story," she'd say.

As part of the treatment, she would have me write down the recurring nightmare and add on several alternate endings. You're working overseas in the middle of the night, only you unlock a door and find . . . a field of butterflies. The endings have to come from the patient, so that the same part of your subconscious that originated "butterflies" in the first place can kick in during REM to diversify the plot. Hopefully that field of butterflies eventually replaces the nightmare portion of your dream.

We didn't work together for long, but the nightmares did eventually taper off. I also picked up some insights on how my childhood family dynamic might have created some trust issues for me, particularly around women. Unburdening yourself to a complete stranger who's sworn to protect your secrets has its merits.*

NICoE and the therapist weren't my first experiences with counseling. Carrie and I had been to couples therapy a few times over a two-year period prior to that. Like most couples, by the time we went, it was too late. The fact that we kept switching shrinks didn't help. Carrie would accuse me of trying to seduce the therapist with my version of the story, get them on my "side." I'm either a master manipulator or just a charming motherfucker, depending on who you ask.

---

* The *Deadly Skills Puzzle and Activity Book*, published in 2018, was designed to lower anxiety and increase brainpower for those suffering from PTSD and TBI. This message brought to you by the Navy SEAL Association for Self-Promotion and Monetary Gain.

We'd switch therapists, and it would happen again. We couldn't have been further away from a united front.

After fourteen years of marriage and the two-year therapy experiment, we'd decided to finally call it quits in 2011.

Unfortunately I was away on a deployment when the papers came through after we'd already been living apart for some time. Virginia requires a one-year period of legal separation that kicks off with the serving of the divorce papers, and I wanted to get the clock ticking so we could both start the process of moving on. So I asked a friend to hand off the papers for me. Neither of us paid much attention to the date. That's how I came to be the guy who served his wife divorce papers on Valentine's Day.

I'd seen a lot of marriages in our community hang on for twenty or thirty years, only to fall apart, like clockwork, as soon as the guy retired. All the stress that had been building up during those years of deployments would come crashing down, or maybe they'd figure out just how far apart they'd grown. Or maybe they'd figure out they never even liked each other all that much in the first place. With my retirement looming in the near distance, we were just a bit ahead of schedule.

22
ESCAPE
THE WOLF

YOU CAN'T COUNT ON DRUM CIRCLES TO GET YOU THROUGH RETIREMENT. And you definitely can't count on the military for career counseling. Or in my case, even a pat on the shoulder.

It helped that I'd had a head start on the transition, even if it nearly cost me my retirement. Long before the dustup with the command, I'd pegged my lottery ticket to a concept called Red Teaming, a threat assessment technique pioneered by Dick Marcinko near the end of his military career.

After Marcinko was forced to hand over the command of DEVGRU under pressure from higher-ups, just before being permanently forced out of the Navy, he assembled a team of SEALs to test the security of naval facilities around the world. "Red Cell," his name for the new unit, would help pinpoint the military's defensive vulnerabilities—and they'd do it by staging simulated attacks on the Navy's infrastructures. The evolution to Red Teaming made sense. DEVGRU had been conceived as a counterterrorism assault force. Now Marcinko and his team would play the part of the terrorists they'd previously trained to hunt. The threat of terrorism was very much alive in the mid-1980s, and nobody was more perfectly suited to testing the weaknesses of the Navy than a guy who took serious pleasure in rattling the establishment.

Ted and I had started using Red Teaming as a training tactic back when we stood up that advanced program around 2007. To get more real-world context and practice, we'd regularly volunteer our services to the military and intelligence community. Our pitch was pretty straightforward: let us see how much proprietary info we can gather right under your noses, and after we're done we'll advise you on how to strengthen your defenses. Anytime we ran into technology or physical obstructions we hadn't prepared for, we'd circle back to study up.

One of the places we infiltrated once we retired and started working together was a multibillion-dollar conglomerate with dozens of subsidiaries in the military, aerospace, and technology sectors. A friendly out-of-house loan to a civilian company we had a vested interest in keeping secure.

We gave ourselves a ninety-six-hour window to crack the code to the CEO's suite, and we spent the first thirty-six watching his pattern-of-life and casing the company's shiny glass office tower. At close of business, a high volume of traffic moving out of the building was guaranteed. There were plenty of employees absentmindedly rushing home and holding open doors for a couple of guys in button-down shirts and slacks. At rush hour in this particular building, the automated barriers in the lobby happened to be unlocked. That meant we didn't need to deploy our backup plan—stealing badges from the cleaning crew. Instead, Ted and I just breezed right through the lobby with cups of coffee in one hand and phones held up to our ears.

That's a little social engineering trick that keeps our hands busy and encourages strangers to open doors for us. Dead simple, incredibly effective, and there are lots more like it.

Once we got into the building we needed to kill some time. Internal alarms wouldn't be disabled until 9 p.m., when the cleaning crew started working, so we camped out at the top of the stairwells and waited. Any employee taking the stairs for exercise at that time of day would be heading down to the lobby.

Around 10 p.m., we made our way toward our destination, a suite on the northwest end of the building on the twenty-fourth floor. The motion detectors used in many office buildings are PIRs, passive infrared sensors that work by detecting levels of infrared radiation. A change in temperature caused by a warm body coming and going trips the sensor. So does a stream of cold fog emitted from an upside-down can of compressed air.

We played a game of cat-and-mouse with the cleaning crew for a while before accessing the CEO's multiroom suite.

Inside his office was a big three-ring binder with a dozen tabs. Each tab represented a subsidiary company, with documentation on every important deal or issue of the week—his executive briefing on all the company's assets. The first piece of paper was an aerospace contract for hundreds of millions of dollars, a piece of competitive intelligence that could have been sold to the right bidder for a large chunk of cash.

Some of our best finds came from his assistants' desks. One hadn't logged out. That gave us access to the CEO's emails. Another had copies of his family members' passports and credit cards in her desk drawers.

We owned his ass within five minutes of accessing the executive suite.

Just goes to show, you can have the best firewalls in the world and the greatest security systems on the market. But hands down, your biggest security liability is your employees. Unwittingly or by design, it's the innocent people who work for you who will fuck you over long before your systems fail.

Before we slipped back out the door and back to the stairwell, we placed a digital picture frame on the CEO's desk. Displayed on the screen was a rotating assortment of photographs of the CEO's family. We'd tweaked them a bit before uploading them.

Maybe Photoshopping red crosshairs onto surveillance photography of his wife and kids went a step too far. When the CEO's executive assistants came in the next morning to open up the office, they saw the photos and immediately called 911. The company's general counsel (the only individual on the premises who knew what we were up to) had to let the cops know that this was all part of a vulnerability test.

Hopefully the results of that stress test made up for how much we terrified his secretaries.

By that point Carrie and I had gotten to be on better terms after working through some of our issues post-divorce. We'd always been great coparents, and there was no reason for either of us to stay on the East Coast once I'd cut my ties to the command. So we'd made the mutual decision to move back to Texas, a homecoming for our modern family.

My formal exit from the Navy a few months after the move hadn't exactly been triumphant. I skipped the official ceremony where you walk across the quarterdeck one last time and they blow the whistle as you leave the stage. Instead I flew to Virginia from Texas and was in and out of the Navy personnel department in about fifteen minutes. It boiled down to having my picture taken, signing a piece of paper, and handing in my active-duty card. After twenty years attached to an elite community of warriors, I walked out of that office and suddenly I was just . . . a guy. According to a signature on a piece of paper, a guy who used to be someone.

It's like the Superman pills wore off and I'd been turned back into Clark Kent. Only I didn't get to keep the cape.

In that first year I lost around twenty pounds and spent a lot of time mentally replaying the way the admiral had fucked with me, when I wasn't bingeing action movies and dumb comedies in my den. When you're moving at the speed of light for twenty years and it all comes to a screeching stop, the baggage has no choice but to come forward. Any habits or addictions you have are definitely at risk of bubbling back up.

And any shit you didn't want to think about is practically guaranteed to come crashing through your synapses.

One memory that sometimes stopped me in my tracks went all the way back to Iraq. My brain had buried it somewhere deep, until a master chief brought it up half a dozen years after the fact. It happened in the middle of the night, a few days after we got to An Nas. My platoon had set up some tents, but the marines were sleeping between their vehicles, in spaces wide enough for a tank to move through. The camp was deliberately kept dark through the night, to protect us from the ambushers sneaking around An Nas. And in the dark, several tanks had plowed through an opening between two parked vehicles, killing four of the sleeping marines. Four nineteen-year-old kids crushed under sixty thousand pounds of metal, an accidental noncombat death the public would never hear about.

The hardest memories were the ones I'd been trying to suppress. It wasn't until I had the time and space that I finally started grieving my friends. My mind always goes to the lives they could have been living or to the kids they left behind. Where they'd be, what they'd be doing.

Social media can be a land mine. You learn to steel yourself on anniversaries, when every SEAL's feeds are flooded with pictures of the friends we've lost. Some of those pictures I'd taken myself.

Once I was ready to get moving again, I turned my focus back to building up the high-end corporate security company I'd bought back from Louis Freeh for fifty cents. We would offer a range of services, from training employees on active-shooter response to developing airtight security protocol. In terms of price point, Red Teaming would be at the top of the list—it's a resource-intensive process that requires additional manpower. Depending on the needs of the company, we would either emulate the actions of random criminals or impersonate a sophisticated, state-sponsored crime ring in search of foreign intelligence.

The name of the company, Escape the Wolf, was inspired by a parable about wolves, sheep, and sheepdogs that you might remember from the movie version of *American Sniper*. The original source is a book called *On Combat,* by a retired lieutenant colonel named Dave Grossman, and the story came out of a conversation between the author and a Vietnam vet.

Society is composed of three kinds of people, the veteran told Grossman. The vast majority are sheep, "kind, gentle, productive creatures who can only hurt one another by accident." A very small but dangerous minority are wolves. The wolves are the criminals, the violent portion of the population who "feed on the sheep without mercy." To protect the sheep from the wolves, you need sheepdogs—alpha types capable of controlled violence who "live to protect the flock and confront the wolf."

People like me.

I liked the idea of flipping that paradigm. The average civilian might not be able to get through BUD/S, but that didn't mean there couldn't be a valuable exchange of information between those born with the freak DNA that caused us to excel at violence and the segment of the population deserving of our protection. Or the companies whose interests are vital to our economy.*

One of the first big jobs I landed had me securing the CEO of a significant tech company during a high-stakes business trip overseas. The chairman was flying to Beijing to close a multibillion-dollar deal with another American company and a Chinese firm. He'd been pushing back on his general counsel's suggestion of a security escort, but the counsel had pressed his case, and the company jet took off with two former FBI agents on board. They'd be checking in with me daily while I monitored

---

* Escape the Wolf is now a leader in crisis management, providing custom policy and workforce education on areas from active-shooter scenarios to cyber-threat awareness for organizations all over the world.

the situation from afar, ready to deploy my diplomatic connections if the situation took any unexpected turns.

In this instance I'd probably be more useful in that capacity—since the Chinese state happened to have my fingerprints, my Social Security number, and my full name and alias on file. Just like 22 million other federal employees and contractors (along with their friends and families), my ass had gotten swept up in a giant security breach in 2015, when the U.S. government discovered that a group of Chinese hackers had installed a piece of malware in its employee database. The spyware had been sitting there sucking up data for a year before it was detected. In that time, the Office of Personnel Management (OPM) breach—unofficially attributed to the Chinese military's cyber-espionage division—had compromised the security clearance files of several million people who'd gotten a U.S. government background check or knew someone who had. It was a shit show. Or, depending on who you ask, business as usual. Those mother-fuckers are as shameless as they come. The twist was the scale of the attack. How or when the data would be used was anybody's guess.

Being one of those millions of people who got a letter telling me that the Chinese government had obtained access to my personal files, I wasn't too interested in having my name pop up on their computers as I went through customs. Going over to China as a compromised for-mer member of the military would practically guarantee me a personal surveillance detail. Luckily I happened to know a couple of guys who were perfect for the job. I'd collected a badass list of freelancers since I got out of the Navy, from former special operators and retired federal agents to hackers with NSA and CIA backgrounds.

The two retired FBI agents I'd selected for the gig briefed the chair-man on some ground rules as the jet prepared to take off.

"There's a high probability that audio or video could be running in your hotel room, so please do not discuss anything sensitive if you can help it."

It's a safe bet that any Chinese hotel room about to receive some

Western guests, particularly the high-profile kind, would have been wired by the state. My guys did a quick check of the room once they were on the ground, but it wasn't in our best interest to ruffle feathers by disabling any surveillance equipment they might have found. Give the Chinese any reason to call you a spy and you'll find yourself in a jail cell faster than you can boil a pot of rice. Anything we did had to be overt.

They also told him to refrain from accessing his company's network while in China—too much of a risk. Intellectual property theft isn't just a black market enterprise over there. It's practically a national sport, and it siphons off hundreds of billions of dollars from the American economy every year.

"One last thing," they added. "Let us know anytime you plan to leave your laptop unattended."

Sure enough, the first thing the chairman did in his hotel room was log into the company network via a VPN connection. Then he left his laptop running, still connected to the company network, and went off to the hotel gym without notifying my guys.

Five minutes later, two Chinese nationals showed up at his door. The smaller one worked the lock on one knee while his hefty older brother stood watch.

"Can we help you?"

My two retired feds had caught their approach through a hallway cam they had affixed to the wall outside their room. The installation was *meant* to be obvious, but these two IT specialists hadn't been paying attention.

"Sorry, sorry," the bigger one said, waving his hands around like he was clearing up a simple misunderstanding. "No English."

Riiiiight. And you're just out here delivering room service.

"Wǒmen kěyǐ bāng nǐ ma?" one of my agents repeated.

No English, no problem. He'd spent fifteen years reading intelligence reports in Mandarin while stationed at the Bureau.

Jiǎnchá duìyǒu, niáng.

Or as we say in Texas: *Checkmate, motherfuckers.*

"Ahhh, sorry sorry," the husky bodyguard type answered in Chinese. "Wrong room!"

Sure, that made sense. There must have been a lockpickers' conference down the hall.

"Well, let's see if we can help you find your way," my multilingual communications expert countered helpfully. "What room are you looking for?"

"Wrong floor, wrong floor! We supposed to be on five!"

"No problem," he said gallantly. "Let me show you to the elevator."

My guys went so far as to escort them all the way to the elevators and even press the down button. Then they watched the lights go straight down to the lobby.

Wrong floor, my ass.

On the way home, the agents told the chairman: "Do not discuss anything remotely sensitive or related to the deal on the aircraft." Corporate executives tend to treat their jets like mobile SCIFs—Sensitive Compartmented Information Facilities designed to repel any attempt at spying. By then they'd won the chairman's trust, and everyone on board kept their commentary to themselves. When they swept the jet on the ground, my guys found two battery-operated GSM listening devices installed behind panels at the front and rear of the aircraft. They wouldn't have transmitted after the flight took off, but any chatter on the runway would have been fair game. No wonder the Chinese transportation authorities had declined our request to have one of our guys stay behind and watch the jet. They wanted some private time with the upholstery.

23
SOCIAL
ENGINEERING

SILICON VALLEY, 2014

MY BEST RED TEAMING STORY SO FAR INVOLVES A JOB WE FIGURED WE'D never be able to crack. The target was a multibillion-dollar data center in Silicon Valley, and the security was airtight. On the virtual side of the house, the company's digital assets were protected by a cadre of top-of-the-line security engineers. The fence lines and firewalls they'd erected would foil even the most sophisticated hackers. But they wanted assurances that their physical facilities could withstand a potential intrusion. From our vantage point the setup looked pretty solid. The property was surrounded by a double fence line outfitted with razor-sharp wire, fortified by the best seismic motion detectors money could buy, and watched by dozens of well-placed cameras. Three guards were permanently stationed at the main security kiosk, eyeballing drivers as they scanned their badges at the front gate. Between the two fences, armed guards in Humvees patrolled an area the size of several football fields. Jocked-up ex-military types armed with semiautomatic rifles, a no-shit defense contractor rotating a crew twenty-men strong in eight-hour cycles for round-the-clock coverage. The contract probably numbered in the multiple millions of dollars.

Beyond the fence lines, two massive warehouses held racks upon racks of servers and hangers full of hard drives. Every day the hard drives and fiber cables inside those warehouses supported billions of data searches and a significant quantity of valuable personal information. More important, they enabled vital pieces of civic and government infrastructure whose malfunction could tip entire cities into chaos. In other words, the site was a gold mine for any cybercriminal ambitious enough to take on the challenge.

Throwing a chunk of carpet over the wire and shimmying our asses over the top wasn't going to cut it. It didn't take long for me and Ted to determine that social engineering would represent our greatest chance at surreptitious entry. Our best bet would be a female, ideally single. A young, unattached employee who would be more likely to meet up with friends or coworkers for drinks—and who might be open to being chatted up at the bar by a couple of clean-cut professionals.

Rotating between three inconspicuous rentals, we set about staking out the exit to the parking lot.

On night number three we hit payload. A blonde, early thirties, no visible wedding ring. Better yet, several coworkers who followed her out.

Happy hour. Operation "Romeo" was a go.

Ted and I tag teamed it to a bar within a mile of the facility. We spotted the group as we walked in, four women and two men already loading up on mixed drinks. This crew didn't look like they were going to be sitting around nursing beers for hours on end, so we sped up our timeline. Their two sidekicks, standard IT pocket-protector types, looked a little crestfallen as we moved in on their dates.

"So," I said, pulling up a stool. "How would you feel about being hit on for a little while?"

It was a goofy line with about a 40 percent chance of success. Maybe less. But the clock was ticking on our ninety-six-hour window. Besides, the blonde was cute, with a nice little round ass. Twenty years in the military will definitely mess with your sense of what's considered appropriate as far as humor and small talk. And I'm still figuring out the whole single-life thing. But sometimes being rough around the edges can work in your favor.

Eliciting actionable information from a target really comes down to being a good listener. Within a few beats, our new friends had revealed the name of their employer, the nature of their work, their relationship status, and the general location of their homes.

"So what's it like over there?" I asked our new acquaintances. "You guys got a Ping-Pong table?"

The blonde laughed.

"It's not really that kind of tech company," she said. "We're sort of on permanent lockdown."

"Yeah," her friend joined in. "We always joke about the fact that security is so tight, you'd practically have to sneak your boyfriend into the trunk of your car to give him a tour."

Bingo.

The security guards weren't checking for surreptitious cargo, like they do on some military bases.

"Here's what I'm thinking," Ted whispered as we leaned into a two-man huddle a few feet down the bar. "You take her home, hook up with her, and sneak into her trunk."

A rear entry, but maybe not exactly the kind you're thinking about.

My date was a few cocktails in. I'd already been priming the pump with a few friendly instances of physical contact, even playing on her sympathies with a little material on how my latest relationship had just bitten the dust.

After I told her I'd had a few too many, she offered me a ride to her place, a duplex a couple of miles away.

Free of charge, safer than an Uber, and it would give me access to her private, covered garage. I watched her set the alarm on her mobile device for a bright and cheery 5:30 a.m. before getting down to the business at hand. I didn't cut any corners, if that's what you're wondering.

SEALs have a reputation to live up to in the bedroom, and most of us take it pretty seriously.

Around three o'clock in the morning I spliced in a few yawns, went to "sleep" with one eye open, then waited until I heard her breathing go slow and deep. Another few minutes and she'd be in REM. Once I spotted that telltale movement of her eyelids I slipped out through the kitchen and into her garage.

Her car keys were still on the kitchen table where she'd tossed them when we'd come in, but she'd left her car unlocked. A pop of her trunk release latch granted me access to the first-class storage compartment where I'd be spending the next two and a half hours.

I wedged my right arm into a pillow and settled in for some quality personal time.

I didn't hear any audible cursing coming from the house around 5:30, so it seemed like she took my early exit in stride. After an hour and a half of puttering around inside, she slid into the driver's seat.

"We're moving," I texted Ted.

Just a couple of genuine NoCal environmentalists carpooling to work.

There was a quick muffled call I could only assume was a girlfriend-to-girlfriend review of the night's events. Then I felt the S-curve that meant we'd turned onto the access road leading to the guard shack.

Ted was already positioned outside the fence line with a clear view of the parking lot, waiting for any employees to make their way out of the immediate area. A few minutes later he sent me the all-clear text. Time to move. I popped the hatch and quickly rolled to the ground, the moment with the highest possibility of failure. Impossible to mistake for anything but a criminal act. But easy to miss because it happened so fast. We were counting on the second possibility. Pulling the trunk closed behind me, I crawled over into the space between the cars, slowly rose to full height, then pretended to fiddle with the lock on the driver's-side door of the neighboring vehicle.

Nothing to see here but an employee parking his car.

I walked over to the main building but veered around to the side. Just as we'd assumed, the side doors were locked. The only way into the compound was through the two main entrances, requiring a verified badge and some face time with security. Ted and I have successfully breezed past security in Fortune 500 companies with stolen badges around our necks. But when it comes to the hardware and data of our biggest technology companies, you're talking about an entity so vital to the public interest that it's been designated an official national asset. The large men with rifles weren't working for the U.S. government. But if they happened to be trigger-happy, they'd have the full force of the Justice Department on their side.

Time to fold.

The mission was over. We'd accomplished our goal.

I walked back out through the main pedestrian gate and hopped into the passenger side of Ted's waiting sedan. We hightailed it out of there, our signed and sealed get-out-of-jail-free letters from the company's general counsel untouched in our breast pockets.

That sure made for an interesting debrief.

"I'm not sure you want to know about this," I told the general counsel in private.

He didn't.

We left the particulars and the employee's name out of our report. Too many liability issues for the company, along with a few obvious reputation concerns for me. That particular technique wasn't anything I'd be looking to repeat, though the lessons are there for the taking.

It's an open secret that Silicon Valley is crawling with spies. But business travelers or employees working in sensitive areas in any location should be reading carefully. That clean-cut guy who starts chatting you up over after-work drinks might be interested in nailing you—while simultaneously nailing down the details of your company's security plan. And the attractive female giving you her undivided attention at the hotel bar could be taking you for a ride. Only she might be taking your entire company along, too. The risk of getting caught up in a scam is exponentially higher when you're traveling to countries where intellectual property theft is a known hazard. But you never know what kinds of honeypot or Romeo traps could be lurking closer to home.

EPILOGUE

TOWARD THE END OF MY MILITARY CAREER I STARTED WONDERING whether it might be time for us to stretch our conception of what Rumsfeld's "Find, Fix, Finish" catchphrase could look like.

The special operations community had been quietly developing its capabilities in that direction ever since 9/11, using smaller teams and more specialized operators like me. So why were we spending millions a pop to have Hellfire rockets rain from the sky, when someone like me could take out a target with a ten-cent 9mm round?

Compared to dropping hundreds of pounds of explosives off a remotely piloted aircraft, a bullet to the head would be a hell of a lot more discreet, and the risk of collateral damage or mistakes would be radically reduced. But a flyover from a $20 million Predator fails to contradict the official U.S. position that says we're not at war in countries where we don't have boots on the ground.

It also looks a lot less like a mob hit.

"No employee of the United States Government shall engage in or conspire to engage in political assassination."

Those seventeen words don't appear until more than halfway through the executive order President Gerald Ford passed in February 1976, in a section called "Restriction on intelligence activities." But Executive Order No. 11905 would go down in history as the piece of paper that, for the first time, formally prohibited any corner or member of the U.S. government from plotting a political assassination.

The executive order came on the heels of a congressional investigation chaired by a senator named Frank Church. The Church Committee had gone fishing for evidence of overreach in the intelligence branches because they suspected their spook friends of eavesdropping on U.S. citizens without warrants—but when they blew open the vaults of the NSA, the FBI, the CIA, and the Internal Revenue Service, they turned up some unexpected finds. Namely, a whole bunch of crazy-ass CIA plots to bump off Fidel Castro, from those famous exploding cigars to an outsourced mob hit and a booby-trapped seashell. The list of potential and attempted hits crashed through the news cycle like a tornado with a giant turd at its center.

A secret assassination squad wasn't a good look for the leaders of the free world, especially not in the Watergate era. And it could open us up to all kinds of hijinks from the world outside our borders. Giving the nod to assassination would be giving the nod to potential assassins targeting *our* president.

Future leaders would find ways around those seventeen words without publicly overturning them. They had to. They used military orders to classify terrorists as "enemy combatants," as President George W. Bush did in the aftermath of 9/11. Or called on the National Security Council to reclassify an American citizen as a military enemy who posed an imminent threat to the country, as Obama did in the case of Triple-A. The new era of warfare wasn't pitting us against armies in traditional theaters of war. It was based around a hunt, for lone assassins or small groups of fanatics plotting against ordinary U.S. citizens. And sometimes that hunt looked a lot like a hit.

That 1976 prohibition against assassination wasn't as binding as it sounded. Only no one ever wanted to be caught holding the bloody knife.

Getting so close to the bad guys, within arm's length at times, became a kind of operational tease. And I started to think maybe there was something to be done about it—not just planting a tracking device but actually carrying out the mission. SOCOM, particularly within the team I joined during my final years in the Navy, had always encouraged the enlisted men in its ranks to think outside the box. I'd already built several training programs within the spec ops community from the ground up, and seen a few others get their start through the ranks of the enlisted. It wasn't outside the realm of possibility that I could build another.

This one would build on the specialized curriculum I'd been building throughout the second half of my career. It would also include a discreet kill component. A covert targeted-killing program with the lightest possible footprint and greatest possible chance of accuracy was a logical evolution on the path we were already on.

Here's one way to think about it: cutting off terrorism at the kneecaps might make a legitimate target of a well-heeled financier hiding out in a four-star Paris hotel. But you can't launch rockets in fucking France.

That's a completely hypothetical situation, of course, from the location, to the target, to the question of whose responsibility that financier would fall under. The United States wasn't about to stoop to the level of Vladimir Putin or Kim Jong-un's nerve-agent-wielding goons. But chasing bad guys all over the globe might put us in situations where body armor wasn't an option, and capture was impossible.

Creating potential protocol for a totally unsanctioned spec ops assassination program was treading on sensitive and potentially illegal ground. The topic of targeted killings has a way of churning up controversy—as well as unpredictable weather events loaded with fecal matter. Outside of our locker rooms, that is. Lawmakers and talking heads up on the Hill might have spent their days debating terms like *extrajudicial overreach*, but the topic didn't really come up in the hallways of the command. Not at my pay grade, anyway.

After jotting down a few ideas in the middle of the night, I casually broached the subject with a few of my peers. Their response came down to just two words:

"FUCK YEAH!"

That was all I needed to hear. The approval of my peers didn't constitute anything near authorization, and my budget was only imaginary.

But over the next year the project I'd describe as a "nonkinetic capture or kill program" became my main hobby.

The term *nonkinetic* won't make too much sense if you consult a dictionary. But in the military, a "kinetic strike" describes a bomb ferried to its final destination by a rocket. That rocket-and-bomb combination can take several forms, but the basic idea is a projectile weighted down with explosives, kinetically traveling over some distance to accomplish its goal. It's all about the machines and the tech.

In contrast, the "Violent Nomad" program would be all about the human touch.

Basing the program around a character helped me think about the kind of traits we'd have to train and select for. Also, it sounded fucking cool.

We'd start with the most seasoned, national-level operators and screen potential candidates from within that pool. SEALs were already trained in combatives, from jiujitsu to knife work. The fundamental technical skill sets were in place, and discretion wouldn't be an issue. When it came to psychological profile, however, they weren't necessarily a match.

Most men who make it to the top of the heap as special operators are fundamentally team players. These shadowy Violent Nomad operatives would work alone, potentially sneaking in and out of foreign territory with little to no institutional backup (a risky-as-shit setup designed to minimize potential traces of governmental involvement). Once they reached their targets, they'd need to be able to commit something that looked a lot like full-on murder. The kill would take place in an intimate context, without the distancing effect of a sniper rifle's scope and three hundred meters of space between the shooter and his target. They would need to be able to recover without developing lasting trauma or requiring extensive counseling, or the whole thing would be DOA.

The potential long-term effects led me to seek some off-the-record advice from a couple of military shrinks. Along with research of my own,

those conversations started to point me toward a catalog of traits that would insulate an imaginary fighting force against emotional and psychological fallout.

The men who'd fit the profile of a lone assassin would have blood the temperature of ice and titanium nerves. They would be intelligent, aggressive, coldly calculating. Disregarding of the law, their own safety, the safety of others. That much was obvious. Most important, they needed to be immune to remorse or fits of conscience.

In other words, these operators needed to demonstrate a lineup of psychological traits that looked a lot like a familiar prototype—the figure commonly known as a "sociopath."

Psychology technically lumps sociopaths together with psychopaths into the general category called "antisocial personality disorder," but sociopaths are generally understood to be a step short of total psychopathy. What it boiled down to was that in order for such a program to work, I'd need to locate a bunch of high-functioning freaks who would have been candidates for some degree of incarceration if they hadn't found their way into military service.

Obviously I spent a good amount of time pondering where exactly on the spectrum a clinical diagnosis would locate me.

The selection process would be baked into the program, with a hypothetical test I began to sketch out on paper. Its setting was probably inspired by the labs where I'd done some of my medical training. The rest came from an extremely fucked-up place inside my head.

A seasoned operator would enter a sanitized room. Inside the room he'd find a table with a hammer on it. Also, a live goat.

In under two minutes, the operator would have to use the hammer to coldly, expertly crush the animal's skull, while a panel of experts observed his performance through two-way glass.

The kill would be bloody, senseless, gruesome, explosively violent, and perversely intimate. And it would be only the beginning of the operator's trial.

With the task completed under the panel's watchful eyes, the operator would immediately be pulled into a simulated interrogation testing him on the cover he'd been assigned. Had the intimate act of brutality affected his nerves or his ability to lie on command? This moment would be critical. It would reveal any potential aftereffects of what most normal human beings would consider a traumatic experience. Unless they'd been brought up on a farm where goat death by hammer happened to be the norm.

Once he passed through an interrogation aimed at getting him to give up the operational details he was briefed on, the operator would be directed to another small, bare room. Only in this room, he'd find nothing but a small kitten.

I know, this looks bad.

But I swear, this scenario wasn't born out of a vendetta against felines, and no kittens or goats were harmed in the writing of this chapter. After the age of fourteen I became a friend to the animal kingdom and eventually spoiler-in-chief for a sweet, lazy golden doodle.

The test was designed to stimulate empathy by presenting the operator with a completely defenseless victim. Following the thrust of my imaginary program to its logical endpoint, an operator might be enlisted to sneak into a secured compound and dispatch an impossible-to-capture target in his sleep. That's a completely different scenario from anything you might encounter in combat. Curled up in his blankets, the target would be utterly vulnerable, posing zero immediate threat. Would an operator be able to carry out the mission under such intimate, human circumstances? My expectation was that only a few men would be able to proceed. The test, particularly in its final step, would weed out the normal operators from the guys who'd have been an equally good fit for a placement inside Israel's Mossad.

When I took the idea to a couple of officers and they told me my passion project didn't have a chance in hell of ever getting off the ground, I shrugged them off and privately carried on. Maybe I just hadn't found the right audience.

Anyone who made it through the selection process would go on to a training program covering improvised weapons and explosives, tradecraft, and deception operations. With terrorists and their networks very aware of our presence on their turf and our lawn mowers in the sky, the game of cat-and-mouse was getting more involved. In the face of a hard-to-track target, increasingly threatening acts of vandalism and sabotage against known accomplices might be one way to roust terrorists from their hiding spots.

The grand finale would be the section on discreet, nonkinetic methods of accomplishing an unattributed kill. A bullet to the head might be the most efficient way to dispatch a target, and a special operator certainly wouldn't need any training on how to use one. But a bullet could also create the kinds of potential forensic issues that tend to bring on unwanted attention.

You're probably picturing syringes and poison darts, or the nerve agents recently favored by our Russian friends. An extraction of 100 percent nicotine, delivered via a lethal injection between the toes, or a dose of poisoned toothpaste that induces an untraceable heart attack. Or a technique I once heard about, attributed to a Japanese assassin, where a chemical is poured down the drain of a hotel bathroom sink. The drain is plugged, and then a second chemical, lethally reactive with the first, is poured on top. When the target enters his hotel bathroom, he empties the sink, inadvertently mixing the two chemicals together in the drain. The gas kills him instantly, leaving only traces of the chemicals behind.

But the more complex the method, the higher the risk of failure. An injection might be reversed by the right medical team, and fancy chemicals are likely to show your hand. Bashing someone's skull in is forever, and it might at least give the appearance of a random street kill.

Which is why the tool most likely to be used in both Russian mob hits and Kremlin-sponsored retirement parties is a simple lead pipe.

My favorite back-of-the-napkin concept was the airbag method. You take about a dozen strips of duct tape and overlap them, sticky side up, to form a square. Dump a bunch of broken ball bearings and screws onto your sticky death platter, cover that up with a second layer of duct tape, and insert it inside the steering wheel. Trigger a car accident by shutting down the fuel pump, and complete chaos ensues.

The Violent Nomad would have many uses for duct tape, along with other everyday items like condoms and tampons. He was a self-reliant, resourceful type. No black boxes being parachuted his way in the middle of the night. Covert infiltration, by any means necessary, would be a particular specialty. On the ground, he'd go dark, staying in shitty hostels and hotels where the odds of a camera in the lobby were slim to none.

If this all still seems completely nuts, consider the context: as far as I know, there wasn't a single capture of a high-profile target during the entire course of Obama's eight-year presidency. For high-value targets, the spec ops community and intelligence agencies had defaulted, by orders from the Oval Office, to those multimillion-dollar long-distance strikes that placed minimal American boots on the ground. I wasn't the only one putting more emphasis on the first part of the "kill or capture" equation than the second.

Here's my personal theory as to why: After the CIA got into hot water over its interrogation techniques, Obama didn't particularly want the words "detainee" or "torture" bubbling up into public consciousness again. Killing meant no pesky Gitmo prisoners to handle. No prisoner, no crime. No crime meant a better chance of reelection. Seemed kind of obvious to me. But I never shared that with anyone or heard anyone else voice that opinion, so who knows if there's any truth to it.

It probably won't surprise you to hear that my imaginary assassination program never made it past the notebook stage inside the Navy. But it didn't exactly die on the vine. Eventually I turned the bones of Violent Nomad into a two-book survival series called *100 Deadly Skills*.

Check it out at a bookseller near you, along with the survival edition that followed soon after.* At the very least you'll find some enlightening material on how to use an aluminum cigar tube to hide stuff in your butt. You might even pick up a simple tip that could save your life, or somebody else's.

There are a lot of folks out there hoping for a chance to be that good guy with a gun. But those stories tend to involve a guy like me—former military, off-duty cop, someone with special training. Instead of counting on that random hero in the checkout lane, or the state trooper who pulls up just in time, wouldn't it be nice to have a little extra insurance?

There will always be wolves in the social order, and natural-born sheepdogs are the exception to the rule. But if enough civilians start practicing more vigilance, maybe the criminals in our midst will think twice about whatever the fuck they're planning.

In the meantime, I'll be that guy sitting in the back of the restaurant, scanning the exits. Who knows, maybe I'll get lucky.

---

* Or go to violentnomad.com and buy my damn T-shirts .

ACKNOWLEDGMENTS

Most SEAL authors would love for you to believe that they actually wrote their book from cover to cover—that makes me laugh out loud. I certainly did not. I had the help of family, friends, Tom, and Savanah.

To my family: Thank you for the unconditional love and support throughout the process, recalling memories, collecting stories, and taking countless phone calls and answering random questions. Most of all, thank you for each and every memory, experience, and lesson learned—good or bad—I love you.

To my friends: Thank you for filling in multiple gaps with fact-filled lies based on true stories that I failed to remember. Each of your contributions made this book far more informative and entertaining, for sure.

To my illustrator: Tom, you are a master of your craft. You turned my stories into incredible works of art. There is no doubt in my mind that the illustrations are just as valuable as the words written, making this one of the most unique military memoirs published.

To my coauthor and friend: Savanah, you and I both know you were the architect, project leader, and author of this book. I appreciate every bit of your patience, creativity, research, interviews, and talent from beginning to end. Thank you.

To my readers: Thank you for your support, and don't forget to write your congressmen about the fucked-up subjective redactions! I hope you enjoyed the book!

INDEX

INDEX

ABOUT THE AUTHOR

CLINT EMERSON is a recently retired Navy SEAL with twenty years of service with the Special Operations community. He spent his military career serving under various Naval Special Warfare Commands as a Special Operator (SEAL). He is also a graduate of the American Military University in Virginia with a B.A. in security management.

Emerson is also the founder and managing partner of Escape the Wolf, LLC. His company focuses on crisis management for small-to-large global companies. He is also author of the New York Times best-selling book *100 Deadly Skills, The SEAL Operative's Guide to Eluding Pursuers, Evading Capture, and Surviving Any Dangerous Situation.*